BUILDING WRITING CENTER
ASSESSMENTS THAT MATTER

ELLEN SCHENDEL
WILLIAM J. MACAULEY, JR.

UTAH STATE UNIVERSITY PRESS
Logan, Utah
2012

© 2012 by the University Press of Colorado

Published by Utah State University Press
An imprint of University Press of Colorado
5589 Arapahoe Avenue, Suite 206C
Boulder, Colorado 80303

The University Press of Colorado is a proud member of

 The Association of American University Presses.

The University Press of Colorado is a cooperative publishing enterprise supported, in part, by Adams State College, Colorado State University, Fort Lewis College, Metropolitan State College of Denver, Regis University, University of Colorado, University of Northern Colorado, Utah State University, and Western State College of Colorado.

All rights reserved
Manufactured in the United States of America
Cover design by Barbara Yale-Read

ISBN: 978-0-87421-816-9 (paper)
ISBN: 978-0-87421-834-3 (e-book)

Library of Congress Cataloging-in-Publication Data

Schendel, Ellen.
  Building writing center assessments that matter / Ellen Schendel, William J. Macauley.
      p. cm.
    ISBN 978-0-87421-816-9 (pbk.) — ISBN 978-0-87421-834-3 (e-book)
1. English language—Rhetoric—Study and teaching (Higher)—United States. 2. Writing centers—United States. I. Macauley, William J. II. Title.
  PE1405.U6S34 2012
  808'.042071173—dc23
                              2012023988

For Amorak, Zoe-Kate, and Eli—a family of writers.
—ELLEN SCHENDEL

For my mother, who taught me that everyone knows something worth listening for, and my father, who taught me that hard work is both an honor and its own reward.
—WILLIAM J. MACAULEY, JR.

CONTENTS

BUILDING WRITING CENTER ASSESSMENTS THAT MATTER

ACKNOWLEDGMENTS

Throughout the process of writing this book, we've been touched by the work of a number of scholars and the kindness of colleagues and loved ones whose contributions have been profound. Both of us have been influenced by the assessment work of Brian Huot and Neal Lerner, scholars whose thinking has permeated our own scholarship and assessment practices. We want to thank MaryAnn Crawford for helping us to shape and plan this project. We appreciate the lively participation and comments from IWCA and ECWCA writing assessment workshop participants, whose perspectives and questions helped us to shape the outline for this book. We are grateful for the useful feedback two anonymous reviewers gave to an earlier draft of this book. And we have benefitted greatly from the suggestions and support of the Utah State University Press staff, particularly those from Michael Spooner. But there are many others who have been there along our assessment and book-writing journeys.

From Ellen:

In addition to having the privilege to have my thinking about assessment stretched by Bill Macauley, I'm grateful to have had the experience of working on assessment projects with energetic colleagues at Grand Valley State University. Wendy Wenner, Julie Guevara, and Dan Royer have taught me much about leadership and innovation when it comes to assessment and program development. Many thanks to Patrick Johnson, Lisa Gullo, Michelle Sanchez and the incredible writing consultants I've worked with over the past decade—your enthusiastic and creative work on assessment and strategic planning have made lasting impressions on our center's work. And I must acknowledge the incredible support offered by the participants of the Faculty/Staff Writing Retreats from 2009-2011, when drafting and revision of this book were in full swing. Finally, hugs and high fives to Zoe-Kate and Eli for their patience and support, and to my husband Amorak for listening intently, offering sound writing and editing advice, and championing this project from the very beginning.

From Bill:

I want to acknowledge first and foremost my coauthor, colleague, and friend Ellen Schendel, who really carried this project as I made a complex transition from Ohio to Nevada. I also want to thank my friend and colleague, Nick Mauriello, who literally taught me how to design, sustain, and complete a book project. I must also thank another friend and former colleague, Simon Gray, who developed with me the first iterations of the process described in chapter two of this book. I also have to thank my colleagues at the University of Nevada, Reno, who have been absolutely and consistently supportive of my work, especially Maureen McBride, Wade Brown, Jane Detweiler, Heather Hardy, and Eric Rasmussen. And, as usual, I am eternally grateful to my wife and partner, Debi Stears; I am always better because I know you (and because you know me so well, too).

INTRODUCTION

YOURS, MINE, AND OURS
Changing the Dynamics of Writing Center Assessment

Ellen Schendel
William J. Macauley, Jr.

When we started this project, we had one idea in mind: to help our friends and colleagues make sense of and use assessment in their writing centers. We have been acting on this idea by providing a range of conference sessions and workshops over the past four years. This book project continues that work and benefits from what we have learned from so many of our colleagues through our conference meetings.

Through these shared experiences, we felt as though we had found a clear idea of what writing center directors (WCDs) were looking for, what they wanted to learn and know, and what we could offer to support them in their assessment efforts. Once we had that clarity of purpose and audience, we started talking with folks about our book project ideas. We received only support and encouragement from our friends in writing centers, writing assessment, and writing program administration. Based on our workshop experiences and the support from multiple "camps" within our field, we started writing. We finished the first couple of chapters . . . and realized we had a problem.

Throughout the writing process, we were surprised by how frequently we could come to contrasting views. And it didn't happen all at once or even early in the project. These differences arose even as we completed the second half of the book and sought feedback from others. Our readers sensed some fundamental differences in our approaches to assessment and the kind of conversation we wanted to have with other WCDs. We understood the differences as primarily a function of Ellen's background in writing assessment and Bill's longer experience as a writing center director.

We knew we agreed on one essential idea, however: both perspectives were necessary because they informed not only the project at hand but how we got to it. The contrasts of perspective were at first problematic; even so, we recognized that the tensions between our respective views created a heightened expectation to support our individual claims and interpretations. In short, we were pushing one another harder than we would have had we agreed at every turn.

As you'll see in the pages that follow, we have written our own chapters. This structure may be deceiving, making it appear that we have dealt with our contrasting perspectives by simply avoiding them. However, we have shaped (and reshaped) each piece together while preserving the different perspectives that have informed our thinking about writing center assessment.

DIFFERENT BACKGROUNDS

Ellen has been thinking about assessment for at least thirteen years and wrote a theoretical dissertation on writing assessment as social action—thinking that informs her current assessment work in the classroom and the writing center. A number of metaphors about assessment permeate her scholarly and practical work: assessment as social action; assessment as research; assessment as reflection; assessment as rhetoric. For Ellen, assessment isn't just practical, local work—although it starts there. It's one very important way that writing specialists and WCDs communicate their values and philosophies to high-stakes, external audiences—and to each other.

Bill's dissertation focused on empowering student writers, using studio pedagogies to do it, and adapting those studio pedagogies to first-year composition courses. His experience with assessment spans writing centers, writing programs, and general education programs. An interest in assessment came long after he had become immersed in both the promise and lore of writing centers as locations of empowerment and student ownership of their work. In fact, Bill's interest in writing center assessment evolved out of questions related to the agency of tutors and writing centers as well as student writers working within tutorials. Bill has felt for some time that writing centers have done a great deal to empower student writers. What assessment means for Bill now is the empowerment of writing center participants.

DIFFERENT INSTITUTIONAL FOCUSES

Ellen is one of several composition and rhetoric faculty in an independent writing department; she and other faculty who direct the various writing programs at the university are not "permanent" program directors—the work can rotate as needed. The Writing Department has a long-standing interest in program and outcomes-based assessment, and the university's assessment structure includes an administrator in the provost's office who manages assessment university-wide as well as a university assessment committee that is a standing committee of faculty governance. The writing center itself is an independent unit; as director, Ellen reports directly to the dean of Interdisciplinary Studies.

The institution that Bill just recently left is a traditional, private, undergraduate liberal arts college, one that many would describe as a "private elite." In this context, writing is essential to the mission and reputation of the college. The curriculum there assumes that students will be successful writers when they arrive, and the need for the kinds of writing curricula and resources other schools need are not the norm there. Bill, the director of writing, was the only faculty member on campus formally trained in rhetoric and composition. He participated in assessment committees, departmental assessments, and the development of assessment plans for multiple campus constituencies. The program in writing, which includes the writing center, is a stand-alone program that exists between academic departments and divisions. As you can imagine, these very different institutional contexts for writing center work, WCD support networks, and institutional support for assessment have shaped our perspectives on and experiences with assessment within our centers.

You'll see that in this book we talk quite a bit about the collaborative nature of writing center assessment. We both take that to mean that the staff of the writing center can (and should) participate in assessment processes. But collaboration in Ellen's context means working with other writing program administrators as well as others beyond the writing programs; in Bill's former context, collaboration outside the writing center meant working entirely with people outside of the fields of writing centers and composition studies. How we feel about collaboration— whether we view it as the opportunity to draw energy from others or a tax on our own; whether it means standing some ground or opening ourselves to what other perspectives have to offer—is shaped by our very different experiences and support networks.

THE DIFFERENT STORIES WE WANT TO TELL

As a result of our different perspectives, Ellen's orientation to this project was to work toward big-picture concepts from the local level, showing how writing center assessment is connected to lots of resources and thinking about assessment in other fields. Bill's approach was to work from what serves the needs and interests of a writing center, showing WCDs that assessment could be their own, built from the goals and values of writing centers. Ellen wanted to inspire WCDs to engage with broader goals: to think of assessment as a means of shaping both a writing center and the field of writing center scholarship. Bill wanted to enable practical work that begins from concerns at the local level. Ellen wanted to engage writing centers with assessment writ large. Both of us wanted to show how assessment can change internal and external understandings of writing center work.

Despite our different experiences with assessment and goals for this book project, we have always agreed on one fundamental principle: assessment, when done thoughtfully and pragmatically, serves the work of writing centers in both small and profound ways. Increasingly, assessment is an institutional mandate for writing centers, but we are best served by understanding writing center assessment from the inside out, crafting assessment plans, processes, and reports with an eye toward the possibilities they hold for writing center work. In the rest of this introduction, we want to show you why and how writing center assessment can matter—and why we WCDs should embrace it.

The Relationship between Writing Centers and Assessment

In writing centers, we are used to counting things. We count visits by department, by identity markers, by class level, by faculty recommendation—we are experts at telling ourselves and others how much we are doing and at slicing and dicing that information in innumerable ways. We are good at this. In some ways, counting is necessary to our centers' well-being and continued funding; at certain moments, it may well be the only necessary assessment.

But these data, while helping us to understand traffic patterns, student satisfaction with our services, and visitor demographics do not help us to answer richer questions about our writing centers' work: Do writing centers help make better writers? What kind of differences do writing centers make in students' writing? How does the work of the writing center contribute to the university's mission and strategic plan? Answering these questions requires us to understand the effects of the writing center for individual students and also for the institutions where our centers live. It's the kind of information that can help us to improve what we do in fundamental ways: our pedagogies, the services/

programming we offer, the ways tutors are trained and compensated for their work, and the development of new tutoring technologies.

And, increasingly, this information helps us communicate with others—administrators, colleagues across campus, students, the larger public—about what writing centers value and why. Assessment is, by and large, the *lingua franca* of education right now and will continue to be so, but it can be so much more useful and meaningful to us than simply filling out forms or meeting benchmarks. Assessment can mean much more than counting visits and the number of satisfied students, though those are important aspects of assessing a writing center's work too. It can help us to understand much more tangibly the work that we do, what works best, why it works, and how we can make that work accessible to as many as possible.

Finally, if we can use our own knowledge and expertise to conduct assessment that is meaningful to our work, that we know will bring understanding and valuing of that work by those to whom we are responsible, we will have changed the context for our centers and, thus, the work itself.

In their book *Reframing Writing Assessment to Improve Teaching and Learning*, Linda Adler-Kassner and Peggy O'Neill show how discussions about what and how we assess students' literacy practices reflect much more than the teaching and learning we observe in our classroom and writing center contexts:

> Those discussions that we as two- or four-year college writing teachers or program directors might have about assessment—with other instructors in our program, with colleagues in our department, with campus administrators, or with people outside of our institution—aren't *just* about writing assessment. Instead, they exist within an ever-expanding galaxy of questions about what people need to know to "be successful" in the twenty-first century. These questions are inexorably linked to other items that populate the galaxy, as well—ideas about what it means to be a part of "America" as a country; ideas about how America develops as a nation and what is necessary for that to happen; ideas for how the nation's youth become "productive" citizens and what "productive" means. (5)

In other words, when we share our assessment results with others—when we make decisions about what information to gather and how to gather it—we engage in larger conversations about what writing centers value. We articulate how our work fits within the institution and within the field of writing studies—within the whole idea of empowering people through writing and education.

Adler-Kassner and O'Neill's argument is pressing and perhaps even overwhelming for us to consider as we begin the assessment process, in part because the passage above doesn't begin to represent the complexities of the writing center world. Writing centers are a global phenomenon. They are in two- and four-year institutions and exist entirely online or as brick-and-mortar locations. They are funded within for-profit and nonprofit entities, housed in high schools, set up in libraries, and operating in community literacy contexts. Writing centers might offer credit-bearing courses. They might include classroom-based fellows programs. They might offer other writing services or programming such as poetry slams, community writing workshops, and faculty writing retreats. They might be administered by faculty or staff who may come from very different backgrounds of study, and they might include tutors who are paid, those who tutor for course credit, or those who volunteer their time. The tutoring staff may be students or graduate assistants, professional staff, community or parent volunteers, or faculty. Writing centers can be independent units or parts of other units (such as a larger tutoring center) and may even have somewhat fuzzy reporting lines. So how can we even approach writing a book about writing center assessment when writing centers themselves are so many different things, and given the seeming chasm between the kinds of assessments that are familiar for us and those expected elsewhere?

Our answer to this question might be somewhat familiar to you, a bit like how you'd answer the question, "How can your writing center meet the individualized needs of writers from so many different disciplines and backgrounds?" We want to start where you are and help you articulate what you already know and what you need to find out. We want to provide a framework for thinking through your local context so that you might build an approach to assessment that satisfies your local needs while connecting you to larger conversations about literacy and learning. We'll show you examples of how we've developed assessments in our local contexts and used what we learned from the data to make decisions and shape the futures of our writing centers. But, like the modeling tutors might use in a writing consultation, these are just examples to show you how the two of us have worked through these processes and applied important assessment principles to our own contexts. What *you* do will be based on your own needs and institutional context.

To push the writing center metaphor a bit further, there are a number of rather obvious ways that the practices of tutoring, which should be very familiar to us, and assessment are comparable as well as a number of ways in which good assessment reflects the values inherent in writing center theory. When we sit down with writers, we tend to ask a lot of questions that help us to understand the writer's purpose, audience, and context such as:

- What are you working on?

- What concerns do you have?

- Where are you in the process of building this project?

- Where do you want to go with this work?

Likewise, assessment begins with your questions, then moves to finding answers and acting upon the information available. There are a number of additional ways in which writing consultations and writing assessments align with each other:

- Consultations and assessments are context-sensitive.

- Sometimes all a writer needs is one trip to the writing center. Sometimes a writer needs many visits. Similarly, some assessments are one-shot and quick while others take time to unfold.

- A writing consultation is aimed at improvement of the writer as well as the piece of writing under discussion that day. Likewise, assessment is intended to enhance the tutoring and learning going on in the center, as well as those who conduct the assessments, rather than simply make isolated changes in practice.

- Writing center consultations and assessments are back-and-forth dialogues—collaborations, not one-way monologues.

Read on, and we think you will see that the best of tutoring aligns very nicely with the best of assessment.

What This Book Does

Throughout this book, our goal is to be consultants to our readers, much as writing tutors act as consultants to the writers who visit a writing center. Our premise is that outcomes-based assessment is important both locally—to our schools, centers, tutors, and students—and globally, given the political landscape of assessment and the ever-increasing call for demonstrable efficacy, which is concurrent with the call to serve more and diverse populations. We draw upon what we consider the best that educational assessment and writing assessment theories, research, and practices can offer to the construction and application of effective assessment plans for writing centers. By including and explaining sample assessment projects, we illustrate the kinds of processes you might try as you devise outcomes, collect information, and make decisions based on that information. These are examples to illustrate processes rather than solutions intended to work in all contexts.

Assessment is not a bureaucratic task but an enactment of principles, theories, and practices writing center professionals already embrace. The principles of assessment that we believe in are:

1. Good assessment is a kind of inquiry or research (O'Neill, Schendel, Huot 2002). It's an opportunity to ask and find answers to questions that will help us do our work better or learn how others perceive our work or ask "what if" regarding our processes, pedagogies, and policies.

2. Good assessment is rhetorically sensitive in two ways (Huot 1996). Our assessment plans—what questions we ask, what methods we use to collect and analyze information—are constructed in response to internal or external conversations about our work or an opportunity to "set the stage" for a conversation about the writing center's value. And our assessment reports, typically submitted to administrators and other agencies, are storytelling opportunities.

3. Good assessment is collaborative. It draws upon information others have already learned in a given context, and it can draw upon the work of others in the field for its shape. Reciprocally, a writing center's assessment should contribute to strategic goals and help monitor a center's role in achieving its institutional mission, or the community's understanding about learning and literacy, and/or a discipline's understanding of what writing centers do.

4. Good assessment drives positive change. An assessment doesn't end with the analysis of data. In some ways, that is just the beginning. Assessment allows us to see possibilities for the future and build sound strategic plans.

5. Good assessment is an open invitation to greater relevance. It's an opportunity, to use Adler-Kassner and O'Neill's argument, to help frame for others what writing centers, good writing, and good teaching and learning are all about.

To this end, we describe the ways that writing center assessment is necessarily collaborative, involving many (if not everyone) on staff as well as other stakeholders and units on campus. We show how, as a rhetorical act, writing center assessment is an opportunity to articulate in a public way the values informing everything the writing center does and to shape the perceptions of the writing center held by stakeholders and others. In fact, we think writing assessment can—and should—become a site of collaboration and convergence, a means of connecting what *we* (writing centers) do with what *we* (institutions/professional communities) collectively can do. We show how the process of assessing the work of writing centers is a scholarly, knowledge-making activity. And we show that the products generated via the assessment enable effective decision making and the opportunity for a feedback loop to refine values and outcomes.

We start by surveying the concepts already written about writing center assessment. Chapter 1, "The Development of Scholarship about Writing Center Assessment," is a discussion of the published scholarship related to writing center assessment. As you can see from the way Bill taxonomizes the existing literature, there are a variety of contexts, connections, and methods to draw upon in constructing writing center assessment plans. We hope you find the accompanying annotated bibliography—see the appendix—useful as you dive into the scholarship that can guide and inform meaningful writing center assessment.

Chapter 2, "Getting from Values to Assessable Outcomes," begins with the very practical work of orienting oneself and making a plan. As any tutor knows, the very best and most successful consultations begin by getting to know the writer, because the writer needs to know himself before producing good work. So in this chapter, Bill begins the larger process by helping readers to articulate answers to the following kinds of questions: What are your values? What do you want out of assessment? What is your context? Then he helps readers move from what they know to what they want to learn, creating clear and assessable outcomes to serve as goals or targets. These will become the basis of an assessment plan and ensure that assessment projects and process stay rooted in a reflective process of inquiry and discovery.

Chapter 3, "Connecting Writing Center Assessment to Your Institution's Mission," describes the role of institutional mission statements in the development of assessment plans. Bill shares what he's learned by surveying the mission statements of writing centers across America. These mission statements demonstrate collectively how the field describes its work, and he shows how writing centers are "sticky ideas" that serve important roles in the ways institutions achieve their missions.

In Chapter 4, "Moving from Others' Values to Our Own: Adapting Assessable Outcomes from Professional Organizations and Other Programs on Your Campus," Ellen elaborates on Bill's methodology to show how writing centers can tap into rich resources from professional organizations to better tie assessment plans to issues in higher education, issues that administrators and faculty across the university care about deeply. This chapter shows how linking writing center assessment to larger conversations about writing instruction and student support can help to create the linkages between writing centers and the core goals of institutions or larger communities. Reciprocally, by deliberately engaging with national and global conversations on learning and literacy in the way assessment plans are built and findings are reported, the writing center's work will be informed by best practices and new knowledge created by several fields.

We pause between chapters 4 and 5 for an interchapter from writing center scholar Neal Lerner, who shares thoughts on the roles of qualitative and quantitative data in writing center assessment. In "Of Numbers and Stories: Quantitative and Qualitative Assessment Research in the Writing Center," Neal shows that each kind of data has an important role to play as we learn about our centers' work and communicate what we learn to others.

The book returns to the very practical work of assessment with chapter 5, "Integrating Assessment into Your Center's Other Work: Not Your Typical Methods Chapter," and grapples with two common stumbling blocks: determining which methods to use in gathering information for your assessment and figuring out how to work assessment into the already busy life of directing a writing center. Although this chapter does not provide a silver bullet to solving either issue—so much of assessment, we keep saying, is context-dependent—we intend for this chapter to help you align methods of data collection and analysis to the priorities of the writing center rather than seeming like a labor-intensive layer of bureaucracy that masks the "real work" of that center. Ideally, assessment work *is* or will become some of the "real work" every center does.

Chapter 6, "Writing It Up and Using It," seemed the right way to bring our practical advice to closure. Providing specific strategies for writing effective assessment reports, it shows that the process and the finished products themselves, enable WCDs to do other kinds of work more efficiently and effectively as well as to strive for excellence.

We have an afterword from Brian Huot, an expert in writing assessment and a veteran WCD, and Nicole Caswell, a new scholar in writing assessment, about what it means for assessment work to be rooted at once in the practical and the theoretical. In "Translating Assessment," they show how assessment is scholarly, professional work that positions writing center directors as leaders on campus.

We provide some last observations about writing center assessment work in the "Coda." The idea of a coda, not unlike the discussions of "what comes next" at the end of a writing tutorial, invites readers to think about writing center assessment through lenses that are not strictly related to our field. We reflect on the leadership issues inherent in doing writing center assessment well.

We suspect that readers may have very different reasons for picking up this book. You may be motivated by curiosity. You may be worried because an accreditation visitor is coming to your campus soon. You may have questions about your writing center's work that counting simply will not answer. We hope that this book's combination of theoretical and practical approaches to writing center assessment will help you to construct assessments that are useful to your particular needs at this moment.

To put it plainly, we want to discuss writing center assessment with you—its political and oftentimes problematic role in the university; its process as an articulation of values; its products as written reports; and its occasion for strategic planning. Most importantly, we share how we think assessment isn't something to fear but is something to embrace, because it holds great promise in helping you—the WCD—discover your writing center's potential and exceed it.

REFERENCES

Adler-Kassner, Linda, and Peggy O'Neill. 2010. *Reframing Writing Assessment to Improve Teaching and Learning.* Logan: Utah State University Press.

Huot, Brian. 1996. "Toward a New Theory of Writing Assessment." *College Composition and Communication* 47 (4): 549–66.

O'Neill, Peggy, Ellen Schendel, and Brian Huot. 2002. "Defining Assessment as Research: Moving from Obligations to Opportunities." *Writing Program Administration* 26 (1/2): 10–26.

1

THE DEVELOPMENT OF SCHOLARSHIP ABOUT WRITING CENTER ASSESSMENT[1]

William J. Macauley, Jr.

After most of the writing center assessment workshops, sessions, and talks Ellen and I have done together, participants have shared their high levels of frustration with not finding scholarship to support assessing their writing centers. Coupled with the increasing assessment pressure that so many writing center directors (WCDs) are feeling, these worries have only escalated. Workshop participants have often found little scholarship on writing center assessment in the usual library databases. Another concern is that the scholarship on writing center assessment is interesting but doesn't really answer the right questions. These frustrations make writing center assessment increasingly problematic, even as the pressure mounts to develop, conduct, and complete meaningful writing center assessment.

If we step back from these particular conversations, though, this has been a field-wide issue for some time. In fact, the frustration and confusion surrounding writing center assessment has been a concern for WCDs for several decades. Back in 1982, Janice Neulieb pointed out that the first problem in evaluating a writing center is that:

> there is no established method for going about the evaluation. . . . The director is faced with the prospect of creating a new research design that somehow anticipates all the possible questions that will be asked by those who read the finished report. (227)

This is apparently still true for many WCDs. Assuming that the concerns Ellen and I have heard directors voice are at least minimally representative, it seems as though the field has not yet overcome this problem.

---

1. Any reference not included in the bibliography at the end of this chapter can be found in the annotated bibliography at the end of the book.

In fact, because WCDs are now moving out into their campuses and participating in institutional discussions and decision making, this limitation is more frustrating and becomes a higher stakes issue for the center and its director. Inexperience with assessment also becomes "a weakness" in the director that is easier for others to see. Making the right assessment choices seems even more important now that assessment is more than a campus conversation but also a public and political one.

However, there actually is quite a bit of writing center assessment information that directors can use to educate themselves and think through their own assessment plans and procedures. Thirty years ago, Mary Lamb (1981) surveyed all of the writing centers she could find (120 at that point) in order to find out what assessment practices were most frequently in use. She identified basic counting, questionnaires, pre-/post-tests, external evaluation, and professional staff publication/ activity as the most frequent writing center assessment methods, findings that share a great deal in common with the bulk of practices we hear and read about today. A year later, Joyce S. Steward and Mary K. Croft, in *The Writing Laboratory: Organization, Management, and Methods* (1982), wrote:

> A lab director can choose from several kinds of evaluation: internal (reactions of tutors and tutees), school or campus-wide (reactions of referring faculty and departments), and external (use of a professional consultant); and can collect data through questionnaires, surveys, interviews, discussions, and case studies. (92)

Stephen North (1984), only two years later, argued that "writing center research has not, for the most part, been formal inquiry by which we might test our assumptions. It has tended to fall, instead, into one of three categories," which North identified as "reflections on experience," "speculation," and "survey" or questionnaire-based methods (24–5). James H. Bell (2000) reiterated this critique more than a decade later: "Writing centers should conduct more *sophisticated* evaluations" (7, emphasis original). While North named three specific methods that seemed to dominate writing center research in the 1980s, Bell's comments in 2000 suggest that the sophistication of writing center research methods had not progressed. Reflections, speculations, and surveys may have become so familiar, so commonplace, that their appropriateness or limitations aren't even questioned anymore. And these common understandings among professionals in the field may have removed the need to explain why these methods figure so prominently in the way we track the successes of our centers and push our centers to grow and change. For the WCD trying to understand and choose assessment methods, the absence of such discussions only complicates an already significant set of challenges. Likewise, there may be little scholarship that helps even a seasoned WCD articulate the "why" behind assessment choices. This omission is especially problematic when the audience is people outside of the writing center who receive, read, or act on writing center assessment reportage.

But the field's blind spot may not be borne out of simple familiarity. A number of scholars have also pointed to quantitative reluctance and inexperience as limitations on writing center assessment (J. Bell 2000; Donnelli and Garrison 2003; Field-Pickering 1993; Henson and Stephenson 2009). Frequently cited among these scholars is Cindy Johanek's 2000 book, *Composing Research: A Contextualist Paradigm for Composition and Rhetoric*, where she argues that researchers in composition studies tend to appreciate narrative and literary types of research methods over quantitative ones. In addition, Johanek writes, numbers rouse math anxiety and are too frequently accompanied by dry writing that argues from a position of objectivity that few in our field would support or accept. In Peter Carino and Doug Enders's "Does Frequency of Visits to the Writing Center Increase Student Satisfaction? A Statistical Correlation Study——or Story" (2001), the authors claim that their statistical research enabled them to "stop fearing numbers and love the interpretation of them," and celebrate that change as a significant shift in their thinking and work (83). Even so, within that same article, they note some concern that their writing could become dry or boring because of the introduction of numbers and statistical analyses. Who wants to produce that kind of writing?

Luke Niiler (2005) comments, "Our field needs to complement its abundantly rich qualitative research with work that can be transferred from one site to another," proposing the kind of formal inquiry that North discussed in Gary Olson's *Writing Centers: Theory and Administration* (1984) (14). Niiler goes on to suggest, "Perhaps statistically grounded research will begin to move us in that direction" (14). Given that North also called for more sophisticated methods of inquiry (formal, transferable) more than twenty-five years ago, it is somewhat disheartening that current researchers are still hoping to see that development. But it's not hopeless. Writing center scholars have at least come to acknowledge that quantitative methods can support and/or complement qualitative assessment practices. Johanek writes:

> Numbers alone won't reveal everything we need to know. Stories alone can't do it, either. But, when researchers stop defining their work by method only . . . then the full power of any data, be it story or number, will truly blossom into the knowledge our field seeks and the discipline we hope to become. (209)

For the new-to-assessment director, these circumstances create a real problem. As thinkers and researchers who largely came up through the academy within composition studies, literary studies, or allied fields, our field's preferences for literary, narrative, and qualitative methods may be very strong. However, it seems as though the primary qualitative methods available for writing center assessment may be so fossilized within the field that the scholarship no longer explicitly articulates their foundations. We don't see detailed discussions of why firsthand experience should be such an integral part of a scholarly argument in writing center research. Scholars in our field seem to feel quite comfortable with speculation as an outcome of research, and there are only a handful of published articles that demonstrate continued inquiry that moves beyond speculation. There is no denying the prominence of survey- or questionnaire-based inquiry in writing centers, even though the limitations of these methods are clear. In short, informed choices among qualitative methods for writing center assessment may be hard to come by. Quantitative methods may be no better an option. Our collective resistance to them is undeniable, and many WCDs are not trained in these particular data-gathering methods or analyses.

FINDING RESOURCES USEFUL TO BUILDING WRITING CENTER ASSESSMENTS

And yet, despite the present conversation about writing center assessment focusing on what we may not know, a simple Google search for the phrase "writing center assessment" reveals a wide range of writing center assessments being done at a variety of institutions. Our lack of expertise or familiarity with numerical research has not stopped us from generating assessment data. Of the seventy relevant hits generated by that Google search, the first thing that becomes apparent is the variety of venues sponsoring conversations about writing center assessment. The Web provides information on institutes/conferences focusing on writing center assessment ("East Central"; "2011 Summer Institute"; "MAWCA 2011") as well as special interest groups at other conferences (Ballard), descriptions of individual workshops (Caswell and Werner), and materials supporting those presentations (Law).

One might also be surprised by the variety of writing center assessment documents available online, which WCDs can adapt to their own contexts and purposes:

- Entire writing center assessment plans ("Caldwell Community College"; Paoli, Silver, and Koster; "The University Writing Center (UWC)"; "University Writing Center Assessment Plan"),

- Examples of writing center assessment reports (Andrews and Kelly-Riley; Modey; Smith and Talavera; "Assessment Report"; "University Writing Center, University of Wisconsin-Platteville"),

- Combined plans/reports ("Institutional Support Area Assessment Report"; Copas; "Salt Lake Community College").

- A number of other less-familiar writing center assessment documents include a tutor self-assessment form ("Tutor Self-Assessment Form"), a program outcomes assessment worksheet ("Program Outcomes Assessment Worksheet"), a writing center assignment sheet that invites professors to articulate their goals and objectives for assignments that students will bring to the writing center ("Writing Center Assignment Sheet"), and a heuristic for developing writing center assessment plans (Lerner and Kail, "Heuristic").

There are also a variety of materials intended only as digital texts that can help directors shape their thinking about assessment approaches and the instruments and methods used to collect assessment data. One of the most prominent of these digital resources is The Peer Writing Tutor Alumni Research Project website (see appendix to this volume), which assesses the long-term impacts of working as a peer writing tutor as well as invites writing centers and writing center alums from all over the world to contribute to the growing data available through the project (Kail, Gillespie, and Hughes). Another valuable digital resource is the Writing Centers Research Project, housed at the University of Louisville's website. It includes results from several international surveys of writing centers as well as data about director salaries, tutor wages, number of sessions conducted per year, and other basic information about writing centers that can help directors with benchmarking data. The journals *Praxis*, *Writing Lab Newsletter*, and *Writing Center Journal* all have web presences, and simple searches at those websites will reveal a number of scholarly articles about writing center theory and practice. The University of Wisconsin–Madison Writing Center provides a series of podcasts on writing center assessment (three including Harry Denny and Lori Salem and one including Jill Pennington, Neal Lerner, and Jason Mayland).

And there are a host of useful bibliographic resources, as well. A wiki on writing center assessment was started through Wikia ("Writing Center Assessment Wiki"), and the Northern California Writing Centers Association provides a discussion forum on writing center assessment that includes a useful bibliography (Griffin and Dennen). A particularly thorough resource is Neal Lerner and Harvey Kail's "Writing Center Assessment Bibliography," which is both annotated and available online. Their annotations provide insight into not just the content of the included sources but also the historical significance and unique qualities of pieces that can be useful in connecting writing center assessment to other fields. "A Selected Bibliography on Empirical Writing Center Research," available at the International Writing Centers Association (IWCA) website, although not focused specifically on assessment, does bring together in one place a wide variety of research methods and discussions that are immediately relevant to writing center assessment. Lerner's "Dissertations and Theses on Writing Centers" and the "IWCA Bibliography of Resources for Writing Center Professionals" could also be mined for useful and relevant scholarship. Finally, a thorough (maybe *the* most thorough) annotated bibliography on writing centers is Christina Murphy, Joe Law, and Steve Sherwood's *Writing Centers: An Annotated Bibliography* (1996), a collection of more than 1,400 entries, which includes a section focused specifically on writing centers research. Although these bibliographies may not be entirely up to date, they provide discussions of evaluation, research, and scholarship in writing centers that can be readily adapted to current writing center assessment purposes. The connections these resources make to other fields and areas of study can be very informative for writing centers and their assessment, as well.

However, while all of these online sources and bibliographies include materials that can be very useful to WCDs, the concerns raised earlier still hold. Without some access to foundational ideas informing writing center assessment, much of this literature can seem only remotely relevant or useful. How to build a coherent, workable assessment plan that draws on these various methods is what seems to be lacking. Without a strong foundation in the goals, options, and processes for planning, implementing, and reporting on assessment, making sense of the rich resources already available is a challenge. There is no doubt that writing program assessment, educational assessment, and writing assessment more broadly defined have a lot to offer WCDs, but without deliberate guidance that is grounded in writing center theory, pedagogy, and practice, these adjacent fields remain provocative but remote for the new writing center assessor.

A TAXONOMY OF WRITING CENTER ASSESSMENT RESOURCES

As my search for writing center assessment resources unfolded, three general types of sources emerged. The first category includes "context" pieces. Scholarship in this group works to provide some sort of larger idea related to composition studies (loosely defined) that can support and inform writing center assessment. The second category consists of "connections" pieces; articles and chapters in this group focus on what other fields and disciplines have to offer writing center assessment. The third category is made up of "methods" pieces that focus on the nuts and bolts of writing center assessment—research articles that demonstrate methods that would be useful for collecting information as part of a writing center assessment.

As I read everything I could about writing center assessment, I put each piece into one of these categories. When each of the categories was fully populated—in other words, when each article and chapter had been distributed to a scholarship category—an interesting phenomenon emerged. About half of the pieces included in this review were methods pieces. These pieces were often research articles whose relevance to this review were the processes and methods they described for gathering or analyzing data, rather than an explicit focus on writing center assessment. The next largest grouping was context pieces. Finally, the pieces "connecting" with other fields formed the smallest group.

My strategy for taxonomizing the literature on writing center assessment is by no means the only way of characterizing the themes of this scholarship. However, because I defined the context and connections categories much more broadly than the methods category, I would have expected comparatively fewer methods pieces when compared with context, connections, or context and connections combined. Be that as it may, the distribution I found does roughly support the larger argument being made here: that the literature relevant to writing center assessment does offer a great deal of information on methods while there is much less on context or connections. In other words, the literature available to writing center assessment does not seem as focused on "global" discussions as it does on the "local." An overemphasis on the local and anecdotal is not a new criticism of writing centers research and scholarship, but it does make clearer why the new-to-assessment WCD might find the literature disembodied, decontextualized, not readily transferrable to his or her own writing center.

Scholarship That Works to Contextualize Writing Center Assessment

Context scholarship can be very helpful in any kind of research and literature review; writing center assessment is no exception. What may be unusual is the combined questions of how far outside of the field one wishes to go and which "outside" holds the greatest promise. This review limits contextual discussions to that scholarship found within writing or composition studies because these are the most readily comparable contexts for any writing center work.

If one were looking for a detailed history of writing assessment as an industry, there would be no finer choice than Norbert Elliott's *On a Scale: A Social History of Writing Assessment in America* (2005). This book chronicles the rise of psychometrics and its intersection with writing assessment in the United States. Most interesting may be the discussion of aptitude testing for military service around World War I. Elliott's book allows a potential writing center assessor to make much more informed choices, especially when she feels pushed to use quantitative methods or standardized tests. The knowledge made available here can be very useful in making methodological choices in the richest possible way. Patricia Lynne's *Coming to Terms: A Theory of Writing Assessment* (2004) provides a scaled-down historical overview while challenging the influence of positivism, particularly the concepts of reliability and validity, on the development of current writing assessment. Lynne's work makes compelling arguments for a humanistic approach to assessment that does not uncritically default to quantitative or standardized methods. Although not directly focused on writing center assessment, these two books can help a writing center assessor to consider/discuss where quantitative methods come from and argue more articulately for assessment measures that are reflective of writing centers' theoretical traditions.

Several other sources are also useful in contextualizing writing center assessment, even while their scope is more focused. Marie C. Paretti and Katrina M. Powell's *Assessment of Writing* (2009) provides a broad discussion of the issues and concerns influencing and shaping writing assessment including assessing writing across the curriculum and the use of electronic portfolios. Brian Huot's *(Re)Articulating Writing Assessment for Teaching and Learning* (2002) builds a functional, rational, and applicable new paradigm for writing assessment, the principles of which resonate easily and meaningfully with writing centers and their assessment. Huot argues that "any writing assessment theory will need to be considered a work in progress as new procedures and the theories that inform them continue to advance our theoretical and practical understanding of writing assessment" (105). So even as Huot articulates that writing assessment must be site-based, locally controlled, context-sensitive, rhetorically based, and accessible, he also acknowledges that we make the path as we walk it. This is a particularly engaging perspective for WCDs who are looking to begin assessing their centers. In a lot of ways, this book meets the folks who have shown up at our writing center assessment workshops where they are, eager to get started and looking for a guide.

Willa Wolcott and Sue M. Legg's *An Overview of Writing Assessment: Theory, Research, and Practice* (1998) is a discussion of writing assessment methods most popular at the end of the 1990s. What is most useful here is the selection of specific, popular methods that can be easily adapted to writing center assessment, along with detailed discussions of each methodology. In each section, the method is described, explained, and illustrated thoroughly. Eleven years later, Peggy O'Neill, Cindy Moore, and Brian Huot published *A Guide to College Writing Assessment* (2009), which focuses less on individual methods, pays more attention to programmatic contexts and assessment situations, and provides a full complement of writing assessment documents as appendices. For the WCD ready to select methods, these can be useful resources. These books include a great deal of useful discussion of specific methods and their applications so, as a general resource for WCDs, they can be useful. At the same time, these sources are not written specifically for WCDs; thus, they are somewhat removed from our work, revealing a gap between the larger discussion of writing and writing program assessment and the specific work of writing centers.

In many ways, Bob Broad's *What We Really Value: Beyond Rubrics in the Teaching and Assessing of Writing* (2003) makes a plain argument: we need a new, more sensitive and context-specific way to think about writing assessment. Broad argues for what he calls DCM or "dynamic criteria mapping." Responding particularly to the predominance of rubrics in writing assessment—and by extension the desire to use them in a one size-fits-all manner—Broad lays out a process for something of an emergent design/constant-comparison process that allows writing assessors to not only critically analyze writing but continually develop more specific and accurate criteria for that process. For a WCD, reading about how results of an assessment feed back into an understanding of writing more generally can be useful in the reconception of writing center assessment as an opportunity for sustained, meaningful knowledge creation.

Other writing and writing program assessment scholarship turns its attention to issues other than methodology. In their 2010 article, "Responsibility and Composition's Future in the Twenty-first Century: Reframing 'Accountability,'" Linda Adler-Kassner and Susanmarie Harrington concentrate on destigmatizing writing assessment by rethinking the purposes that frame it. Instead of assessment being high-stakes accountability that can carry with it so many liabilities and hazy outcomes, these authors argue that a shift in our thinking can put us—those informed about composition and writing-related programs—back into a role that we can work with. Rather than thinking of ourselves as victims of assessment, we can instead become the informed drivers of writing-related assessment. These reframing efforts are extended and continued in Adler-Kassner and O'Neill's recent *Reframing Writing Assessment to Improve Teaching and Learning* (2010). While these sources argue for a more meaningful understanding of assessment, Cornelius Cosgrove, in his 2010 article, "What Our Graduates Write: Making Program Assessment Both Authentic and Persuasive," argues that we should be training our graduate students to write about the questions and issues that matter most to us, and in ways that make those discussions accessible to audiences outside of our immediate areas. Together these pieces make a cohesive argument for our taking on a more decisive, empowered role in writing center assessment.

Chris W. Gallagher's "What Do WPAs Need to Know about Writing Assessment? An Immodest Proposal" (2009) argues for another form of responsibility by articulating what he thinks every administrator of a writing-related program should know about assessment. Tacit in his argument is that we who are charged with this work must prepare ourselves responsibly for assessment. That kind of preparation leads to understanding some of the traps in which others have been snared. Edward White's "Language and Reality in Writing Assessment" (1990) helps assessors to understand one of those snares when he describes the deep differentiations between educational assessment and writing assessment. Meanwhile, a responsible writing center assessor must consider the substantial difference White often argues for between writing programs and writing centers, throughout his work, in order to appreciate appropriately his body of scholarship.

In addition to these books and articles, there are a number of other resources that survey the literature related to writing center assessment and can help orient directors. For instance, Terese Thonus has generated a number of useful articles related to non-native English speakers (NNES) working in writing centers. One of the most useful is also one of the most focused. In 2004, Thonus published a meta-analysis of NNES writer studies that used discourse analysis as their primary methodology. Casey Jones (2001) did a similar analysis of the literature on the impact of writing centers on writing improvement. Although Lerner's 2003 chapter in Michael A. Pemberton and Joyce Kincaid's *The Center Will Hold* is not a typical literature review, "Writing Center Assessment: Searching for the 'Proof' of Our Effectiveness" creates a rich context for current writing center assessment by providing historical context, discussion of earlier assessment work, and specific examples of current writing center assessment efforts. As one takes on the responsibility of writing center assessment, the rewards of consulting this type of scholarship can be a great support and help to avoid the foibles others have already experienced. In some ways, although there are few pieces of this type focused specifically on writing center assessment, those that do exist can help to create the kind of context that so many writing center assessors need for useful, meaningful, and informed choices about their assessment plans and methods.

However one might choose to approach writing center assessment, no matter the methods chosen or plans made, the front-end decisions in the process can be some of the most important. Scholarship on writing, writing center, and writing program assessment offers important advice on these issues. Asao Inoue, in "Engaging with Assessment Technologies: Responding to Valuing Diversity as a WPA" (2010), makes a convincing argument that writing assessors can be more sensitive to issues of diversity by carefully considering the biases that assessment technologies (methods, etc.) inhere. Gallagher's 2010 article, "Assess Locally, Validate

Globally: Heuristics for Validating Local Writing Assessments," provides a set of heuristics for writing assessment—guidelines that enable assessors to think beyond the assessment itself and toward the outcomes and decisions that might be made based on those assessments. This kind of through-put thinking can help to keep an assessment on track and to minimize drift.

There is no shortage of scholarship that works to help assessors move away from defensive assessment postures and toward more productive orientations; Gallagher's 2011 article, "Being There: (Re)Making the Assessment Scene," argues exactly this from a Burkean perspective. In terms of writing center assessment specifically, Nancy Grimm's 2003 chapter in *The Center Will Hold*, "In the Spirit of Service: Making Writing Center Research a 'Featured Character,'" argues that we must shift away from research that explains writing centers and toward research that focuses on the writer in context. Steve Sherwood's 1993 article, "How to Survive the Hard Times," is an argument aligned with Grimm's that discusses proactive assessment as a way of being ready when budget cuts seem eminent. Together these authors argue that we gain a great deal by working more proactively with writing center assessment and stand to lose a great deal if we continue in familiar, comfortable patterns.

Many articles and chapters also focus on more specific assessment interests—targeted to a specific aspect of a writing center's work. Tara Cushman, et al.'s "Using Focus Groups to Assess Writing Center Effectiveness" (1995) concentrates on focus groups as an assessment method. In a 1968 conference address titled *Evaluation as Enlightenment for Decision-Making*, Daniel Stufflebeam, who worked in educational assessment, proposed CIPP, a systematic series of assessments that examine context, input, process, and product. This is a resource that many writing center assessors might appreciate as a way to develop long-term plans. There are other arguments to be made about what a writing center assessment can enable, as opposed to what it should be providing or creating. Law and Murphy's "Formative Assessment and the Paradigms of Writing Center Practice" (1997) makes a compelling argument for the writing center as a site for investigating student writing processes in action. Carol Severino's "The Writing Center as Site for Cross-Language Research" (1994) argues that the writing center is a vital site for writing center and second-language researchers to not only collaborate but learn from one another's accumulated disciplinary knowledge and research methods. Isabelle Thompson's "Writing Center Assessment:

Why and a Little How" (2006) even goes so far as to argue that imposed writing center assessment can "bring us to the table" of institutional assessment. Along with this invitation comes a caution: counting visits simply won't be enough. Thompson provides a model for the development of writing center assessment plans that could help make the move away from basic counting. She provides a working taxonomy of writing program assessments that foregrounds her guiding the reader through the development of an assessment plan. Following that, she provides detailed discussions of putting writing centers' usual counting practices to good use, using comparative studies as writing center assessment, and sampling methods that would enable very different types of assessment outcomes.

In all of these cases, scholars argue for and provide ideas that help us to see writing center assessment from another perspective, whether a larger context or a specific point of contact. All of them draw on a deliberate selection of resources and experiences to characterize writing assessment in a unique way, toward developing a deeper understanding of what it is and has been. Their only shortcoming, for our purposes, is this: when they do focus specifically on writing centers, they tend to do so from an abstract and relatively distant theoretical vantage point. For the WCD, the missing context remains problematic here. So while these kinds of big-picture discussions can be useful, they remain somewhat removed from actual writing center assessment theory, knowledge, work, and practices.

Scholarship That Connects Writing Centers to Other Campus and Public Communities

While the scholarship outlined above helps to paint a big picture for writing center assessment, other pieces have focused on connections that writing centers have or could have with the rest of the university community. Colleen Connolly, et al's "Erika and the Fish Lamps" (2003) focuses on the changing physical space of one writing center, examining specifically how tutors' decorations of the writing center reveal something about their conceptualizations of the writing center's relationship to the rest of the university. More to the point, Connolly and her colleagues question whether the writing center's physical appearance is a rejection or reflection of the larger university. In very real terms, this is a question of the connections between the writing center and others. This piece is somewhat unique among the connections pieces because it is not about what relationships with others can/might do for writing centers or vice versa. Instead, it is about how the staff of one writing center displayed their (changing) ideas about their center's connection to the rest of the university through the ways that they constructed their writing center environment. Although there have been a number of pieces published on writing centers' physical spaces, this is one of the few I could find that assessed the physical space of the center as an inward reflection.

Karen Rodis's "Mending the Damaged Path: How to Avoid Conflict of Expectation When Setting up a Writing Center" (1990) discusses an essential and deceivingly complex question: Do we want to use writing center assessment to confirm or counter the expectations of others? In some ways, Rodis's questions are part of the larger discussion provided by Robert W. Barnett in "Redefining Our Existence: An Argument for Short- and Long-term Goals and Objectives" (1997), which argues for statements of goals and objectives because they can be useful in demonstrating commonality with other constituencies on campus and developing shared mission statements and objectives.

Other scholarship extends these kinds of ideas. John N. Gardner, Betsy O. Barefoot, and Randy I. Swing's *Guidelines for Evaluating the First-Year Experience at Four-Year Colleges* (2001) provides a list of questions that could easily be used by WCDs working toward supporting the first-year experience on their campuses. As acknowledged in both Phillip E. Beal and Lee Noel's *What Works In Student Retention: The Report of a Joint Project of the American College Testing Program and the National Center for Higher Education Management Systems* (1980) and Gary Griswold's "Writing Centers: The Student Retention Connection" (2003), there is a great deal of common ground for writing centers and retention efforts, and awareness of those commonalities can be very useful in designing writing center assessments. Other scholars have focused on the ways that writing centers prepare future educators. For example, Irene Clark's "Preparing Future Composition Teachers in the Writing Center" (1988) shows that writing center work provides developing teachers with insights into student writing that no other context does; the savvy WCD would be mindful of these connections in deciding which directions to take in documenting assessments relating to tutor training programs and peer tutors' experiences on the job. Still other pieces focus on teacher evaluation, such as Clyde Moneyhun does in "Performance Evaluation as Faculty Development" (2009). The relationships between teaching and tutoring are extended when the kind of open, community-developed teacher evaluation practices advocated by Moneyhun—specifically, the shared development of evaluation criteria and procedures designed to enable continued development rather than punish flaws—are considered as writing center assessment methods.

Perhaps the most important connection a WCD can make is with his or her own field. "NWCA [now IWCA] News from Joan Mullin, President" (1997), argues that, no matter how much WCDs wish it to be otherwise, writing center assessment happens within institutional contexts that include a wide array of values that both cohere and contrast with our own. This was much less of an issue when writing centers remained marginalized, but things are changing. We have to find ways of successfully engaging with our colleagues and the rest of our campus communities. Rather than surrender to assessment efforts that do not reflect our values, Mullin argues that WCDs must find ways of bringing their own values, evidence, and methods to the fore.

Mullin makes a compelling argument that can bring clarity to the work of writing center assessment: finding and acting on the possible connections to be made with other disciplines, other campus offices and programs, and other research traditions. In essence, Mullin argues that we must take *to* those relationships no less than we intend to take *from* them. By contrast, William Yahner's 1993 article, "Explaining and Justifying Writing Centers: One MORE Example," focuses on using writing center data to develop and make cogent arguments about the value and impact of the writing center. He seems to suggest that we should bring *more* than we take.

Writing centers work from their own histories, bodies of knowledge, and values; they have something to offer others. WCDs must carry this knowledge into working collaborations with others. If the WCD does not have this knowledge—cannot connect the field's assessment values, methods, or practices with the research of other fields—he or she cannot be a full collaborator. Thus, these discussions of connections are meaningful in terms of possibility for the new-to-assessment WCD, and they certainly provide a sense of the scope of assessment commonalities there can be with other fields and programs. Meanwhile, these potential connections also bring into sharp focus how necessary it is for WCDs to have a solid foundation within their own field and to adapt that foundation to multiple, varied contexts and collaborations.

Scholarship That Connects Writing Center Assessment with Research Methods

Jaime Hylton published "Evaluating the Writing Lab: How Do We Know That We Are Helping?" in 1990 and presented a useful argument relative to writing center assessment methods: "The goal of program evaluation is to provide data for informed decision-making. . . . It addresses the need for accountability within the University and provides feedback" (6). Part of that informedness is the thoughtful selection of research methods. Again, the new-to-assessment WCD is at a decided disadvantage in this regard; even the more experienced WCD can find these decisions difficult because there are no discipline-wide protocols for assessment or consistent research traditions that would be easily adapted to assessment.

Writing center scholars have provided some guidance, however, in how WCDs might think about assessment. In "Conducting Research in the Writing Lab" (1982), Harvey Kail and Kay Allen provide a wonderful walk-through of the methodology decisions a director might make, sharing important differentiations among exploratory, experimental, case study, and survey-based research. However, by and large, methods pieces did not provide nearly as much discussion of "why" as they did "how" and "what happened." That said, the variety of methods scholarship found in this review is extensive and, thereby, worthy of further discussion.

One group of methods articles and chapters tended to focus on sequences of research or assessment activities, versus focusing on individual practices. Matthew Ortoleva and Jeremiah Dyehouse's "SWOT Analysis: An Instrument for Writing Center Strategic Planning" (2008) discusses the role of analyzing the writing center's strengths, weaknesses, opportunities, and threats in a program assessment. The results of this kind of analysis can foreground meaningful writing center assessment choices by providing both focuses and context. Bené Scanlon Cox's "Priorities and Guidelines for the Development of Writing Centers: A Delphi Study" (1984) describes a survey-based research project that used the Delphi technique to achieve "expert consensus on ranked priorities for future planning of writing centers and to construct guidelines for establishing new writing centers and developing existing ones," which involves a series of increasingly focused surveys and/or questionnaires (77). David Hodgdon's "Assessing a High School Writing Center: A Trek into the Frontiers of Program Evaluation" (1990) deployed

Stufflebeam's CIPP protocol (discussed above) to develop a multifaceted assessment plan for understanding the overall quality of the writing center from multiple perspectives. A thorough plan that includes multiple stages of assessment is one approach, and there are other ways to use an iterative strategy to great effect.

Another group of articles and chapters took the idea of iterative assessment in another direction. Instead of focusing on a comprehensive plan for assessment or research, these pieces argued instead for multiple, small-scale assessments that together point toward more holistic understandings of what is being assessed, in this case writing centers. James Beebe's "Basic Concepts and Techniques of Rapid Appraisal" (1995) argues for multiple, small-scale assessments based in systems assessment, which means using a range of independent assessment methods to both understand individual features of a writing center and develop a more informed sense of the whole. Malcolm Hayward's use of surveys in "Assessing Attitudes Towards The Writing Center" (1983) was designed around understanding multiple perspectives on the teaching and tutoring of writing. Beth Kalikoff's "From Coercion to Collaboration: A Mosaic Approach to Writing Center Assessment" (2001) argues that there is a richness of information and many more opportunities to engage with potential collaborators from outside of the center when a "mosaic" strategy is used, as opposed to single or dual assessment methods. Jon Olson, Dawn J. Moyer, and Adelia Falda's "Student-Centered Assessment Research in the Writing Center" (2002) takes this idea of multiple assessment activities in yet another direction, deploying a "rapid assessment process" (described in detail by Beebe) that involves multiple assessors working as a team, focusing their attention in distinctly different areas. The takeaway here is the idea that multiple smaller assessments may not only be easier to manage but also more informative when they are brought together.

Among the methods included in such multi-pronged assessment plans are those that focus on students in the center. Authors like Anne DiPardo (1992) make effective use of case studies. Historically, case studies have been popular methods in both writing and writing center research. However, other student-focused methods have also developed. Cathy Leaker and Heather Ostman's "Composing Knowledge: Writing, Rhetoric, and Reflection in Prior Learning Assessment" (2010) focuses on assessing students' prior learning as part of a larger effort to understand how writers negotiate their discursive places within institutions of higher learning; certainly, the writing center is a most appropriate space for just these kinds of negotiations. Beth Rapp Young and Barbara A. Fritzsche, in "Writing Center Users Procrastinate Less: The Relationship between Individual Differences in Procrastination, Peer Feedback, and Student Writing Success" (2002), pursued the relationship between writing center use and procrastination and found that writing center users do procrastinate less. This article demonstrates a smart use of correlation methods to answer an interesting question. Julie Bauer Morrison and Jean-Paul Nadeau, in "How Was Your Session at the Writing Center? Pre- and Post-Grade Student Evaluations" (2003), move in yet another direction, working to clarify the impact of grades on tutorial satisfaction. The students' initial ratings of writing center tutorials was not related to grades while students' perceptions of their writing center tutorials did change after their graded papers were returned.

Researchers who focus on students in the writing center have chosen other emphases as well. David Roberts's "A Study of Writing Center Effectiveness" (1988) compared the impact of group (classroom) instruction with the impact of individual (tutorial) instruction on student writing improvement and found that classroom instruction may have been more effective in "promoting syntactic maturity" (57). Stephen Newman, in "Demonstrating Effectiveness" (1999), found that students who used the writing center had significantly lower SAT and ACT scores than those who did not, even while students who used the writing center were much less likely to earn failing grades in first-year composition (FYC) courses when compared with those who did not use the writing center.

Students visiting the writing center are not the only students impacted by the work of the center. Scholarship also investigates the impact of writing centers on peer writing tutors. Steve Whitney's "Down and Dirty Assessment" (1997) argues that peer tutors can become essential informed participants for writing centers assessment through activities completed during tutor training, which can be used to develop both short- and long-term planning. Moneyhun's protocol for shared development of evaluation practices and processes (mentioned earlier) could certainly be used to engage peer tutors as more formal assessment participants by asking them to participate directly in the evaluation of the writing center staff, including the faculty and professional staff who direct their centers. Olson, Moyer, and Falda (also mentioned earlier) formalized the roles of peer tutors as writing center researchers by inviting them to participate in rapid assessment teams that looked at writing center activities from multiple perspectives.

Students are significant participants in writing centers and writing centers assessment, but they are not the only assessable features of a writing center. There is always a text of some sort, in some stage of development, and many writing center researchers have focused their attention there. Nancy McCracken, in "Evaluation/Accountability for the Writing Lab" (1979), focused her attention on error analysis through pre- and post-testing as a measure of the influence of the writing center. Niiler's "The Numbers Speak: A Pre-Test of Writing Center Outcomes Using Statistical Analysis" (2003) used numerical rating and statistical analyses to identify changes in student writing before and after tutorials, when students could decide whether to use the center. Jessica Williams, in "Tutoring and Revision: Second Language Writers in the Writing Center" (2004), focused this kind of research specifically on NNES writers working in writing tutorials, finding that directive methods were more successful for sentence-level revisions with English-language learners.

One of the significant variables in Niiler's 2003 study was student perceptions of the writing center. Students decided whether to use the writing center based on the grades they had earned on a particular paper, based in no small part on their perceptions of what the writing center was and what impact it might have. These perceptions can be an important part of writing center assessment, and they are not limited to students. Both Rodis (1990) and Thonus (2001) used multiple perspectives to focus their studies specifically on perceptions of writing center and writing tutor roles, respectively. These studies found that institutional constructions of writing centers and writing tutor roles (whether constructed for or by the writing center) can create dissonance for writers. This dissonance can interfere with effective writing center work when the contrast is too great.

Perception has other implications as well. When Carol Severino, Jeffrey Swenson, and Jia Zhu (2009) compared native-speaker requests for help in online environments with those of NNES, they found differences that they could act on, that they could respond to, that they could feed back into their centers. Thonus (2002) worked with a similar idea and a different focus; she analyzed the discourse within tutorials themselves to both understand what the talk was like in tutorials with NNES students and to identify which discursive practices seemed most helpful.

MAKING SENSE OF IT ALL

My overall perception of this larger body of scholarship on and related to writing center assessment has changed significantly over time. Where I assumed a dearth of information, I now see an abundance of information, methods, and influences. Where I had assumed that this abundance of scholarship was sufficient, I now recognize key and missing characteristics. Within this corpus that considers students, texts, tutors, centers, and perceptions, there are two small segments of the scholarship that are of particular note, despite their small numbers. The first of these two groups includes research that not only reports on research but also demonstrates clear efforts toward improved methods. These kinds of studies are of particular use for new-to-assessment directors. They not only describe a process and show what that process can do as a research methodology, but they also demonstrate why and how directors might continue to develop methods as their thinking becomes more focused and their focuses become clearer.

Many WCDs use satisfaction surveys, and when the data come back consistently high, the directors accept that their centers are succeeding. However, these kinds of results, though useful and appreciated, don't allow the director to continue to develop the writing center from those data. Linda Ringer Leff (1997) took this as a weakness in her own assessment tool and developed a more discriminating questionnaire that would give her something to work with in improving the writing center. Two changes developed from her revised survey: training tutors to be less directive and to be tougher in their responses to student writing. The revised questionnaire allowed Leff to see contrasts between the center's theory and practice as well as between tutor practice and student expectations.

Lerner's famous pair of articles, "Counting Beans and Making Beans Count" (1997) and "Choosing Beans Wisely" (2001), demonstrates this same kind of diligence and persistence in making sure that assessment efforts are doing everything they can. After all, who wants to do assessment that is not as useful as it can be? In his 1997 article, Lerner presents an assessment based in grades, test scores, and writing center use to see what impact the writing center had on grades in first-semester composition. Within this first "Beans" article, Lerner acknowledges problems such as the limitations of numbers in accurately representing human beings and students not clearly starting from similar points (essential in a discussion of progress). In his second "Beans" article, Lerner focuses much more attention on the assumptions he made earlier and how they influenced his findings. Writing that he didn't really solve the problem of whether students were starting from similar places, Lerner went on to question three warrants inherent in his earlier research: a strong relationship between SAT verbal scores and final grades in FYC, final grades in FYC as indicators of writing ability, and the null impact of the teacher in FYC (and thus the comparability of grades among sections).

In 2005, Niiler published "The Numbers Speak Again: A Continued Statistical Analysis of Writing Center Outcomes" as a follow-up to his 2003 study. He acknowledged shortcomings in his 2003 methodology and, in 2005, presented a strengthened methodology and thereby a more credible outcome. These kinds of follow-up pieces underscore the utility of continued questioning and development in assessment processes and practices. They also demonstrate that no methods or researchers are beyond improvement. So if experienced researchers benefit from these kinds of review practices, the new-to-assessment director should expect nothing more or less for herself.

Meanwhile, directors new to writing center assessment do have needs that more experienced directors may not have, and a handful of pieces filled those needs. New WCDs need scholarship that not only provides discussion of commonality with other fields and disciplines but that articulates a context that is specific to writing center assessment. There is no question that there is a rich and vibrant body of scholarship available that describes research, evaluation, and assessment methods that can be useful and meaningful in writing centers. However, without a clear sense of a writing center assessment context from which to choose those methods, these kinds of decisions are like whistling in the dark. New WCDs know there is something out there, in the dark. They can't quite see assessment fully, but they can make out a shape and know it is big. Still, they must at least provide the impression that they remain optimistic, even while they may be scared to death.

Harvey Kail has understood and worked to address these needs for more than thirty years. It is no coincidence that his name appears on most of the articles that work to provide not only guidance in beginning an assessment but also context for doing assessment well. Beginning in 1982, Kail and Allen took an important step forward by working carefully through and explaining the context for a range of research options while they also argued for getting help from others when needed, even providing an example of how they themselves did this work. Kail took another step forward with "Evaluating Our Own Peer Tutoring Programs: A Few Leading Questions" (1983), where he worked to help writing center assessors make methodological choices and think about the kinds of questions that inform those choices. In that piece, Kail asks good questions but also helps readers understand why they are good questions for writing center assessment. In 2004 Kail collaborated with Lerner to develop a heuristic for writing center assessment. This document provides a substantial list of writing center assessment questions paired with sources and methods for answering them. But these are not the only pieces that do this kind of progressive, contextualizing work for writing center assessors. North, in 1984, argued that we need to test our assumptions and provides a rich discussion of not only why but how. Neulieb (1982) provides another rich tool for contextualizing writing center assessment through her overview of writing center assessment focuses, methods, and reporting, along with a thoughtful discussion, again, of as well as to make use of them.

But these few pieces are not enough. As useful as they can be, only the Lerner and Kail heuristic is newer than 1984. These materials are outdated and increasingly difficult to find, if for no other reasons than the ongoing expansion of published materials and the databases through which we often find them. The WCD scrambling to find these kinds of resources may simply not have the time for a full-on literature review such as this one. Colleagues in the field may not have thought about these pieces for a very long time and may not think to recommend them. Even if these pieces are remembered and recommended, their scope, form, and historical placement will not allow them to carry the entire field forward.

Ellen and I have built this book to address exactly this problem. Our book will seem strange to some because it is not a catalog of assessment methods or questions. It is not a theoretical discussion of what is at stake or who stands to benefit most/least from the writing center assessment practices that are in current use or might be in the near future. Neither is this book a walk-through of an assessment process that argues for a single method or outcome. Instead, this book is a thorough discussion of the processes and decisions a writing center assessor experiences as she builds an assessment. This book shares our experiences as writing center assessors, both productive and otherwise, as illustrations of assessment choices and their outcomes. Finally, we provide readers with ideas, options, and enough writing-center-specific context that they can feel confident when they go forward from here with their assessments. As far as we know, no other monograph attempts what we have. And it's about time.

REFERENCES

Andrews, Wesley, and Diane Kelly-Riley. 2010. "The Washington State University Writing Center, Pullman, First Findings: June 2008–May 2010," accessed August 17, 2011, http://universitycollege.wsu.edu/units/writingprogram/units/writingassessment/reports/WCReportfinal2010.pdf.

"Assessment Report for Writing Center, September 1, 2002 to August 3, 2003," last modified March 25, 2004, http://www.tamiu.edu/adminis/iep/data/admin/sp03/WritingCenter2003.pdf.

Ballard, Donna Kim. "Writing Center Assessment Special Interest Group Meets at the IWCA-NCPTW Conference," accessed August 17, 2011, http://writingcenters.org/2010/10/writing-center-assessment-special-interest-group-meets-at-the-iwca-ncptw-conference/.

"Caldwell Community College & Technical Institute: Quality Enhancement Plan," accessed August 17, 2011, http://www.cccti.edu/QEP/assessmentplan.htm.

Caswell, Nicole, and Courtney Werner. "Across the University: Developing Effective Writing Center Assessment Projects," accessed August 17, 2011, http://writing.msu.edu/ecwca/proposal/across-university-developing-effective-writing-center-assessment-projects.

Copas, Leigh Ann. "Utah Valley State College Assessment Record, Program: Utah Valley University Writing Center, Assessment period: 2008–2010," last modified April 1, 2010, http://www.uvu.edu/owl/strategic/Assessment%20Record%202008-2010_1.pdf.

"East Central Writing Centers Association Conference 2011," accessed August 17, 2011, http://business.intuit.com/directory/info-western-michigan-university-writing-center-kalamazoo-mi.

Gallagher, Chris W. 2011. "Being There: (Re)Making the Assessment Scene" *College Composition and Communication* 62 (3): 450-76.

Griffin, Susan, and Leslie Dennen. 2011. "NCWCA Discussion: Writing Center Assessment," accessed August 17, 2011, http://norcalwca.ning.com/forum/topics/ncwca-discussion-writing.

"Institutional Support Area Assessment Report for AY 2010–2011: Program: Writing Center," last modified July 19, 2011, http://ir.columbusstate.edu/assess/Writing%20Center%202011%20ISS.pdf.

"IWCA Bibliography of Resources for Writing Center Professionals Updated 2009," last modified December 15, 2010, http://writingcenters.org/wp-content/uploads/2010/12/bibliography_of_resources.pdf.

Law, Joe. "Talking about Assessment," accessed August 17, 2011, https://www.sinclair.edu/centers/wc/pub/owcc/assessment/frame.htm.

Lerner, Neal. "Dissertations and These on Writing Centers," last modified December 15, 2010, http://writingcenters.org/wp-content/uploads/2010/12/WC_Dissertations_and_Theses_RevJuly2010.pdf.

Lerner, Neal, and Harvey Kail. "A Heuristic for Writing Center Assessment," last modified April 24, 2008, http://web.mit.edu/nlerner/Public/AssessmentHeuristic.pdf.

———. "Writing Center Assessment Bibliography," last modified April 24, 2008, http://web.mit.edu/nlerner/Public/WCAssessmentBib.pdf.

"MAWCA 2011: The Writing Center and the Campus Context," accessed August 17, 2011, http://www.wcupa.edu/_academics/writingcenter/mawca/program-by-theme.asp.

Modey, Christine. "Assessment of Tutoring Best Practices," accessed August 17, 2011, http://www.lsa.umich.edu/sweetland/research/tutoring/assessmentoftutoringbest-practices.

Mullin, Joan. 1997. "NWCA News from Joan Mullin, President." *WLN* 21 (7): 8, 16.

Paoli, Dennis, Marcia Silver, and Jo Koster. 1997. "A Proposed Self-Study Questionnaire for Writing Center Accreditation," accessed August 17, 2011, http://faculty.winthrop.edu/kosterj/scholarly/NWCA/proposal.htm.

"Program Outcomes Assessment Worksheet: Writing Center for 2006–2007, Lock Haven University of Pennsylvania," accessed August 17, 2011, http://www.lhup.edu/planning-and-assessment/program/0708/ProgramOutcomes/WritingCenterProgramOutcomes0607.doc.

"Salt Lake Community College Community Writing Center Assessment," accessed August 17, 2011, http://www.slcc.edu/cwc/Assessment.asp.

"A Selected Bibliography on Empirical Writing Center Research," last modified July 22, 2010, http://writingcenters.org/wp-content/uploads/2010/07/A-Selected-Bibliography-on-Empirical-Writing-Center-Research.pdf.

Smith, Kimberly, and Esteban Talavera. "Gavilan College Writing Center: Report to the Campus Community," last modified April 22, 2007, http://www.gavilan.edu/writing/documents/WCReport2007.pdf.

"Tutor Self-Assessment Form (Individual)," last modified January 5, 2006, http://www.csustan.edu/WritingCenter/FormsPublications/TutorSelfAssessment-Indiv.pdf.

"2011 Summer Institute," accessed August 17, 2011, http://writingcenters.org/links/iwca-summer-institute-2/.

"University Writing Center Assessment Plan," last modified February 24, 2005, www.wright.edu/assessment/plans/uwc_plan04.doc.

"University Writing Center, University of Wisconsin-Platteville: Mission/Purpose Statements, Learning Outcomes, Assessment Tools for University Writing Center," last modified July 6, 2004, http://www.uwplatt.edu/stuaffairs/files/Assessment/WritingCenter.pdf.

"The University Writing Center (UWC): Assessment," accessed August 17, 2011, http://www.stu.edu/Academics/UniversityWritingCenter/Assessment/tabid/2322/Default.aspx.

"Writing Center Assessment Wiki," accessed August 17, 2011, http://writingcenters.wikia.com/wiki/Writing_Center_Assessment_Wiki.

"Writing Center Assignment Sheet," accessed August 17, 2011, http://legacy.bluegrass.kctcs.edu/fileadmin/files_writingcenter/ASSIGNMENT_SHEET_REVISED.pdf.

2

GETTING FROM VALUES TO ASSESSABLE OUTCOMES

William J. Macauley, Jr.

Even while writing center directors (WCDs) usually know a great deal about what tutors and clients in their centers are doing and why, they can also worry that they don't know enough about assessment to accurately represent that work. Writing center directors may worry that assessment won't show the good work their centers do because assessments haven't been designed or implemented properly, or because assessment designs found in the literature are not tailored specifically to writing centers. At other times, WCDs can worry that an assessment will be imposed from the outside, which will either inadequately measure some things or miss the boat and assess the wrong things altogether. Those who wait for a reaccreditation visit or the institutional research officer to knock on the door are particularly vulnerable in these scenarios. These are real concerns, and these concerns can become real outcomes, especially when WCDs are not intimately involved in writing center assessments. Meanwhile, these worries often originate, in one way or another, from the same root problem: a lack of confidence, experience, or opportunity to accurately discuss the work of a writing center through assessment, especially within the context of institutional and programmatic assessment on the local campus. Frankly, writing centaurs (a term used to describe those involved in writing centers, used especially to address those who participate in WCenter)[1] suffer something of a double whammy in this regard because (1) writing center work can be so isolated, given that there is typically only one writing center director per campus, and (2) there simply isn't a great deal of current scholarship focused on how to do writing centers assessment.

---

1.   If WCenter is unfamiliar to you, it is a listserv that is probably the most prominent means of communication within the writing center community. So much good information comes through that list; anyone serious about writing centers has to be a participant, IMHO. Any internet search using the term "wcenter" will get you the information you need to join.

Although those of us in writing centers can so often feel a sense of discomfort when we are thinking about assessment, we generally feel certain of our writing center work. Even while WCDs must accept these less-than-perfect conditions, we must also acknowledge our own expertise and efficacy as substantial to the development of writing center assessment on multiple levels. We, who work every day in writing centers, are actually the best people to take on these challenges because we know what our writing centers value, what our writing centers accomplish, what we want them to achieve, and what we want (and want others) to know about our progress toward those achievements. We know anecdotally what our centers are producing, and we know empirically who is using our centers, how often, and for what purposes. So we are in a unique position of doing work that is relatively new and quite familiar at the same time, and we are the only ones who can do that work.

A primary challenge in building writing center assessment is finding a suitable foundation. WCDs might simply look to prior writing center assessment scholarship but, as our introduction argued, there is decidedly little scholarship available on writing centers assessment. What is available falls generally into two categories: broad arguments that writing centers should be doing assessment and writing center research that could be adapted to assessment. Joan Hawthorne's "Approaching Assessment as if It Matters" (2006) is a good example of the former category and makes a strong argument for meaningful writing center assessment, from several perspectives. Peter Carino and Doug Enders's "Does Frequency of Visits to the Writing Center Increase Student Satisfaction? A Statistical Correlation Study—or Story" (2001) is a smart and useful quantitative study of the relationships between data sets to which many WCDs often have ready access. Although Carino and Enders work to explore relationships between visits and satisfaction, and the methods might be adapted to assessment projects, their work is not assessment because it is not focused on an assessment question. There is a significant gap between an argument for assessment and assessment itself—between research that studies writing centers and research that assesses them. These latter types of scholarship are appearing slowly and will continue to develop. By conducting assessment within our writing centers, we can both build on and build toward that developing scholarship.

Frameworks and methods for assessment exist in other writing fields, and those fields have been working with assessment for decades. For example, there is a wealth of scholarship on the assessment of writing programs. This body of work draws not only on ongoing research in the teaching and learning of writing but also on educational assessment and psychometrics more generally. With that strong foundation, writing program assessment is becoming more accessible, more user-friendly. There's less that must be explained at the front end because the scholarship is becoming more familiar and abundant. As a result, current writing assessment scholarship can start from a very different place than would be the case for a field less familiar with the topic. A good example of recent scholarship focused on writing program assessment, that is very accessible to writing center assessors, is Linda Adler-Kassner and Peggy O'Neill's *Reframing Writing Assessment to Improve Teaching and Learning* (2010). Instead of beginning with an argument for writing assessment or with a historical context for assessment, these scholars can begin with a very straightforward and simple claim:

> Regardless of the end point or process used, three very broad questions can be asked about assessments:
>
>   What is the purpose of the assessment?
>
>   Who is (or are) the primary audience(s) for an assessment and its results?
>
>   What decisions might, or will, result from an assessment?
>
>   Within these broad questions, a number of others are also present. . . . With so many different processes, programs, tests, and options, these discussions can be overwhelming and confusing. (3-4)

Certainly these questions can inform useful writing center assessments, and a WCD should be able to answer them, but it may be quite difficult for a WCD to answer these questions in meaningful ways when assessment is new to her, her center, or her institution. In "Responsibility and Composition's Future in the Twenty-first Century: Reframing 'Accountability'" (2010), Adler-Kassner and Susanmarie Harrington argue for reframing writing assessment away from assessment as accountability and toward assessment as taking responsibility. Viewed through this lens, a WCD would not simply comply with institutional demands for assessment; she must make informed and productive decisions toward the best possible assessment choices. Given that writing center assessment is comparatively underdeveloped, how does a WCD choose an appropriate purpose? How does he learn what audiences are possible and likely? How can he adequately anticipate the kinds of decisions that might result? WCDs don't have the context and body of scholarship that other fields have; as a result, these questions can be much

more difficult for a WCD to answer. The responsible writing center assessor must take more time to ground his work, before he can reasonably
undertake an assessment project.

There is relevant literature; a number of studies of writing centers have
been conducted over the years, designed to answer questions about our
centers and how they work. Comprehensive collections of research and
scholarship on writing centers can provide a range of options for writing
centers research, which may be applicable to writing centers assessment.
Gillespie, Gillam, Brown, and Stay's *Writing Center Research: Extending the
Conversation* (2002) is one such collection in which readers can see an
array of studies using multiple research methods including participant
observation (Lerner), rhetorical analyses (Carino), grounded theory
(Neff), and portfolios (Thomas, Bevins, and Crawford). Another comprehensive collection is Christina Murphy and Byron Stay's *The Writing
Center Director's Resource Book* (2006), which includes discussions of writing center history (Lerner), strategic planning (Childers), working with
administrators (Simpson), and dealing with plagiarism (Howard and
Carrick). However, only one of the pieces in these two collections discusses assessment specifically, and it is a discussion that WCDs should be
having more frequently (Hawthorne).

For many WCDs, being overwhelmed by the prospect of assessment
is understandable. It can be very difficult to find a way through the
processes of developing and constructing writing center assessments.
However, as the demand for meaningful assessment increases, so do the
needs for data sources, assessors, and further insight into what students
are and are not learning about writing. The questions before us are
whether we will pursue answers to these questions and, if not, who will
meet the assessment demand and how they will do so.

One recent answer came from Richard Arum and Josipa Roksa,
in their most controversial book, *Academically Adrift: Limited Learning
on College Campuses* (2011). Although these authors used recognized
national tests, surveys, and data sets to reach their conclusions, as
well as respectable methods of data analysis, there is no evidence
that the National Council of Teachers of English, Conference on
College Composition and Communication, Council of Writing Program
Administrators, or International Writing Centers Association played
any role in their research, even though these organizations are directly
involved in the teaching and learning of writing across the United States
and elsewhere. This can be read as bias, as a choice in focus, or as a

methodological flaw. Regardless of the explanation, these researchers made an argument that has gathered significant public attention. And make no mistake: studies such as Arum and Roksa's have traction and impact on campuses too.

So we do have skin in the game, so to speak; but so do others, and their agendas may not align easily with our own. That is not to suggest that an adversarial relationship is in place or needs to be. It is simply to say that our writing centers being marginalized may have created limitations for others, outside of the center, as well as for us. Others may be assuming that we just correct and edit, that we don't keep detailed records of our work. We have a lot to offer in this arena (and sometimes a lot to learn too), and others may need what we have to offer more than they know (at least what they know right now). They—whomever "they" might be at any given moment—may simply not know what writing centers do, what those centers have to offer, or what kinds of meaningful information an engaged center can provide for assessment. Anne DiPardo (1992) wrote long ago that "we must serve as models of reflective practice—perennially inquisitive and self-critical" (126). Our work is unique, which means that others cannot reasonably be expected to handle the assessment of that work. In order to assess and accurately represent that work, we cannot work from lore or anecdote alone. When we conduct meaningful assessments that make our work more understandable, we are deepening our ability to ask important questions about our work as well as help others to know that we are not fix-it shops, not the grammar police. And shaping those understandings in ways that are accessible to others serves us better than not doing so. In many ways, reshaping our ideas for other audiences promotes inquiry and self-critique because it forces us to not only resee our ideas but rearticulate the connections and arguments around them:

> It behooves us rhetorically to construct our arguments on grounds that match the concerns and perspectives of our administrative audiences. . . . Rhetorically, this seems like such a simple decision: it doesn't mean changing what we do or what we value, the nature of *our* trust market, but how we *talk* about it. We tell our tutors and our tutoring clients this all the time. (Koster 2003, 155, 158)

This chapter, as well as the rest of the book, begins from the argument that writing centers operate within a world that is focused on assessment, and if writing centers are to continue their development, assessment will have to be a prominent feature of that development. Meanwhile, because writing centers are comparatively late to the assessment party, WCDs don't have the wealth of resources available to other fields in developing their own assessments. WCDs must explore and try on the rhetoric of others in order to make their assessments accessible and meaningful to those others, but these moves have to have a functional basis, as does writing center assessment more generally. We must build writing center assessment on a solid foundation; we have only a few options beyond the values and goals that guide our centers. WCDs are the people to do this often groundbreaking work because they have the intimate knowledge of writing centers necessary to meaningful writing centers assessment. Writing center assessments are necessary because of the contexts within which writing centers operate, but they are even more important as continuing efforts are made to more deeply understand and explain what writing centers do, how they do it, and how well they are meeting their own goals. Finally, writing center assessment must be presented in ways that break it out of the writing center community and into others; this helps those of us within the field to re-see our own work and enables those outside of writing centers to appreciate the unique and multiple ways that writing centers contribute to learning, curricula, and institutions.

This chapter will do two relatively straightforward things that support taking on these challenges. First, it argues for the importance of writing centaurs' firsthand and empirical writing center knowledge. This may seem obvious, but there are multiple conditions under which writing center assessments might not start here: centralized campus assessment offices, administrative marginalization, writing centers segregated from curricular assessment, writing centers included in larger academic support systems and their assessments (or lack thereof), the comparative institutional status of the would-be assessors, and so on. The point is that WCDs can and should be the ones leading writing center assessment efforts. Second, this chapter will describe a systematic process for moving from broad writing center values to assessable outcomes. Writing-centaur expertise will be particularly important in this process because the process calls for both theoretical and functional knowledge of not only the local center and its context but writing pedagogy, writing center practices and users, and tutorial methods.

Expertise is not the only factor, however. The reality is that we, in writing centers, have to balance a number of concerns when we are designing and conducting assessments, as we do in all of our work. Assessments must be meaningful, and not just to we who are working in those centers. They must provide some information that can be used to carry forward the development of writers and writing. Assessments must be useful. They must be functionally relevant to writing centers that are working in cooperation with the institutions where they are located. Assessments must be informed. Like any credible argument, an assessment worth the effort must be built out of knowledge. There is no reason to reinvent the wheel with every research project, but there is also a lot of room for innovation in writing centers assessment.

WHERE DOES WRITING CENTER ASSESSMENT START?

Nationally known assessment expert Barbara Walvoord, who has traveled the country teaching administrators, staff, and faculty from all parts of the university how to devise outcomes-based assessments of student learning, articulates a reasonable and workable assessment model in *Assessment Clear and Simple: A Practical Guide for Institutions, Departments, and General Education* (2004). Her process is a wonderful place to start for several reasons, not the least of which is that it makes assessment work easy to understand. Walvoord admonishes her readers that one need not assess everything all the time—this is a biggie because the assess-everything-all-the-time model is nothing short of a nonstarter and, unfortunately, way too frequently where newer assessors (or administrators who can mandate but don't have a lot of experience with assessment) begin. One thing at a time makes a great deal of sense and enables more focused and careful assessment; the richness of a successful assessment comes of quality rather than quantity. Walvoord's process goes something like this:

- *Choose a small number of goals you want to assess.* This is an essential concept. Remember that each assessment is part of a larger assessment agenda, whether that assessment agenda has been clearly defined or not. Each project works to answer a question or two—but not all of them—and may inform directly the next assessment questions. One mistake that newer assessment designers often fall into is the idea that they want to get as much out of each assessment as possible and, as a result, try to do too much in one project. Making the most of assessment is not a bad idea, except when it makes the assessment so complex and convoluted that it cannot be successful. So do one thing at a time. Be thorough and thoughtful with a few questions, and then move on.

- *Develop direct and/or indirect measures of your success in meeting those goals.*[2] Walvoord is clearly thinking of assessment as a formative practice here. In other words, rather than assessment saying that a goal was or was not reached (summative), this approach sees assessment as locating performance on a continuum, as part of understanding progress toward specific goals. Mixed measures (direct and/or indirect, quantitative and/or qualitative, etc.) provide a broader range of data as well as varied perspectives. Differentiated measures provide opportunities to compare data, too.

- *Assess your progress.* Individual assessments are not often ends alone; they are usually means, too. They are designed with the understanding that assessment is ongoing research, and that each assessment can provoke new questions about a topic or begin to address a completely new topic. Writing center assessment is no exception. Assessment can be summative (Have we met our goals?) or formative (Where are we now in relation to our goals?). Walvoord focuses on the latter.

- *Integrate what you have learned into your program, completing the feedback loop.* This is the part that so many attempted assessment projects forget or dismiss, which only serves to increase both the stress around assessment and the seemingly all-or-nothing nature of individual assessments. What is learned from an assessment should be used to improve that which is assessed. What is learned from one assessment should inform and improve the next assessment, as well. After all, assessment is about change, about growth and development. So if the results and learning from one assessment are not fed back into the work of that which has been assessed (including future assessments), what's the point?

---

2.   What follows are gross generalizations that will do for the time being: Direct measures look at actual activity or work done; indirect measures look at secondary information such as perceptions of activity or work. Quantitative methods focus on numerical outcomes/data; qualitative methods focus on more social, situational data.

The clarity of Walvoord's model is due, in no small part, to the purpose that it is designed to serve. To be fair, this model is as stripped down as it can be for purposes of accessibility, and, for the newer assessor, this simplicity can be somewhat misleading. The model, as presented, assumes that the assessor has assessable goals ready at hand. For many writing centers, this is simply not the case. Although not an insurmountable problem, developing and setting assessable goals must be done carefully and thoughtfully. If the first step is wrong, the rest of the project will be, too. Another seeming assumption in Walvoord's model is independence in selecting goals. As part of an institution and a curriculum, writing centers are not independent operators. So, the selection of goals is oftentimes more complex than Walvoord's model would indicate.

The Walvoord model also makes some assumptions about the assessments themselves. It takes time to conduct a meaningful assessment project. The development of assessment goals should be careful and well planned. The design of the assessment project takes time too; reviewing options, trying on multiple methods, and pilot studies can all be important options that make a big difference in the quality of an assessment project. There is also a high level of optimism embedded in Walvoord's last step, the feedback loop. It is not always easy for a WCD to decide how to apply what has been learned, especially when the results of her assessment indicate a need for change outside of the writing center. There are other voices that must be considered, other stakeholders.

This is why the expertise of the WCD is so essential as a foundation for writing centers assessment: a simplified model provides a place to start, like the five-part essay. And, like the five-part essay in relation to college-level writing, a basic plan like Walvoord's is necessary, but not sufficient, to a meaningful assessment within any single unit. Beyond a simple plan, the relationships that a WCD has built across campus are essential to a successful assessment. The importance of her knowledge of the values and priorities of not only the writing center but the curricula, campus community, and institution cannot be ignored. Her deep understanding of campus resources and institutional plans can be an essential part of assessment efforts, as well. (We'll talk more about connecting with and pooling resources with units across campus throughout the rest of this book.)

One of the gifts of assessment is that it emphasizes systematic inquiry based on clear goals and objectives; that emphasis helps us to work carefully, one step at a time, and in ways that our institutions can recognize as meaningful, useful, and informed. It also helps assessors make important decisions about developing assessments, improving assessment procedures, revisiting methods, and/or redesigning assessments to fit new contexts and questions. If nothing else of use is found in this chapter, I hope that this idea will stick with the reader: the opportunities to learn and lead via assessment based on our expertise as WCDs far outstrip the liabilities of designing and conducting new assessments.

WHAT ELSE SHAPES THE DIRECTION OF WRITING CENTER ASSESSMENT?

In so many institutions, assessment is directed by an office of assessment, an assessment committee, or someone whose title includes a phrase like "institutional research." These folks are usually experts in assessment of many kinds, and they can be great collaborators/supporters of writing center assessment. However, it is just as often the case that assumptions about the work of the writing center and the students who use it are wrong, even while they are pervasive. There is no shortage of faculty who work directly with student writers and send their students to the writing center to "clean up the grammar" in their papers. Even those who require their students to make use of the writing center can do so for a variety of reasons, both meaningful and not. Although writing centers in so many institutions have been rescued from the storage room beneath the stairs, there is still a great deal of misunderstanding about what writing centers do. In other words, like so many others on our campuses, institutional research officers, whose direct contact with the work of student writing can be sorely limited, may not have the expertise or a working knowledge of writing centers. In a context such as this, writing center assessment can go wrong very quickly because those involved are frequently working out of misguided assumptions rather than expertise. And assessment is no exception.

Brian Huot, in *(Re)Articulating Writing Assessment for Teaching and Learning* (2002), identifies one of the struggles of writing assessment in general with which WCDs must wrestle as well. He writes,

> For the last two or three decades, writing pedagogy has moved toward process-oriented and context-specific approaches that focus on students' individual cognitive energies and their socially positioned identities as members of culturally bound groups. In contrast, writing assessment has remained a

contextless activity emphasizing standardization and an ideal version of writing quality. (104)

Writing centers have participated actively in this movement, though our field has not always communicated its accumulated knowledge as successfully as it might. However, what is important here is that Huot offers an alternative for writing assessment that is much more reflective of these essential turns in writing pedagogy and, by extension, the theories that have been informing writing center practice for some time. Acknowledging these turns, Huot identifies five specific principles for a new theory of writing assessment: writing assessment must be site-based, locally controlled, context-sensitive, rhetorically based, and accessible (105). One might argue that the context described above, where assessment is informed by misguided local assumptions, could potentially meet these five principles. On a campus where a WCD is not available, where writing center scholarship is not accessible, part of the learning and feedback loop of an assessment could necessarily, then, involve learning a lot of what writing centers have already learned, such as focusing on content first, the application of the Socratic Method, and many other well-established features of current writing center pedagogy. However, a campus with a writing center, a WCD, and other writing centaurs should not need to start in the past; misguided local assumptions should not determine the work or assessment of the writing center. It would seem logical to seek out that context in which the most workable and accessible knowledge of the site, locality, context, rhetoric, and access meet, which in this case would be the writing center itself.

WHO SHOULD BE INVOLVED IN WRITING CENTER ASSESSMENT?

Huot goes on to explain, "The procedures should honor the instructional goals and objectives as well as the cultural and social environment of the institution or agency and its students, teachers and other stakeholders" (105). Along with assessments being site-based and locally controlled, this principle clearly points right at the writing center as the place to start in designing a meaningful writing center assessment project. Writing centers have long been collecting syllabi and writing assignments, developing deeper understandings and richer materials around discipline-specific writing, as well as liaising with faculty, administrators, staff, students, and others on their campuses, in order to support writing in the most successful possible ways. On many campuses, the writing center is the best place to see the array of writing that students might be asked to do across disciplines, departments, programs, and levels. By extension, the writing center is often also the best place to understand the fullness of "instructional goals and objectives as well as the cultural and social environment of the institution" and its participants (Huot 105). WCDs can often, therefore, have a more informed understanding of writing and writing instruction on their campuses because they are working at the collection point of so much of the work on student writing.

Huot's assessment principles emphasize local stakeholders as well. Assessment must be developed out of the "resources and concerns of an institution, department, program or agency and its administrators, faculty, students or other constituents" while it also responds to "the concerns of all those affected by the assessment process" (105). As stated above, the writing center is a nexus/collection point that is usually readily accessible by all constituents. While local participants seem the only reasonable choice, there are simply too many people involved in the teaching and learning of writing—at various levels of engagement with that work—on any given campus to involve most of them in a writing center assessment project. Writing center assessors must be selective about who is involved in terms of expertise, interest, and availability. The reality on most campuses is that the WCD and her staff are necessarily the most invested in writing center assessment because they will do the bulk of the assessment work, if not all of it. In most institutions, writing center assessment is understood as the responsibility of the WCD anyway, when it is done at all. Truth be told, although there are numerous potential contributors on most campuses, there is seldom an abundance of human resources available outside of the center with the required expertise in writing centers. That doesn't mean that the involved WCD knows everything necessary to put together a good assessment plan and carry it out. It does mean that WCDs must make strategic use of those other human resources when their specific expertise is really needed.

But what kind of expertise is important? When in the process should we seek it out? William L. Smith (2009) analyzed multiple-rater writing placement at the University of Pittsburgh, and his findings are particularly useful here. In his analysis, he found one especially compelling result: "almost all of the disagreements between the raters happened when the raters had most recently taught different courses." Smith goes on to write, "The raters' expertise, the expertise which comes from working with their students, might be more powerful than any training session in which they are told about the various courses and read essays prototypic of those courses" (183). In short, Smith's research argues that those who are working most closely with student writers in various contexts have the greatest expertise in assessing those students' writing from within that context.

I'm arguing, then, that expertise within writing centers, especially hands-on experience with the work of writing centers and the writers who rely on those centers, makes writing centaurs best choices for writing centers assessment. This extends beyond simply assessing writing samples to understanding student writers within the context of the assessment, the ways that they engage with that context, and what they hope to get out of those interactions, as was the case with Smith's teachers. But there is another reason that firsthand experience with the writing center is essential to meaningful writing center assessment, and that has to do with the theoretical and pedagogical knowledge base necessary to making informed decisions throughout the assessment process.

This kind of assessment work, which must be differentiated from the usual types of counting that writing centers have been doing for years, is relatively new to many writing centers and WCDs. Therefore, it is that much more important that those with the greatest expertise and experience in writing centers be in charge of writing center assessments. Seek help where it is needed, even if it is at the earliest stages of the project. However, because one desired outcome of writing center assessment is developing the richest, most useful information that can be fed back into the work of the writing center, expertise in writing centers is a must for those who will be collecting and analyzing the data. In *What We Really Value: Beyond Rubrics in Teaching and Assessing Writing* (2003), Bob Broad argues that writing assessment is undergoing a significant shift in moving away from more traditional educational assessment:

> The interplay between two forms of educational inquiry, writing assessment and qualitative research, has gained increasing attention lately in books and journals devoted to improving postsecondary teaching and learning. Scholars in a variety of fields—composition and rhetoric (Huot 1996), evaluation theory (Moss 1996), and qualitative research (Guba and Lincoln)—have directed researchers' attention to the benefits of integrating qualitative methods into educational evaluation. (13)

Broad goes on to advocate for "dynamic criteria mapping" (DCM), a new process by which changes/developments in assessment criteria are mapped and developed as the assessment work unfolds. In other words, instead of paying attention only to what is in the rubric, or not, from the start of the project, DCM confirms the developing understandings that evolve during an assessment project and uses those developing understandings to refine and more tightly focus the ongoing assessment. So not only is Broad pointing out the importance of expertise at the outset of an assessment project, but he is also arguing for the ongoing importance of expertise in the development that occurs as an assessment project is being carried out. The important idea here, for writing center assessment, is that the mapping of criteria, and how those criteria continue, drop out, and/or change over the course of the assessment, cannot be done well by researchers whose empirical experience with what is being assessed is limited or nonexistent. For example, an assessor who does not understand that the tutor training emphasizes higher-order concerns (HOCs) before lower-order concerns (LOCs) will obviously struggle if looking at tutorials where errors are not addressed. Context matters, and it cannot be fully understood without experience within that context.

Writing center assessment that is going to be the most fully developed will reflect the contexts within which it is conducted. Only those who are part of that context can adequately appreciate that reflection and its accuracy/impact. The value of experience and expertise in what is being assessed is beyond question; writing center assessment is no exception. Finally, expertise is not only necessary at the start of the assessment process but throughout. Informed participants must be engaged in the process of data collection, and especially analysis, as well as the ongoing work of refining goals and objectives. In this case, the informed participants are writing centaurs. We who are directing, tutoring, and otherwise working in writing centers can be the best options for meaningful writing center assessments.

A PROCESS FOR DEVISING ASSESSABLE WRITING CENTER OUTCOMES

The goal of the rest of this chapter is to lay out a process by which readers can build meaningful writing center assessment. Here the process will focus on building an assessment project out of writing center values; later chapters will build from elsewhere. And as I describe this process, which draws heavily upon Walvoord's process for designing outcomes-based assessments, I will use my own experience in working with the assessment committee at the College of Wooster to devise assessable outcomes for writing as a means of illustrating the process—outcomes that the writing center used as the basis for its assessment activities. No matter what sources an assessment is built from, or toward which goals that assessment is directed, it is imperative to remember that assessment is research. It works to answer a question. Writing center assessment can address any number of different questions: What are tutors doing in their sessions? How does the writing center support the teaching of writing in the first-year composition course or program? How are students from different disciplines using the writing center? How are student writing practices altered by working with writing tutors? However, before the question can be considered, a clear understanding of context is necessary—in this case, the context is the values that guide the center.

Step One: Identify What Your Center Values

The first step in the process is to identify very broad, big-picture kinds of statements about the goals you work with in your center. These statements tend to be comprehensive, summative, and/or cumulative. Think about end results and broad-stroke ideas. It may be helpful to think of these values or goals as the outcomes of your center's work. In some cases, it might be work that you want students to do when they are finished with a tutorial. It might also be statements of certain broad understandings or generalized competencies developed over time by the tutors in the writing center. The key, at this stage, is to not worry about assessibility or about specificity. That comes later. Just get the big ticket items on the table.

There are a number of ways to get at these broad values. One might invite staff members to discuss and develop a set of goals for the work of the writing center. This is a useful practice in the service of assessment, and it also involves the staff in assessment, provides assessors with a variety of perspectives, and coheres a sense of what is being done in the center and why. In my experience, and that of others with whom I have discussed this approach, the discussions help to not only see commonalities but develop greater clarity about what those broad ideas mean in practice. Many times, ideas come up that are points of consensus, even while they are new or newly articulated ideas that have become so deeply embedded in a writing center that they have gone unnoticed. Another approach works from statements of goals, objectives, mission, and/or vision. When we began our assessment work at the College of Wooster, we found that our own writing center mission statement was a productive point of departure.

There are a number of viable options when you are looking for both values and indicators, and one of the best is mission statements. There are many who dismiss mission statements as unimportant, as vacuous texts of little real value. A former department chair once told me that a mission statement is what you feel like you should be doing and a vision statement is what makes you feel guilty for not doing it. However, in the College of Wooster Writing Center, we felt a real sense of accomplishment in our writing center when we built a mission statement that we really liked. That mission statement was the first thing we built together; it was foundational to our shared work, and it became an essential part of our moving forward as a community. That energy would not last forever, though, so I was quick to follow the mission statement with further developments.

When I began as director of writing at the College of Wooster, there had been a writing center on campus for more than thirty years, though it was very isolated and withdrawn from the rest of the campus. It seemed that only a handful of folks on campus knew where the writing center was, let alone what it did. There were a lot of misconceptions on campus and, frankly, problematic practices within the center too (one of the outcomes of isolation). The center needed direction, a shared direction. A mission statement could provide that collective direction. As you might imagine, with a new director and a number of long-term employees (at least a couple had been there twenty-plus years), this was a process that could be intense at times. The staff and I worked for some time on developing a mission statement, reviewing multiple drafts via e-mail and through discussions in our staff meetings. Although we tended to express our ideas very differently, and act on them with a variety of practices, it wasn't long before we recognized that our commonalities far outnumbered our differences. Eventually we did come to consensus (not complete agreement but consensus) and settled on the following mission statement:

> *The College of Wooster Writing Center is dedicated to close reading, critical inquiry, and thoughtful discussion that improve writing processes as well as written products. Growth and learning are intended outcomes for each and every participant in these processes.* (Macauley)

This became a very useful statement because it is comprehensive. It worked well to articulate priorities. It aligned nicely with developing institutional strategic planning and college-wide value statements as well as later developments in delineating graduate attributes. Within the College of Wooster Writing Center, there had not always been agreement on which part of the statement was the most important or where efforts would be focused most, but there had been agreement that these were appropriate broad goals for the center. Beyond these general points of agreement, this mission statement has specific learning goals:

- Close reading
- Critical inquiry
- Thoughtful discussion
- Thoughtful discussion of writing processes
- Thoughtful discussion of written products

Although not really the focus at the time, these were also good starts at assessable outcomes because they are, for the most part, empirical; they can be seen and measured. Later would come the parsing out of programmatic, learning, and professional goals for the staff, but these goals became a foundation from which the development of writing center assessment at the College of Wooster would continue to build.

At this stage of the process, it behooves readers to think as broadly and generously as possible—in this case, more is more. What should students experience in the writing center? How does one know if a tutorial was successful? What should the participants take away? What impact should a tutorial or a series of tutorials have? The more options on the table, the more informed the choices will be because they will be more deliberately selected. One might also find that goals and objectives can sometimes fold in together, helping to clarify as one major goal what were previously several smaller objectives. The excitement and engagement of this stage of the process are very strong because they allow many WCDs and their staffs to talk openly and deeply about what they value most in their center—maybe collectively for the first time. This engagement with mission and big-picture thinking can be revolutionary in the life and collective work of a writing center.

Step 2: Identify Indicators of Those Values

Once a set of broad values has been identified, the next step is to decide how you can see those values. What tells you that this goal or value has happened? For instance, if one of the goals is that students will think critically, what tells you that critical thinking has happened?

One of the greatest challenges to composition studies has been that so much of the work of writing is internal, in the mind, where we cannot see it. A number of research methods have been used to investigate these kinds of internal activities including speak-aloud protocols, reflective writing, and interviewing, to name a few. However, we have not yet solved the problem of not being able to see into other people's thoughts and minds.

It would seem very simple to ask a writer if critical thinking has occurred. One might argue that the thinker is the best resource in assessing critical thinking because he is the one doing the thinking. However, how might one ensure that the writer's understandings/definitions of critical thinking are consistent with one's own? Might writers be too willing to describe their thinking as critical, since there is such a premium put on critical thinking in so many modern institutions? Remember that assessment is systematic; whatever happens with one subject or observation or sample has to happen with the others. If some subjects define critical thinking more generously than others, or have a strong desire to be perceived as critical thinkers, the results of the assessment could be skewed and, therefore, inaccurate. So it is essential to select indicators that can be as overt, as obvious as possible and to acknowledge their limitations as well.

These indicators can often be described as traits, learning outcomes, attributes, qualities, or skills. This step can be a bit tricky because would-be assessors sometimes assume a consistency of meaning or find themselves thinking that they have to find *the* indicator for each broad ideal or that there is only one valid indicator that will work. It is always smart to consult the literature: see if you can find studies of writing (not necessarily writing assessments alone, but writing research more broadly) that look at the same features or qualities of writing that you are pursuing, or studies of the teaching of writing that you can adapt to your own assessment interests. Check with your colleagues on campus, in regional writing center organizations or via WCenter. We all benefit by the smart questions and informed discussion we find there. Meanwhile, since you know that assessment work will continue, you should do the best you can at each stage; be articulate about why you have made the choices you have, but also remember that each step teaches you something not only about your work but about what you want to know and how to ask better questions about it.

At Wooster, our discussions of indicators helped us to see the complexities of some of our goals. For instance, when we discussed close reading, we found that there were a number of competing concepts at work. One of the staff members said that when she thought of close reading, she thought of received texts, particularly canonical literature, and locating foreshadowing, character development, and the contrasts between the action and structure within a novel or poem. Another consultant said that she was thinking more of the close reading of students' own writing that focused on lower-order concerns. Another said that she thought close reading meant avoiding academese. Because we could not get to consensus about what we meant by close reading then and there, we could not begin to think about indicators for that goal. We moved on to articulating indicators for other goals before we came back to addressing these particular and widely contrasting interpretations of close reading. This experience taught us that picking the low-hanging fruit first was a smart approach. This is especially true when the assessor is new to assessment, as it was for our center. Nothing builds success like successes, and we thought it advisable to build not only an assessment agenda but assessment experience and expertise that scaled upwards in terms of complexity and difficulty.

As you begin to develop indicators, work to find the indicator that works best for you, for now, for your goals and objectives, for your work. If you don't feel comfortable with your decisions, share them with others whose perspectives you appreciate. Mistakes are progress, too, and differences of opinion can be very helpful both in considering other options and in articulating our own preferences/understandings. Remember that assessment is not about getting it right every time (as nice as that might be) but about making progress every time. Remember, too, that a good bit of the value of this work is not only the assessment itself but the impact of that work on the program and the staff development that it often enables simply by bringing about discussions of values and priorities. What matters most at this stage is that the indicator is something that you can see, something you can argue is connected to the values you are pursuing, and something that matters to you and to your assessment.

Three to five indicators should be plenty, at least at first.

At Wooster, as we worked to articulate indicators and prioritize our goals, we seemed to be moving backwards in some ways. Instead of getting more specific, we seemed to be gathering in more and more details of the outcomes we wanted our work to produce. We veered off into how we did our own work, too. We thought about how we defined our writing center and the work we did there:

- Writing across the curriculum
- Writing in the disciplines
- HOCs before LOCs
- Process before product
- Non-directive
- Collaborative
- Individual goals
- Programmatic needs
- Curricular values
- Institutional goals

Although this process became somewhat frustrating because it seemed the focus was expanding rather than narrowing, these were essential steps because they forced us to make differentiations between our practical goals, programmatic goals, institutional goals, and student learning goals, the latter being where we wanted to focus our attention. These steps helped us to focus our thinking, and we found that we could not rely on the list of descriptors above as traits or indicators. Although they were essential concepts that shaped our work, they were not assessable learning outcomes. We couldn't really see them in student work.

It seemed ill advised to make student writing responsible for illustrating all of these big-ticket ideas in the College of Wooster Writing Center. We recognized that if we wanted to get to assessable outcomes, we had to focus more on what we wanted students to be able to do, rather than focusing on the guiding principles we saw behind that work. We eventually did come to a collection of indicators, to accompany the broad values articulated in our mission statement. Notice that these indicators or traits are stated as things students should do; we were deliberate in that because it helped us to avoid further wandering:

1. Students should read closely.

2. Students should inquire critically.

3. Students should thoughtfully discuss their writing.

4. Students' writing processes should continue to develop.

5. Students' written products should improve.

When we submitted these learning goals to our assessment committee, their review and feedback were very helpful but in surprising ways. The committee had a number of suggestions about how we might refine and make our learning goals more focused. They also asked questions about our focuses, which we could see were reflections of their inaccurate ideas about the writing center and its work (namely, that our work was remedial and focused primarily on LOCs, which I will discuss in more depth later).

The importance of this feedback cannot be overstated. Clearly, we welcomed the help with making our assessment as effective as possible, but the benefits did not stop with questions of economy or accuracy. The suggestions made in terms of our learning goals forced our writing center staff to rethink our goals, and this is where we revisited the idea of close reading. For example, when the assessment committee asked us to which reading our first student learning goal referred, it confirmed the lack of clarity we had experienced earlier in the process. However, the question helped us to clarify for ourselves that a lot of the work in the College of Wooster Writing Center involved close reading of so many texts: assigned readings, online and multimedia and hardcopy resources, reference materials, style guides and handbooks, and sometimes assignments themselves. What the staff in the writing center began to appreciate was that our goals did not have to create unrealistic or artificially narrow boundaries on our work; instead, we recognized that we had to make choices within our broad values and, thanks to our experiences with close reading and the feedback from the assessment committee, we felt much better prepared to do so.

While the intention of the assessment committee may have been to narrow our focus—and rightly so—it actually helped us to consider the wider range of reading work we did. In the end, we were even happier with our goals because they allowed us to see our choices within each goal and then selectively articulate much more manageable and discrete goals, which we could then assess directly. Below are examples of the further articulations we developed, each an assessable outcome on its own (some more readily assessable than others):

1. Students should read closely:

    a. Their own texts.

    b. Reference materials.

    c. Assignments.

    d. Review materials.

2. Students should inquire critically:

    a. Into their own arguments, claims, evidence, and warrants.

    b. Into the qualifications and intentions of reference material authors.

    c. Into their own habits and processes.

    d. Into the relationships between perspectives within a topic.

3. Students should thoughtfully discuss their writing:

    a. By describing for themselves and others their purposes and goals in writing.

    b. By describing for writing center staff their intended focuses for sessions.

    c. By articulating both strengths and weaknesses in their written products.

    d. By articulating both strengths and weaknesses in their writing processes.

4. Students' writing processes should continue to develop:

    a. Through conscious decision making in process.

    b. Through breaking down the writing process into manageable stages.

    c. Through informed choices about adjusting the stages of the writing process that are not working.

    d. Through conscious engagement with increasingly complex writing tasks and subjects.

5. Students' written products should improve:

    a. By successful engagement with increasingly complex topics and arguments.

b. By demonstrating greater control over syntax and mechanics.

c. By demonstrating control over increasingly diverse forms.

d. By indicating a greater sense of an author communicating with an audience with care and craft.

A further benefit from the assessment committee's feedback was the perspective it gave us on how members of the committee understood our writing center. From the feedback we received, we could see that the committee was making assumptions about our work that were not entirely accurate. They seemed to be seeing our work as primarily remedial—focused on the weakest of writers while the stronger writers neither needed nor made use of the center. Because the committee was made up of faculty and professional staff from across the campus, we were willing to trust that these views were somewhat representative. We were actually pleased about this realization because we knew that the kind of assessment we wanted to do would confound that perspective.

Another assumption seemed to be that our work was primarily focused on LOCs.[3] We did a great deal of that kind of work, as do many writing centers. However, we found that we much more frequently worked on HOCs, focusing on developing, expressing, and cohering ideas. The assessment committee's responses did not seem to recognize that and, again, we saw this as an opportunity because it encouraged us to conduct assessments that would change this perspective.

The assessment committee was right about our goals even if it was wrong about our work; there is no question that further clarification of our goals was useful and productive. In the end, we at Wooster decided not to change our learning goals because of the richness they afforded

---

3. HOCs and LOCs describe the kinds of thinking involved at different stages of the writing process. As discussed first in McAndrew and Reigstad's *Tutoring Writing* (2001), higher-order thinking ("thesis and focus, development, structure and organization, and voice") focuses on content and the ways that ideas work together while lower-order thinking ("matters related to surface appearance, correctness, and standard rules of written English . . . sentence structure and mechanics") focuses more on the rules and regulations of writing (42, 56). In other sources, such as Gillespie and Lerner's *The Allyn and Bacon Guide to Peer Tutoring* (2004), LOCs are defined as "later-order concerns," meaning that they occur toward the end of the writing process. Although the original source focuses on the kinds of thinking involved, and a later text focuses on when concerns are relevant within the writing process, they both help writers and writing tutors to focus on content first and surface-level issues later.

us. Instead, we chose to focus on specific features within those broader learning goals, leaving the others for later assessment projects.

We continued to think together about what we wanted student writers to accomplish in their visits to our writing center, and we used the mission statement to guide that thinking, along with the feedback from the assessment committee. We knew that we wanted to improve writing, but that could mean so many different things. Meanwhile, one of the gifts of our staff was their diverse perspectives. For example, because we have folks who are trained in reading theory and in working with English-as-a-second-language readers, we didn't lose track of the reading goal we had included in our mission statement.

We also had to clarify what we meant by *improve*. We wanted student writers to be informed consumers of their own literacy practices. We wanted writers to be able to critique their writing processes, break those processes down into manageable stages, and make informed and conscious decisions about their work. Better yet, we wanted students to be able to identify the segments of their writing practices that didn't work for them, learn what other options were available, try them out, and find new steps that would better meet their needs. We wanted the same for students in their written documents: the ability to break them down into manageable pieces in order to focus on efficient development. We knew we couldn't compel students to make changes in their processes, but we did want the writing center to help students develop the critical lenses that would allow them to see where their processes were breaking down, understand that they could ask our writing center for help in addressing those concerns, and know that they could choose other process and product options for themselves. No doubt you recognize the ambition and complexity of these goals.

What we learned from this process of moving back and forth between values and indicators of those values was that these moves were ongoing; eventually, we didn't worry if we didn't get to clarity right away. The work was formative at that stage, not summative. We didn't try to say everything about our work at that stage and, as a result, avoided the rabbit hole of trying to figure out what tutoring writing meant for everyone everywhere. We focused on being articulate and clear about one thing at a time for our purposes and context. Remember, too, that we got a lot further with less frustration by taking a number of small assessment "bites" rather than trying to get it all in one big "gulp." In other words, we explored three to five indicators of the values we identified rather than try to divine a comprehensive assessment of all things writing-centered. Eventually, we could pull together multiple assessments of our writing center's work that would, collectively, provide a rich and deep discussion of our center and the work that was done there. And that context provided more direction for our future assessments as we worked to fill in the gaps between the assessment we would complete.

We continued to further articulate our learning goals and revisit our goals and indicators for the Writing Center at Wooster, but our goals may not resemble yours. Trust yourself, as informed writing center experts, to make good decisions based in what you know. As much as it may seem that we were off and running on expanding our view again, we really saw the work at that point as an opportunity to create even greater specificity and clarity. Our perspective changed along with these greater levels of detail; instead of focusing on numbers 1 through 5 (listed earlier in this chapter) in our learning goals as indicators or assessable outcomes—which would have been problematic because there was such an array of possible interpretations—we began to focus on the lettered items beneath each of the numbered goals. In effect, we were doing exactly what I suggested earlier: we were moving from broader ideas that were statements of values to more tangible outcomes that were potential indicators by paying attention to how our goals and indicators were articulated throughout the process.

Meanwhile, when we worked to further develop our student learning goals, by identifying and clarifying values, as well as the indicators of those values, it would have been easy to err in two very different directions. At the time, it certainly felt as though we had. One direction was to err on the side of expressions too locally defined. Certainly, if we had followed the feedback from our assessment committee, we would have been much more focused—which is a good thing in some ways—but we would have also been excluding a number of important ways that we understood our own work. Although our assessment committee was right that we needed to focus our learning goals, doing so in the ways they suggested would have disabled an accurate representation of what our center was, what our field suggests writing centers should be doing, and what we did.

It is just as easy to err on the side of too global a focus in learning goals. This is problematic because learning goals that are too broad are often too unwieldy to manage. In essence, they are often not assessable. As an example, here is a learning goal that is too broad: *Students will be better writers.* It is certainly a concept that informs our work, guides our practice, and is at the heart of writing center work. However, there are a number of issues with a learning goal this broad. First, what students do we mean? What does *better* mean? Does it mean better grades? Better quality writing? Better command of the writing process? Is better the same for all students?

If one were to pursue this learning goal, one would also have to consider issues of standards or benchmarks. Are we discussing reaching a particular benchmark or making progress toward one? What is good enough? How much improvement do we need to see? Over what period of time? Should that happen in certain courses? At specified levels? The point here is that our assessments have to be meaningful, yes, and they also have to be manageable. If the question is too big, the answer may be too long in coming, if it is available at all; it may require too much preparatory work (articulating learning goals for other programs, getting people to agree to definitions, questions of turf, etc.).

In our writing center at Wooster, we knew that our stated learning goals were broad, and we worked from the assumption that we would focus on a particular facet of each goal when we assessed it. We also understood that the goals would change over time, so we wanted to focus our assessment work on one thing at a time. We wanted our assessments to guide further development of the mission and goals of our writing center rather than try to keep up with them. We really thought of our assessment work as proactive rather than reactive, and that helped us to work productively and informedly thereafter.

My staff and I knew that we could not assess all of these things at once. It was neither realistic nor productive to think that we could. From there, we made a plan. We knew that the bulk of this work had to be accomplished within the normal tutoring schedule because that was where our work and student learning coexisted. We decided to focus on student learning goals 4 and 5 and to choose specific indicators from among the lettered items under each of these broader goals. We chose these learning goals for four reasons:

- Centrality of these goals to our mission.
- Frequency of attention to these goals in our work.
- Assessibility.
- Importance.

We felt confident that under items 4 and 5 were a number of indicators that we could not only see but assess.

Step 3: Identify Assessable Outcomes

From among the indicators that reflect the values of a writing center, which can be measured effectively? Since we have focused our attention on indicators that "show" us that our goals are being acted on, it should be easy enough to just rename them "assessable outcomes." But there is a difference between an indicator and an assessable outcome. An indicator can show you that something related to a value is happening, but an assessable outcome should not be showing you anything else and doing so consistently. For example, we may see multiple appointments as an indicator of students' desire to "thoughtfully discuss their writing" until we discover later that a professor gives extra credit for each tutorial (I do recognize that these are not mutually-exclusive motivations). Multiple appointments could also mean that a student's girlfriend works in the center or he has found a tutor who will edit for him. There are just too many competing explanations. This does not necessarily mean that the student in question is not interested in thoughtful discussion of his writing, but it does mean we cannot say with any certainty that multiple appointments indicates this desire alone. It's not so much about proving something as it is minimizing competing explanations. There is little more embarrassing than to complete a substantial assessment project that someone else can discredit with a plausible alternative explanation that should have been caught.

On the other hand, we at Wooster decided that we wanted to focus on having students' writing processes continue to develop. If, for instance, tutorials with a particular student tended to focus too soon on mechanical issues in earlier sessions but later turned to focus on HOCs first, we might argue that this student's writing process was developing because the focus on mechanics was moving to a later stage of the process, where much of the scholarship suggests it belongs.[4] The challenge, of course, would be to find a way to articulate that kind of change in a way that was not specific only to one student.

The key is to choose indicators that clearly indicate what we assume they do and do so consistently across contexts and instances. These are questions of validity and reliability, upon which there is extensive

---

4.   See *Tutoring Writing* by McAndrew and Reigstad for a thorough discussion of this paradigm.

research and scholarship.[5] Here are three questions you can ask yourself to decide whether something is an assessable outcome:

1. Can it be measured or counted?

2. Can it be measured or counted consistently, both in terms of quantity and quality?

3. Is it clearly a reflection of the value to which you have attached it? Are there any alternative explanations that are as plausible or more plausible than yours?

At Wooster, we decided that the assessment of the College of Wooster Writing Center would focus first on our learning goals 4 and 5:

- Students' writing processes should continue to develop.

- Students' written products should continue to improve.

We wanted to focus specifically on breaking down the writing process into manageable stages and indications of a greater control over syntax and mechanics, respectively. We knew what we wanted to learn, what we wanted to measure, and started our planning around how we would achieve our goals.

POLISHING GOALS AND OBJECTIVES TAKES TIME AND SAVES TIME

The work of establishing and clarifying learning goals takes time, but it is time well spent. It serves your assessment interests, to be sure, but it also accomplishes some things that are very helpful when you get to the stage of designing methods. If the goals are too broad, you may never find appropriate measures because the goals include too many ideas or priorities. If they are too narrow, they may not benefit your center because they cannot be applied beyond a limited context. My tendency has been to ask these questions before I work to develop methods:

- Can I see what I am trying to measure?

- Can I sufficiently differentiate it from other concerns?

- Can I easily connect the indicator to the value?

---

5.   See Huot and O'Neill's *Assessing Writing: A Critical Sourcebook* (2009) for an extensive discussion.

- Can the measure tell me something meaningful about the work I am doing?

If the answer to all of these questions is yes, I will proceed. If not, some review and rethinking is needed.

The development of methods is where Huot's paradigm for writing assessment becomes particularly salient. His five principles[6] are useful for understanding what successful assessment should look like; I apply them to this particular stage of the assessment process because this is the real nuts-and-bolts stage where I can see whether my assessment plans are going to work.

First, locally designed, site-based assessment is just smart. You don't want to try to assess student learning in writing centers everywhere or for all student writers, at least not until after you have seen if your immediate assessment project works the way you want it to. Measures that work elsewhere may not work as well for you. Site-based assessment focuses on what you are assessing, where you are assessing it, with the resources you have available to assess it, and for the purposes that you are assessing it. Keep these ideas in mind; they will help you to both plan reasonably and work productively.

One of the problems of earlier writing program assessments on our campus was that they seemed disengaged from what the writing program and center set out to accomplish. Where one of the goals of the writing program is students' developing facility with a range of genres, none of the assessments had ever looked at that goal. Instead, they had focused on things like the development and exploration of ideas. This latter focus might be meaningful for some humanities writing, as it is often our practice in the humanities to use writing for just this purpose. However, in the other divisions, such as the social and natural sciences, this kind of writing was much less prevalent. This kind of writing would not be recognized as rhetorically based in other divisions and disciplines because it does not adhere to any common constructions of text or uses of writing within those departments.

Accessibility is often understood as reciprocity, but it is also about making sure that those involved understand what you are looking for—and this is directly tied to the construction of methods. In any study, whether assessment or research (an artificial differentiation—they are

---

6.   Writing assessment must be "site-based", "locally controlled", "context-sensitive", "rhetorically based", and "accessible" (105).

both inquiries designed to advance understanding), the design, operation, and results of the assessment must be available to those whose work is being assessed. In our case, that meant that both student writers and staff members had to be able to see the whole thing, the entire assessment process. That does not mean that everyone has to be able to see all of the data, but it does mean that they should be able to pursue any information that will help them to make informed choices about their participation, both before and after the fact.

A few final words: I have a tendency to overdevelop our assessment projects. In other words, I try to do too much, and because the assessments become so convoluted and complex, they also become unproductive. Sometimes the issue is that the assessments are logistically unwieldy. Sometimes the issue is that the data collection far exceeds the question to be answered. Sometimes the issue is that too much is being asked of participants, which discourages participation. Thank goodness, I was able to involve my professional staff to the extent that I could; one of the qualities of good assessment is that potential problems are headed off before they happen. Small successes are much more effective than big failures, and as I stated earlier, remember that each assessment is only a part of a larger assessment agenda. Take your time, make good choices, get the right people involved, and be realistic about what you can accomplish/handle.

Think of assessment not only as an opportunity to learn about your work but as a means of generating interest and energy around that work. See if you can involve faculty in your assessment. Work to engage your staff in the whole process. Get students involved.

Be careful not to overstate your results. If you looked at a small cross-section of students, don't generalize to all students. If you focused on tutoring with science writers, don't assume that your results extend to writers in other disciplines, that all science writers are writing in the same ways, or that all science writing is based in the same values and assumptions. In reporting and discussing your assessments, be sure to include the parameters of your assessment project in terms of specifying the methods you chose (and why), as well as the assessment's limitations, so your audience can see that you are being careful and so they can understand what you did, how you did it, and how the information can be used. We will discuss this much further in chapter 5, but it's worth mentioning in this chapter to highlight the importance of being specific in devising your indicators and outcomes.

Finally, remember that there are a variety of learning opportunities available to you in writing center assessment. The most obvious is your opportunity to learn more about the work that you are doing. Other kinds of learning can happen too. Developing statements of values can be very revealing as to the priorities of your staff and the faculty with whom you work. This work can also build a strong sense of community within your writing center by providing participants with opportunities to influence not only the practices of the center but the values and theories that inform them. Certainly, this kind of assessment allows us to share with our colleagues what we do; there is no question that our field and professional organizations are eager to have accessible, meaningful assessment options. The only real limitation on what we can learn is our own ability to articulate and overcome those limitations.

REFERENCES

Adler-Kassner, Linda, and Susanmarie Harrington. 2010. "Responsibility and Composition's Future in the Twenty-first Century: Reframing 'Accountability.'" *College Composition and Communication* 62 (1): 73–99.

Adler-Kassner, Linda, and Peggy O'Neill. 2010. *Reframing Writing Assessment to Improve Teaching and Learning*. Logan: Utah State University Press.

Arum, Richard, and Josipa Roksa. 2011. *Academically Adrift: Limited Learning on College Campuses*. Chicago, IL: University of Chicago Press.

Broad, Bob. 2003. *What We Really Value: Beyond Rubrics in Teaching and Assessing Writing*. Logan: Utah State University Press.

Carino, Peter. 2002. "Reading Our Own Words: Rhetorical Analysis and the Institutional Discourse of Writing Centers." In *Writing Center Research: Extending the Conversation*, edited by Paula Gillespie, Allice Gillam, Lady Falls Brown, and Byron Stay, 91–110. Mahwah, NJ: Lawrence Erlbaum.

———, and Doug Enders. 2001. "Does Frequency of Visits to the Writing Center Increase Student Satisfaction? A Statistical Correlation Study—or Story." *WCJ* 22 (1): 83–103.

Childers, Pamela B. 2006. "Designing a Strategic Plan for a Writing Center." In *The Writing Center Director's Resource Book*, edited by Christina Murphy and Byron Stay, 53–70. Mahwah, NJ: Lawrence Erlbaum.

DiPardo, Anne. 1992. "'Whispers of Comings and Goings': Lessons from Fannie." *WCJ* 12 (7): 125–45.

Gillespie, Paula, and Neal Lerner. 2004. *The Allyn and Bacon Guide to Peer Tutoring*, 2nd ed. New York: Allyn & Bacon.

Gillespie, Paula, Allice Gillam, Lady Falls Brown, and Byron Stay, eds. 2002. *Writing Center Research: Extending the Conversation*, Mahwah, NJ: Lawrence Erlbaum.

Guba, Egon G., and Yvonne S. Lincoln. 1989. *Fourth Generation Evaluation*. Newbury Park, CA: Sage.

Hawthorne, Joan. 2006. "Approaching Assessment as if It Matters." In *The Writing Center Director's Resource Book*, edited by Christina Murphy and Byron Stay, 237–45. Mahwah, NJ: Lawrence Erlbaum. "Approaching Assessment as if it Matters

Howard, Rebecca Moore, and Tracy Hamler Carrick. 2006. "Activist Strategies for Textual Multiplicity: Writing Center Leadership on Plagiarism and Authorship." In *The Writing Center Director's Resource Book*, edited by Christina Murphy and Byron Stay, 249–60. Mahwah, NJ: Lawrence Erlbaum.

Huot, Brian. 1996. "Toward a New Theory of Writing Assessment." *College Composition and Communication* 47 (4): 549–66.

———. 2002. *(Re)Articulating Writing Assessment for Teaching and Learning*. Logan: Utah State University Press.

———, and Peggy O'Neill. 2009. *Assessing Writing: A Critical Sourcebook*. Boston, MA: Bedford St. Martin's.

Koster, Josephine A. 2003. "Administration Across the Curriculum: Or Practicing What We Preach." In *The Center Will Hold: Critical Perspectives on Writing Center Scholarship*, edited by Michael A. Pemberton and Joyce Kinkead, 151–65. Logan: Utah State University Press.

Lerner, Neal. 1997. "Counting Beans and Making Beans Count." *Writing Lab Newsletter* 22 (1): 1–4.

———. 2001. "Choosing Beans Wisely." *Writing Lab Newsletter* 26(1): 1–4.

———. 2002. "Insider as Outsider: Participant Observation as Writing Center Research." In *Writing Center Research: Extending the Conversation*, eds. Paula Gillespie, Allice Gillam, Lady Falls Brown, and Byron Stay, 53–71. Mahwah: Lawrence Erlbaum.

———. 2006. "Time Warp: Historical Representations of Writing Center Directors." In *The Writing Center Director's Resource Book*, eds. Christina Murphy and Byron Stay, 3–11. Mahwah: Lawrence Erlbaum.

Macauley, W. J., Jr. *Writing Center mission statement and learning goals*. Unpublished worksheet, Writing Center, College of Wooster, Wooster, OH.

McAndrew, Donald A., and Thomas J. Reigstad. 2001. *Tutoring Writing: A Practical Guide for Conferences*. Portsmouth, NH: Boynton/Cook Heinemann.

Moss, Pamela A. 1996. "Enlarging the Dialogue in Educational Measurement: Voices from Interpretive Research Traditions." *Educational Researcher* 25 (1): 20–28, 43.

Murphy, Christina, and Byron Stay, eds. 2006. *The Writing Center Director's Resource Book*, Mahwah, NJ: Lawrence Erlbaum.

Neff, Joyce Magnotto. 2002. "Capturing Complexity: Using Grounded Theory to Study Writing Centers." In *Writing Center Research: Extending the Conversation*, edited by Paula Gillespie, Allice Gillam, Lady Falls Brown, and Byron Stay, 133–66. Mahwah, NJ: Lawrence Erlbaum.

Simpson, Jeanne. 2006. "Managing Encounters With Central Administration." In *The Writing Center Director's Resource Book*, edited by Christina Murphy and Byron Stay, 199–214. Mahwah, NJ: Lawrence Erlbaum.

Smith, William L. 2009. "The Importance of Teacher Knowledge in College Composition Placement Testing." In *Assessing Writing: A Critical Sourcebook*, edited by Brain Huot and Peggy O'Neill, 179–202. Boston, MA: Bedford St. Martin's.

Walvoord, Barbara. 2004. *Assessment Clear and Simple: A Practical Guide for Institutions, Departments, and General Education*. San Francisco, CA: Jossey-Bass.

3

CONNECTING WRITING CENTER ASSESSMENT TO YOUR INSTITUTION'S MISSION

William J. Macauley, Jr.

Chapter 1 focused on looking inward to develop a strong sense of a writing center's values, as a foundation for work in assessing that writing center. There is good reason, which I discussed in chapter 1, to build writing center assessment out of the values that inform that center. However, writing centers don't work in a vacuum; centers live and breathe within institutions, in relation to other academic entities. Writing centers depend on those institutions and those other entities for so much of their work; it behooves writing center directors (WCDs) to acknowledge this reality and work with it. However, negotiating the relationships between a writing center, institution, and other educational offices, academic programs, and curricula is fraught with worries for the WCD: How far should the writing center go in acculturating to an institution and its administration? What can the writing center safely give in order to cooperate with other programs? At what point is the integrity of the center compromised? Writing centers can find themselves in any number of places along the continuum between complete independence and complete assimilation.

The Center Will Hold: Critical Perspectives on Writing Center Scholarship illustrates at least two possible positions on that continuum through Josephine A. Koster's "Administration across the Curriculum" and "Breathing Lessons" by Michele Eodice, which argue for bringing the interests of administrators into the center versus bringing our interests out to others, respectively. Their seemingly contrasting views could certainly be seen as polemical; should WCDs choose to become "administration" and turn away from being writing center people *or* do they make administrators understand the unique work that writing centers do by demanding recognition? Meanwhile, neither Koster nor Eodice argues that this is a real or singular choice. In her discussion of working more effectively with administrators, Koster writes:

> We lose nothing by learning about and employing conventions, disciplinary practices, and linguistic expectations of administrators, just as we have lost nothing by learning about the conventions, disciplinary practices, and linguistic expectations of literary theorists, educational philosophers, cognitive psychologists, and yes, even chaos mathematicians. (164)

Although Koster focuses on rhetorical concerns, her proposition is an expression of a larger idea: we lose nothing by learning about others' values and cultures—and we have to engage with some specific others to get our work done. Eodice extends this idea when she writes that we have much to gain by engaging with others in our institutions:

> professional and social networks are already formed and formidable within the writing center community; these are powerful and productive and ferry our goodies back and forth to each other, but to go beyond this we need to become a "smart mob"—a home grown initiative that utilizes our workaday knowledge to reach others in ways that can impact policy, influence administrative and institutional leaders, and help us grow leaders from among our writing center fellows. (129)

Eodice acknowledges what we can do with our resources within a writing center community; her statement reflects her larger argument that we export collaboration from the writing center and suggests that we may be able to bring the powerful network we have within writing centers to the work we need to do outside of them. She argues that we must build outward from writing centers in order to engage effectively with those around us and, by extension, continue to develop our own work. Certainly, tacit in Eodice's argument is Koster's claim—we have to be participants in the discussions that impact our centers. However, she takes the discussion one step further by arguing that we can and should influence toward writing centers culture the administrators who are making decisions relevant to our centers. In the simplest terms, we have to know what matters to those with whom we work (and want to work) in order to most effectively collaborate with them. Beyond that, we must be deliberate in understanding and engaging others who can impact our work (as we wish to impact theirs).

That idea is at the heart of this chapter: engaging those around us in order to accomplish more for our centers. This chapter argues for making connections with our institutions through not only our assessment results but the careful consideration of institutional objectives when we are developing writing center assessments. More specifically, this chapter will focus on how WCDs can use mission statements, vision statements, institutional goals and objectives, and/or strategic plans from their own campuses to develop useful, meaningful assessments. I will look at this work in three distinct ways. First, I will focus on mining institutional statements and documents for ideas that a WCD might use in writing center assessments. Second, I will discuss WCDs using these same sources to think about priorities for both their centers and their institutions. Finally, I will argue for mining institutional statements about mission, vision, and or strategic planning for language that can be useful in writing center assessment.

WHY INSTITUTIONAL MISSION AND VISION STATEMENTS?

First, when a WCD begins with institutional statements, she is acknowledging Brian Huot's admonishment that writing assessment must be locally contextualized. Second, a WCD who starts with institutional statements can acquire the local language of assessment through these statements, both in terms of outcomes and methods, as recommended by Koster. This language acquisition is part and parcel of what Huot and Nicole Caswell argue is translation work, in the afterword to this book. The WCD can recognize and use local, direct knowledge, as was suggested by William Smith's article discussed in chapter 2.[1] The offices where these statements originate can tell the WCD a great deal about current priorities and their origins, which can make writing center assessments much more timely and useful. This kind of information can also help WCDs to identify those who are making decisions and provide access to the processes by which those decisions are made.

The most concise and pragmatic answer to this question—why look to institutional statements in developing writing center assessments—is of course this: writing center assessors should engage institutional statements, objectives, and goals because institutional mission and vision determine writing center work and resources. If a writing center seems to administrators to be ignoring institutional priorities (and this can happen when writing center assessment goes in another direction or simply when it is not using the language of the agenda for the institution), it is that much more vulnerable to resource reductions,

---

1.   Smith's research found that experience with teaching courses into which students would be placed was an important factor in agreement among teachers' reading/rating student placement writing samples.

absorption into other institutional entities, and even the possibility of elimination. As much of a reality as these responses may be, such a limited answer from a writing center is shortsighted at best. Any academic entity, including a writing center, sustains itself and its work by making that work accessible and relevant, and by showing that the unit is productive. If within writing centers we are no more creative than focusing only on protecting our budgets (not to dismiss the importance of our budgets), that will be obvious to others, and our writing centers' biggest problems will not be in designing assessments. Once that impression is in place, it will be very difficult to displace. However, if WCDs can think a bit more generously, they will find that their institutions can provide a great deal of information, direction, and prioritizing through institutional statements of vision, mission, and strategic priorities.

I want to be clear that I am not advocating the wholesale appropriation of writing centers' work—not even just our assessment work—to accommodate institutional flag-waving. What I am saying is this: there is a lot of information available to WCDs through statements about our institutions' plans and objectives, which is both useful and relevant to meaningful writing center assessment. These statements provide writing centers and their host institutions with opportunities to work together and extend one another's influence, to develop shared understandings of what is useful and possible for both, and to create more options for the writing center to do its unique work. Assessment can help WCDs bring their expertise to bear on institution-wide work as well as help others to recognize and value the unique contributions that can be made only by the writing center.

My discussion of using institutional statements to inform writing center assessment is based on my collection and analysis of institutional, writing program, and writing center mission statements from thirty-seven small, private, liberal arts colleges in the Midwest—institutions like the College of Wooster. The thirty or so institutional mission statements I have collected vary between 28 and 747 words, which indicates both the range and multiple purposes to which these statements can be directed, as well as the richness they can provide to WCDs in thinking through the relationships between their centers' missions and those of the institutions that host them. College and university mission statements are often expected to situate schools within historical contexts as well as school systems (consortia, religious organizations, educational traditions, and so on). They can be used to describe schools themselves, institutional traditions, new programs, old programs, curricula, degree options, philosophies, resources. They can identify learning goals, student qualities, educational environments, graduate attributes . . . I think you get the picture. Unfortunately, they are also often dismissed for a number of reasons. Whatever they do, institutional statements of purpose, goals, or objectives should not be ignored by WCDs who are developing writing center assessments; they are rich resources of information and direction. Why reinvent the wheel?

In some ways, working with institutional statements is like working on higher-order concerns before delving into lower-order concerns (McAndrew & Reigstad 2001). When you are mining institutional statements for ideas, you are working to develop a *focus*; this can be accomplished through institutional statements alone, although it is smart to use them in concert with the focus of the writing center itself. *Developing* that focus further, through consideration of institutional values and statements, allows for a much richer foundation for outlining an assessment project and choosing options for completing it. And a WCD cannot lose track of the voice of the writing center within that larger assessment, either.

Mining institutional statements for priorities is akin to *organizing* and *developing* ideas into a workable and meaningful whole. Because you took the time to clarify your goals, and have found points of commonality between the writing center and institutional statements of mission and purpose, you can make informed decisions about what should come first and why, as well as how, each idea might lead into what follows.

Mining institutional statements for language is like developing *tone* as well as addressing lower-order concerns. For the newest writing center assessor, the language of institutional statements can simply provide options for both the operation of writing center assessments and the reportage that results from it. Shared language can help others to understand the work of the writing center while also providing the writing center with useful terminology that reflects the local context. Commonality of language also allows a WCD to adapt his or her rhetoric, and thereby demonstrate alignment, to those whose decisions can directly impact the writing center.

Altogether, this process of reviewing institutional statements can be an essential part of writing center assessment. In many ways, it can confirm institutional ideas that already exist tacitly in writing center programming. It can make overt connections that might not otherwise have been made (for both the writing center and others in the institution). Finally, if nothing else, it increases the options available to a writing center director who needs meaningful ways to assess the work of her center.

MINING INSTITUTIONAL STATEMENTS FOR ASSESSMENT IDEAS

Obviously, mission, vision, and strategic planning statements are designed to articulate broad-stroke ideas that are important to an institution; these kinds of statements can oftentimes be the only places where those ideas are stated overtly. A writing center and the institution that hosts it can so often share values and objectives, even though those shared ideas are seldom overtly stated. These kinds of statements are important points of contact between them. As a result, institutional statements are a wonderful source of ideas for writing center assessment because they can so often point to such big ideas that already "play well" with the rest of the institution.

The ideas available through institutional statements can provide a WCD with opportunities to explore what is important to the writing center as well as the larger institution. Because those ideas are often so broad, WCDs can find concepts that reflect the values of the institution that do not jeopardize the center's values or purposes. The writing center assessment that responds to those shared ideas can do important work in demonstrating the commonalities between the center and institution. There is also a more pragmatic argument: institutional statements can help WCDs to develop assessments that will "count." This can be particularly important when accreditation visits or curricular reviews are on the horizon.

As valuable as these alignments can be, I would also argue that a writing center can influence the direction of an institution by conducting assessments that challenge the status quo. Because institutional statements so often include such broad ideas, there may be more than one way to understand a particular concept found within them. A good example is the differentiation between what many outside of our field understand as learning to write—producing error-free academic prose—and how those within writing centers might define it: developing process, understanding argument, integrating evidence and outside sources, etc.

It can be very easy for an institution to fall into patterns of practice that are built on assumptions without empirical support. In other words, faculty and administrators can easily fall into a pattern of assuming that something is happening in the curriculum, when there is no evidence to support such an assumption, because they want to believe it and often-times because there is no empirical evidence to the contrary. An assessment from the writing center can challenge that pattern. Let's say that your writing curriculum is based on the assumption that students enter the college with a certain level of writing proficiency. The curriculum reflects that assumption and faculty work from it. An assessment of the kinds of writing issues and questions students are bringing to the center can help to confirm those assumptions or demonstrate that students are generally coming in with better or less developed writing skills. If that kind of finding can be matched with data that show the proportion of the student body served by the center, and/or data on how well or poorly these students have done in the writing curriculum courses, a compelling argument can be made, one that could not be made without meaningful writing center assessment.

When any writing center assessment can use the concepts valued by the institution (so frequently available in institutional statements), it not only serves the writing center but enables the institution to reconsider its own assumptions. It can lead to revisiting former assumptions as well as the goals of the institution itself. The writing center can become an agent of institutional change rather than only a recipient of policies and decisions made from a distance.

Beyond these kinds of alignments and challenges, a productive writing center assessment can provide an institution with further clarification of its own big ideas. Because the ideas found in institutional statements tend to be very broad, they can often be unwieldy. If departments or curricula are assessed in some kind of consistent way, the results and/or reporting can often drift into repetitive compliance. Given the unique work of the writing center, and the perspective that such a unique position enables, a writing center assessment focused on some part of a big institutional idea can provide a fresh alternative to other assessment efforts.

So when a WCD is developing a writing center assessment, how can she actually mine these statements for ideas? An example might help. Below you will find the Albion College mission statement. Although it probably works well to describe Albion, there seems to be little or no overt connection to the ideas that pervade a writing center:

> Albion College is an undergraduate, liberal arts institution committed to academic excellence. We are learning-centered and recognize that valuable

> learning takes place in and outside the classroom, on and off campus. We prepare students to translate critical thought into action.

Even so, a writing center could connect with this statement in several ways. What jumps out first for me is the liberal arts ideal. Certainly, there are few sites where multiple fields are engaged and interact more overtly and consistently than they do in an active writing center. Where else on campus are students collaborating around chemistry, anthropology, English, and art history within the same space? More importantly for the liberal arts ideal, there are few places on most campuses where one field is deliberately brought into what is being learned in another. Because not every writer can work with a tutor who is knowledgeable about the field in question, tutors often have to use their own disciplinary knowledge to understand the work a student is doing in another. For example, Leah is working on a historiography paper related to the civil rights movement in the United States. Terry, who is a psychology major, approaches that work from a psychological perspective. Leah finds that the kinds of questions Terry asks about motivation, emotional impact, mob mentality, and the psychology of resistance help her to think more critically about several authors' arguments and evidence in her historiography. Terry learns more about how historians represent and discuss these impacts. I would argue that this is a productive example of liberal arts education at work. I can point to numerous tutorials of my own, within which a student made a transition from the kind of exploratory writing more prominent in the humanities to the third-person objectivity of the natural sciences, or vice versa. This transition could be as simple as a shift in documentation style or as complex as a lengthy discussion of social construction and the scientific method. Certainly, an argument can be made for the writing center as a vehicle for liberal arts education.

Another big idea for a WCD might be the emphasis on learning-centered work. Writing centers can certainly lay claim to this idea because our pedagogy is based not in having an agenda for teaching but in enabling writers to learn about their writing and to develop their critical thinking skills about that work. It might help others on campus to see assessments address this goal in a variety of ways. Certainly, writing centers could contribute options too: audience analysis, reader feedback/response, one-to-one conferencing, collaborative learning, Socratic method, open-ended questions, and the like.

One key to mining institutional statements for ideas: the WCD and writing center assessment should not expect to define institutional priorities. The common ground of the big idea provides a context for exchange as well as a wonderful opportunity to show what the writing center does and what it can do for the institution. Writing center assessment can certainly contribute to a deeper or more faceted understanding of institutional goals. However, the writing center should not be expected to define values or goals for the entire institution. This is too ambitious and, frankly, can be received as impertinent if not outright inappropriate.

If the campus context reads like an environment that is open to ideas from the writing center, a productive writing center assessment focused on an institutional ideal can help to provide others with options for handling those big ideas. If the campus environment is less open to what is important in your particular writing center, a productive writing center assessment, based in the big ideas found in institutional statements, can begin to build bridges between the center and the rest of the campus. Assessment is, by definition, a cooperative effort.

Let's look at another mission statement, this time from Ohio Wesleyan University. This institutional mission statement has an additional challenge compared with Albion's; it must not only describe the values of the institution but relate them to the university's charter as well:

OHIO WESLEYAN'S CHARTER provides that "the University is forever to be conducted on the most liberal principles, accessible to all religious denominations, and designed for the benefit of our citizens in general." In the spirit of its heritage, the University defines itself as a community of teachers and students devoted to the free pursuit of truth. It develops, in its students, qualities of intellect and character that will be useful no matter what they choose to do in later life.[2]

The "most liberal principles" can be interpreted in so many ways that greater clarification would be necessary for a WCD looking for assessable learning goals. This can be either a gift or a curse. A WCD might decide that his role is to bring about change; he could go ahead and decide on his own interpretation of liberal principles. A WCD could demonstrate the continuity of mission between the writing center and the rest of the

---

2.   This information was originally gleaned from an official Ohio Wesleyan University webpage, which has since been taken down. The URL listed in the bibliography is a secondary source that includes the same text verbatim.

institution by looking for other local definitions of liberal principles. A WCD might choose some hybrid of the two, if the other options seem too risky or too nebulous. This should certainly not be a decision based only in the WCD's own politics but on a careful reading of the institution and the risks/rewards of taking one approach or another.

Defining the school as a community of teachers and students might be an opportunity to challenge the status quo. Taken too literally, that definition could create real difficulties for acknowledging writing tutors within the institution's mission. However, a WCD, by demonstrating both the character and quality of the work done by those tutors, could certainly argue with that exclusion. An assessment of the kinds of work done by tutors, or the valuing of that work by faculty members, could change minds about where tutors fit. There are also contextual issues to consider, such as whether tutors are teaching on campus, whether the writing center is integrated with curricula in a specified way, or whether the center is considered a curricular entity or support resource. This is a rich field of possibilities.

These are simple speculations and easy to make because the work is not high stakes within the bounds of a chapter in a book like this one. The stakes can be much higher when a WCD is making these kinds of decisions in other contexts. The reality is that these negotiations take a lot of patience, finesse, care, and time. Beyond negotiating commonality within institutional relationships, most institutions continue to change and develop. What might seem like a well-established goal for the school may be on its way out. New understandings of those well-established values may be developing. Dialogue with others on campus is essential to making good decisions about values and objectives to pursue, and a degree of flexibility, as well as agility, is necessary.

MINING INSTITUTIONAL STATEMENTS FOR ASSESSMENT PRIORITIES

At their most basic levels, statements of institutional values, goals, and objectives are statements of priorities. Each statement, by choosing focuses, is deliberately not choosing others. Because they tend to be compact, institutional statements can very often be incredibly useful in understanding institutional priorities. In turn, writing centers can use these priorities to develop meaningful writing center assessments that can, again, connect the writing center overtly with the rest of the institution.

There are at least two ways to work through these priorities. One way is to assume that the order of topics included within institutional statements indicates a prioritizing. For example, a small college might create a statement such as this (fictional institution): The College of Chillicothe (CC) provides an educational experience that is accessible, affordable, and focused on productive careers in the arts. If CC is an institution that is new and working hard to build a larger student body, accessibility may be a primary concern. Accessibility can also mean a number of different things: it can refer to geography, to sensitivity to issues of limited mobility, or to engaging students with a range of academic preparation, for example. For the writing center, accessibility is always a primary concern, and a writing center assessment could certainly respond to this institutional goal by assessing usage by non-native speakers of English, by looking into repeat visits, or by investigating the use of online writing center resources for commuter students. The point is that order within institutional statements can indicate priorities, but the WCD working to develop meaningful assessments must think carefully about the institutional context, too, in order to make informed decisions about this approach.

A second approach to mining institutional statements for priorities has to do with repetition. For example, the goal of communicating new knowledge is found in both Wooster's mission statement and its vision statement; certainly, this is a goal that the writing center could embrace easily. When a WCD finds a goal or reflections of a goal repeated, this is a good indication that the goal is important. On the other hand, if a WCD's review of institutional documents reveals that a particular goal appears only in, say, the mission statement for the library or in an assessment plan for the writing curriculum, that may indicate that the goal is less widely accepted. This does not mean the goal is unimportant, but it does mean that, institutionally, it may not be one of the higher priorities.

Looking for repetition is a smart approach for a couple of reasons. First, this approach involves reviewing multiple institutional documents such as mission statements, vision statements, institutional assessments and assessment plans, campus master plans, reports to accrediting agencies, departmental assessment plans, and any number of other institutional documents that outline priorities and plans. The more points of reference a WCD has in choosing a focus for her writing center assessment, the more certain she can be of that focus as a viable option and the better she can argue for that decision. Compare these two statements:

1. The writing center values nondirective tutoring and plans to assess the success of tutoring staff in applying this practice.

versus

2. The writing center values accessibility in many forms, particularly in terms of repeat visits. Accessibility is of primary importance throughout CC and is identified as a priority in the college's mission statement, strategic planning, and multiple recent curriculum review reports. Our proposed assessment will focus on one aspect of accessibility: the use of online writing center resources by commuter students.

Of course, this comparison is somewhat exaggerated, but not much. It is clear that the latter statement has more power and veracity because it is backed up with evidence—evidence that is very familiar to and may have originated with the very entities to which an assessment proposal or plan might be submitted. It is important to support assessment decisions with evidence, and it is probably just as important (in some cases, it will be more important) to demonstrate clear connections between writing center assessments and the big-ticket ideas on campus.

In the first few years of my working at the College of Wooster, there was plenty to do. I started looking for writing center goals and objectives, for institutional goals that I could connect to the work of our writing center (because there were no such statements about our center). I found a few very broad goals for the writing program and some questionable habits of practice in our center. In fact, I found a rich environment of views, opinions, impressions, and claims, but I didn't really find anything concrete. There had been a number of writing program assessments, but I couldn't really see ways to use them in developing assessable writing center outcomes. So I had to figure out how to move from multiple fragments of unsupported ideas to something that was useful and usable in terms of assessing the strengths and weaknesses of our writing center.

My first step was a very familiar one: I worked to find out how our current services were perceived. I generated a session evaluation form, which staff would ask writers to complete after their sessions. Second, I surveyed the faculty and students to see what their levels of writing center satisfaction were. Third, I began assembling the various strands of commentary that I could find.

The Wooster staff continued to use the session evaluation forms. On a scale of 1 to 4 (1 being best), the College of Wooster Writing Center was continually rated overall in the 1.3 to 1.5 range; I saw this as good, with room for improvement. I was only able to survey all of the students and faculty once (concerns about survey fatigue on campus prohibited any follow-up surveys); the results of that survey found that 88 percent of students responding and 90 percent of faculty responding recommended the writing center to others. Although the response rate was pretty low, these data, combined with the session evaluations, steadily and dramatically increasing numbers of tutorials, and increasing departmental interactions told me that our work was seen positively. In fact, I was able to sneak in a short survey of first-year seminar and writing-course faculty one spring and found that they consistently wanted more professional staff available in the writing center, to support their teaching. However, none of this solved the problem of planning an assessment agenda.

So I kept track of every comment and thought about our writing center that I came by. I ran a faculty focus group of both senior and junior faculty to ask what could be done to better support student writing, where I gained a good bit of useful information. If there was a committee meeting where the writing center came up, I made a note. If a department developed goals that included writing, I got a copy. As our new president developed his strategic planning for the college, he also began sharing drafts of the developing plans. Although these plans did not necessarily or directly discuss the writing center, they did include priorities and values to which our writing center's work responded, sometimes very directly.

I then began a mapping process. First, I made lists and worked to align goals and objectives across different constituencies such as the writing program, our first-year seminar, and our writing-intensive sophomore courses. I also reviewed the charges for committees working with writing and other academic programs. I reviewed all of the departmental assessment plans and learning outcomes. I also continued to discuss my work with administrators, as well as my staff, looking for insights that I might have missed or misconstrued. In the end, I found that I had a short list of assessable learning goals that our writing center could act on:

- Create new knowledge
- Clarity: rhetorical sophistication[3] and mechanical control

---

3. Rhetorical sophistication refers to the goals of constructing and sustaining an argument and using evidence as well as range, argument, audience, and coherence. It also refers to engaging the rhetorical triangle as a decisive paradigm toward the

- Appropriate use of sources: academic integrity and documentation style
- Audience analysis
- Disciplinary form/genre
- Specialized (i.e., disciplinary) language

The staff spent a good deal of time thinking about the objectives I had developed in relation to our mission statement and worked to articulate the most familiar focuses within our tutorial sessions. The staff worked specifically from the mission statement because it really captured our work, but also because each item described a range of options that could be pursued independently. Based on our mission statement, the staff settled on the following learning outcomes:

Students should read closely.

Although this was not an objective among the institutional mapping I had done, the staff and I agreed that this was such an essential part of the work that we did in our writing center that it had to be included. We thought of this statement as focused on the texts to which students were responding as well as those that students were generating. Staff members also liked that this learning goal could include the kinds of work done in the peer review sessions they led in many classrooms.

Students should inquire critically.

This feature of our local writing center work informed the writing that students worked on with us, but it was not necessarily a directly assessable outcome within their writing. Staff liked the openness of this learning goal because it could be applied to multiple texts and the text of tutorials, and they were concerned about trying to capture it empirically.

Students should thoughtfully discuss their writing.

Again, this objective was regarded as essential to our writing center's work but not necessarily evident in student writing or institutional statements. Staff members liked that this outcome could be found in spoken or written form and could focus on the production, product, or thinking students were doing about their writing. We also saw this as

rhetorical analysis of the author's role, the media available in any given context, and audience analysis toward the most effective critical thinking and communication.

the development of useful language around writing, an essential and empowering opportunity for student writers.

Students' writing processes should continue to develop.

For us, this indicated that we were not simply correcting work for writers, and enabling them to become dependent on us, but helping them to think critically about how they worked with their writing.

Students' written products should improve.

This was certainly a priority for our writing center and aligned nicely with the overall ideas we had for developing writing center learning goals, even if it didn't show up overtly within the mapped statements.

The staff and I had to think very carefully about how much we could do and how much we wanted to do in relation to our own assessments as well as how those assessments might be used in conjunction with institutional goals. About the time we finished this work, the president's strategic planning had identified working mission, vision, and goals statements for the institution:

> Mission Statement: Our institutional purpose
>
> *Why we exist and what we seek to accomplish*
>
> The College of Wooster is a community of independent minds, working together to prepare students to become leaders of character and influence in an interdependent global community. We engage motivated students in a rigorous and dynamic liberal education. Mentored by a faculty nationally recognized for excellence in teaching, Wooster graduates are creative and independent thinkers with exceptional abilities to ask important questions, research complex issues, solve problems, and communicate new knowledge and insight.

As the staff and I mined this new mission statement for connections with our work, we found several. Certainly, we could see our work in the ideal of independent minds working together; every tutorial is a collaboration between individuals working together to solve problems. Tutorials in the Wooster Writing Center were dynamic because they engaged so many different ideas, fields, problems of expression, and varieties of disciplinary appropriateness. Most exciting was the emphasis on creative and independent thinking. To be honest, we couldn't help but see our work in nearly every facet of that mission statement.

Just about the time that the new mission statement premiered, an additional statement was also introduced to the college community, something we had not before seen or used at the college: a vision statement. While the mission statement focused on what the college was doing at that moment, the vision statement was intended to describe where the college intended to go in the future. The writing center staff and I found our work clearly embedded within this statement as well.

> Vision Statement: The future to which we aspire
>
> Our collective endeavor is to prosper as a distinguished independent liberal arts college, to thrive as a vigorous intellectual community, and to create a reputation that reflects our achievements. We seek to be leaders in liberal learning, building on our tradition of graduating independent thinkers who are well prepared to seek solutions to significant problems, to create and communicate new knowledge and insight, and to make significant contributions to our complex and interdependent world.

Staff more than once remarked that the college aspired to become a successful writing center—out of our shared pleasure in how well our goals aligned with those of the institution, not out of hubris or a lack of humility. We could see our work clearly implicated as a vigorous intellectual community (we never simply fixed things for student writers, even when they or their professors wanted us to), graduating independent thinkers. Figuratively speaking, our teaching our clients to "fish" instead of handing them a fish resonated deeply with the graduating of liberal thinkers. Most overtly, we found our work implicated in students learning to create and communicate new knowledge.

Along with the mission and vision statements, the college published a list of its core values. When we looked at the core values, we continued to feel very much connected with the expressed direction of the college:

> Wooster's Core Values: The values that govern our shared pursuits
>
> Ideas that we hold true:
>
> - Education in the Liberal Arts Tradition
> - A Focus on Research and Collaboration
> - A Community of Learners
> - Independence of Thought

- Social and Intellectual Responsibility
- Diversity and Inclusivity

The staff and I could not have been happier with the values and priorities we clearly shared with the core values of the college: collaboration, learning community, independent thought, responsibility, diversity, and inclusivity. The points of commonality between the college and the writing center were staggeringly numerous. And then we realized something: they were so numerous that we had a problem of abundance. We also had the problem of narrowing these ideals sufficiently to make them assessable. The staff and I were faced with having to choose, so we focused on simplicity; in other words, we strove for goals that we thought would be most readily relatable to the college's new statements and goals but that would also provide the most useful representation of the work that our writing center did.

After much discussion, the staff and I settled on these:

Students' writing processes should continue to develop.

This goal was certainly overt in the work of the writing center. We also saw it as resonating with the writing center's mission statement at least through creative and independent thinking because students had to develop their own productive writing processes that were unique to their own strengths, weaknesses, interests, and training. The connection between this goal and the institutional vision statement revolved around creating and communicating new knowledge as well as the development of rhetorical, syntactical, and disciplinary expertise through writing center tutorials. A core value for both the writing center and the college was collaboration as well as independence of thought; the Wooster Writing Center focused on working together with students toward developing their own ideas, arguments, and texts.

Students' written products should improve.

The missions of both the college and the Wooster Writing Center focused on enabling students to ask important questions and solve problems. Our experiences in the writing center confirmed that students were doing just that in our tutorials. A shared vision included students making significant contributions to the complex and interdependent world around us—understanding and developing texts of many kinds would be essential to those efforts. As was the case for the college, one of the writing center's core values was responsibility, which included everything from students accurately documenting their sources to considering the ramifications of their ideas in the world where those ideas might be activated.

We in the Wooster Writing Center thought that these two goals would serve us best for a number of reasons. Beyond the commonalities we saw with institutional statements, they were the most readily recognizable outcomes of student writer development. Second, they captured some or all of several of the goals I had developed out of my goal mapping work. Finally, they were readily assessable and, as such, well within our resources.

Not long after, a new "graduate qualities" document was released to incoming students and their parents. This document had important implications for the direction of the institution, as well as our writing center, because it described what our institution saw as the ideal in our graduating seniors. These qualities were similar to but not identical with other institutions' statements of graduate attributes or graduate learning outcomes. The differences may seem semantic, but they were not. Instead of focusing only on what the college would like our graduates to be capable of or display to others, institutional planners went a step further and described how College of Wooster alums should engage with the world around them through:

- Independent Thinking
- Integrative and Collaborative Inquiry
- Dynamic Understanding of the Liberal Arts
- Effective Communication
- Global and International Engagement
- Civic and Social Responsibility

Under each of these headings were lists of numerous specific abilities, characteristics, and skills understood to contribute to these qualities and reflective of the designs and learning goals of Wooster's academic programs. The Wooster Writing Center staff and I continued to find a wealth of connections between our work and the aspirations of the college at large: engagement in critical and creative thinking, effective intellectual collaboration, understanding disciplinary knowledge in multiple fields, skill in communication, self-reflective awareness, and appreciating/critiquing values, for example. More to the point, we could see direct connections between the objectives we had chosen to assess and the qualities the college intended for its graduates: devising and completing complex and creative projects, synthesizing knowledge from multiple disciplines, textual literacy, effective discourse, global processes (which we used to describe holistic thinking about large projects like senior independent studies), multimedia writing for diverse audiences, and the like.

These examples of mining institutional statements for writing center assessment priorities have probably seemed like a turbulent and never-ending assessment project. It could have been. A WCD designing writing center assessments must take care not to lose focus in the accumulation of commonalities with the rest of the institution. It is possible to become so interested in commonality that the writing center's priorities can become blurred or lost altogether. The WCD must keep in mind that the purpose of this work is to find meaningful assessments of the writing center, work that is meaningful within the context of the home institution, as opposed to maybe proving that the writing center is committed to institutional objectives or possibly seeking institutional priorities that will stand the writing center in good stead politically. These outcomes can certainly happen, but they should be outcomes of appropriate, successful assessments rather than the purposes out of which those assessments are designed. It is hard enough to do good assessment without complicating it further and blurring the goals of the project. WCDs should also keep in mind that institutional goals, priorities, and focuses change, and so do those of writing centers. So rather than fixing a location for our work in the current published priorities of an institution, WCDs must continue to develop assessments that make sense in the space between what the institution is saying, what it is doing, and the priorities and values of the writing center.

MINING INSTITUTIONAL STATEMENTS FOR ASSESSMENT LANGUAGE

There is no question that the goals and objectives of writing centers can sometimes compare and at other times contrast with those of their host institutions. Ideally, a WCD who is developing writing center assessments would find ideas, priorities, and language that readily represent the work of the writing center. Even if this is not so, a WCD can often find a great deal of common ground between the goals of her home institution and the writing center itself, even when the language is not exactly the same. Sometimes, as Koster suggested, we are simply speaking from contrasting discourses, and it is in our own best interest to put our rhetorical skills to work to bridge these discursive gaps. Sometimes the WCD just has to look a bit harder and think a bit more creatively.

At Wooster, creating and communicating new knowledge was a goal in both the mission and vision statements for the college. Certainly, any writing center could see its own work implicated within these broader goals, and we in the Wooster Writing Center did not miss it. Although we would not have otherwise used these phrases, we recognized the wisdom of doing so and the opportunity that new language provided for developing our own thinking while we simultaneously expanded these ideas for the college.

We in the Wooster Writing Center could easily see these phrases meaning writing. However, if we came at a writing center assessment naming writing as the sole focus of our assessment, we would obviously be working within the purview of the writing center but missing an opportunity to connect the goals of the writing center with the goals of the college. Meanwhile, if our writing center assessment identified communicating new knowledge as a primary goal to be assessed, and then went into assessing writing as part of that work, we could do the same assessments, connect them directly to the goals and interests of the rest of the college, and make our unique interpretation (as well as greater understanding of the work of the writing center) available to the rest of the campus community. So in this case, an adjustment in language that did not require any real change in assessment plans served to make both the writing center and its assessment more institutionally relevant and accessible.

However, it is not always simply a matter of semantics. Sometimes a writing center has to argue for their goals in light of institutional goals. Here is an example. The mission statement from Antioch University Midwest is not focused on writing or a writing center. However, that does not mean that writing center assessment at Antioch could not find common language with the rest of the university in terms of goals and assessment. In this case, an argument might be necessary to connect the values of the writing center with the language in the university mission statement. Here is Antioch University Midwest's mission statement:

> Antioch University Midwest is imbued with an entrepreneurial spirit and strives to provide high quality, socially responsive, flexible, and innovative

educational programs. Antioch University Midwest seeks to pass on to its graduates a legacy of passion for lifelong learning and a commitment to the application of knowledge toward the betterment of our workplaces, our communities, and the wider society.

The low-hanging fruit here are the ideas such as social responsiveness, flexibility, and innovation. The risk here is that these are not the big-ticket items but part of a list of curricular qualities. However, the items at the beginning and end of the mission statement are much larger because they describe the "spirit" of the institution, its "legacy." These may be more difficult to connect to the goals of a writing center, even while they are clearly larger ideas for the mission of the university.

Given this context, I would tend to look for ways to connect with the big ideas in the mission statement. I would want this choice to be as fruitful as possible. Meanwhile, I would also work to engage those whose reading of the mission statement was brief and/or prioritized. In other words, I would try to work with the ideas that others would most readily recognize as part of the university's mission statement. The first ideas in the mission statement would be the most attractive, and I would go after connecting the work of the writing center with the idea of entrepreneurship.

The task at hand would be to define entrepreneurship in ways that would include the work of the writing center. The challenge would not be to find common language but to define entrepreneurship, in institutional language, in a way that allows for the work of the writing center. Entrepreneurs work to bring something new into the world; certainly, student writers who are working beyond their current abilities are doing that. Entrepreneurs assess situations and decide on appropriate responses; a writer working with a tutor often spends time working out the cost-benefit relationships in various options. Entrepreneurs focus a great deal of time and energy on getting the right people to help them produce the right deliverables; a writing center and tutor can certainly be understood in that light. So even if it is not simply a question of semantics, an adept WCD can argue for connections with institutional priorities in the development of meaningful writing center assessment. In this case, finding useful language is about redefining the terminology of institutional values to include writing center work and values.

However, there are other circumstances when the contrasts between the language of institutional statements and writing center goals are simply too great. This is when the clarity of writing center values, indicators, and assessable outcomes are most important because an argument for them can be made. A WCD is much better off to argue from within the center than to try and force a fit that doesn't exist. If an assessment tries too hard to make its goals fit with institutional goals, and forces unusual definitions or turns of phrase to do so, it not only jeopardizes the veracity of the assessment proposal but creates unnecessary challenges for doing the assessment work. When an assessment project seems contrived and then fails, this can do a great deal of damage to the writing center and future writing center relationships.

MAKING WRITING CENTER ASSESSMENT "STICKY"

The idea of reaching out from our writing centers is certainly not new. Within the field, we can see a steady progression from justifying our existence to an increasing sense of ourselves as recognizable participants in the academic project. More importantly, a theme that cannot be ignored is the idea that reaching out to others is not only something writing centers are doing, now that we have greater confidence and presence, but something that has long been appreciated as benefiting writing centers and the institutions that house them.

What has continued to complicate that work is the success of these efforts. The more we reach out, the more options we have—and the more ways we have to access, see, and understand our work and the work that is possible for us. The more we work to make ourselves part of the world around us, the more dispersed our writing centers' missions can become. Writing centaurs (those who work in writing centers and/or participate in WCenter discussions) have to be careful not to become victims of their own successes.

But there are ways of protecting our sanity as well as making informed choices about our assessment priorities. In 2007 Dan Heath and Chip Heath published *Made to Stick: Why Some Ideas Survive and Others Die*. In that book, they set out six principles that describe ideas that stick:

1. Simplicity
2. Unexpectedness
3. Concreteness
4. Credibility
5. Emotions
6. Stories

As they put it, "Here's our checklist for creating a successful idea: a Simple Unexpected Concrete Credentialed Emotional Story" (18). It should be no surprise that these are qualities that describe successful assessment as well. A good assessment is simple in its design, using the most efficient means to answer its questions. It is unexpected in that, being real research, new knowledge is discovered. It is concrete; the relationships between the methods, measures, and outcomes are clear. It is credible in that the reasoning and interpretations are logical and reasonable. Good assessment engages the emotions because it excites the mind and invigorates the work. And good assessment always produces a story worth telling and hearing.

In the first chapter of this book, I argued that the values that inform the work of a writing center are "sticky," so to speak. But looking at those values in relation to the larger institution can make them even stickier. Stickiness is useful in guiding writing center assessors through the seemingly unstable world of mission and vision statements. If we can avoid unnecessarily complex assessments and assessment goals, we necessarily make it easier for ourselves in expressing meaningful outcomes and for others in readily understanding and appreciating those same outcomes. Unexpectedness should be, well, expected when we are making new knowledge about our work, helping others to understand our work in new ways, and relating that work to the goals of the institution. The more concrete our goals, the more integral they can be to the institution. The more we can tie our assessments to the work and priorities of larger, recognizable institutions, including our own, the more credentialed our work will be. The emotional element (as suggested by Heath and Heath) should not inform the assessment itself; rather, it can be the joy of others finding us and our work, the pleasure of knowing that students are well supported, the frustration that we are not enabling the writers we desire. This is not to be feared or avoided; it is a moment of community, an "aha" moment, an opportunity to discover a shared value or objective.

The stories that a provocative assessment can potentially generate are multiple and multivalent. They can be stories of what colleagues have discovered together, through shared assessment results and discussions of institutional objectives. They can be the ongoing story of an institution that values and supports student writing. Those stories can be new tales of what students are actually doing to become the writers the institution and writing center strive to enable. They can be stories of student empowerment, writing center ownership of its own work, and institutions learning just what a rich and resourceful writing center can do for them.

In short, writing centers are sticky ideas, and as they become more concrete in their outcomes and results, they will develop even greater adhesive abilities. Writing centers need not simply attach themselves to an institution; the best adhesives, the stickiest ideas, alter that to which they adhere. And they, too, are altered by the bonding. The chemical interaction does not simply bind one to another; a truly sticky idea changes the surface of both toward creating a new material that is the commonality of the two.

Writing center goals that "stick to" institutional statements are valuable for the writing center that is working to become a more overt participant in the institution. Beyond that, these adherences provide another range of options for the writing center assessor. By considering the widest possible range of values and goals, the writing center assessments that result will be better informed, better conceived, and better designed. In chapter 5, Ellen takes up the challenge of designing assessment methods that reflect the goals and values a writing center might engage. If the values and goals are clear, the development of methods will simply extend the discussion of what is valued and how. If not, the development of methods will be a particularly difficult next step.

REFERENCES

"Albion College's Mission," accessed January 20, 2009, http://www.albion.edu/catalog//about-albion-college/mission.

"Core Values," *About Wooster: Mission & Vision*, accessed January 20, 2009, http://www.wooster.edu/About-Wooster/Mission%20Statement.

Eodice, Michele. 2003. "Breathing Lessons or Collaboration Is." In *The Center Will Hold: Critical Perspectives on Writing Center Scholarship*, edited by Michael A. Pemberton and Joyce Kinkead, 114–29. Logan: Utah State University Press.

"Graduate Qualities," *About Wooster: Graduate Qualities*, accessed November 28, 2011, http://www.wooster.edu/About-Wooster/Mission%20Statement/qualities.

Heath, Chip, and Dan Heath. 2007. *Made to Stick: Why Some Ideas Survive and Others Die.* New York: Random House.

Koster, Josephine A. 2003. "Administration Across the Curriculum: Or Practicing What We Preach." In *The Center Will Hold: Critical Perspectives on Writing Center Scholarship*, edited by Michael A. Pemberton and Joyce Kinkead, 151–65. Logan: Utah State University Press.

"Mission Statement," *About Antioch University Midwest*, accessed January 20, 2009, http://midwest.antioch.edu/about/statement.html.

"Mission Statement," *About Wooster: Mission & Vision*, accessed November 28, 2011, http://www.wooster.edu/About-Wooster/Mission%20Statement.

"Ohio Wesleyan University," accessed January 20, 2009, http://www.americantowns.com/oh/delaware/organization/ohio-wesleyan-university.

Smith, William L. 2009. The Importance of Teacher Knowledge in College Composition
    Placement Testing. In *Assessing Writing: A Critical Sourcebook,* edited by Brian Huot and
    Peggy O'Neil, 179–202. Boston, MA: Bedford St. Martin's.
"Vision Statement," *About Wooster: Mission & Vision,* accessed January 20, 2009, http://
    www.wooster.edu/About-Wooster/Mission Statement.

4
MOVING FROM OTHERS' VALUES TO OUR OWN
Adapting Assessable Outcomes from Professional Organizations and Other Programs on Your Campus

Ellen Schendel

In chapter 2, Bill outlined a process for generating assessable student learning and programmatic outcomes based on your writing center's values and goals. The steps he described and illustrated were:

1. Articulate the values or goals for your center's work.

2. Develop indicators that are expressions of those values and goals.

3. Construct measures that assess those values and goals.

4. Collect data.

5. Analyze data.

6. Complete the feedback loop by applying what you learned from the data to your center's work.

This process is rooted in serious, deliberate reflection on the work of your writing center to discover and articulate what is most valued and to pose questions that reveal your greatest concerns regarding your center's work. Only then can you begin the long-term, recursive work of collecting and analyzing evidence, recognizing and confirming your writing center's strengths, communicating that story of your center's work to others, and shaping new programming.

Moving from values to outcomes is essential to achieving what Brian Huot calls for in *(Re)Articulating Writing Assessment for Teaching and Learning*: an understanding of how our assessment practices can (and should) align with the theories, research, and best practices of teaching writing—and, we'd add, the tutoring of writing. After all, assessment will only be meaningful to the center's work, our campus communities, and the tutors with whom we work if it addresses the issues that they (and you) care so deeply about: Do writing center consultations help build better writers and better writing? And how do you define "better writers" and "better writing"? How will you know those things when you see them? Are tutors adequately prepared to do the work your center requires? Do the various services and programs offered through your center have the positive impact on students, learning, and perhaps teaching and curriculum that you intend? What should you be doing differently?

A tricky aspect of assessment, however, is that it must satisfy two somewhat competing purposes: first and foremost, the assessments you do need to be rooted in your values so that they are useful to you. They must pursue the questions you care about answering and that help you to move the writing center in the direction you've identified is most impactful on your campus. However, assessment reports are read by others, and the data you collect and analyze may be used in decision making about resource allocation by administrators and perhaps even faculty governance. Therefore, the assessment must begin with your values but still resonate with people who are not "insiders" to writing center scholarship and best practices and who may not approach the reading of your assessment report already convinced of the writing center's value. This political reality of assessment is something to keep in mind early on, as you craft outcomes that drive your plan for collecting data—and ultimately the report you distribute.

The rest of this chapter describes how you might map the writing center's values onto larger conversations about writing and higher education that enable you to show the links between the writing center's and your institution's goals to educate and support students.

An important caveat, however: it is only after articulating the values of your writing center as described in chapter 1 that it makes sense to map those values onto outcomes and best practices from outside of your center. Your center's assessment plan must be built upon the bedrock of what you believe to be important and worth investigating via data collection. An equally important caveat: seeing the potential in linking your assessment to outcomes and assessments outside your center requires an open mind and a collaborative stance—and sometimes, a bit more effort. What you stand to gain, however, is profound—both in how others view your center and in the way your center realizes its potential.

MERGING CONTEXTS: WRITING CENTER VALUES AND INSTITUTIONAL REALITIES

Most writing centers are located in educational institutions, within a landscape that is changing rapidly. State funding to public and private institutions is waning; the recent economic downturn has challenged private institutions' endowments; programs and personnel are being cut or reappropriated—all while the government expects the number of college graduates to rise and while institutions seek out nontraditional and first-generation students in greater numbers than ever before. During the writing of this book, core competencies linking K–12 education and higher education have emerged on a national level, and the National Governors Association has released a call for state institutions to produce standardized data regarding retention rates, graduation rates, and success rates in "remedial courses" offered in writing and math. Higher education is now facing many of the complexities and pressures K–12 schools have felt for years: public policy being driven by misinformation and partisan agendas; a lack of experts in the field involved in the decisions that impact the funding and accountability measures devised by government and the private sector; and a rapidly changing context and lack of public support for the delivery of what research demonstrates to be best practices.

The changing role of higher education in a global society pushes on our local institutions in new ways. Strategic plans respond to the latest expectations of state and national governments while referencing—directly or indirectly—global economic trends in financing education and graduating workforces ready to contribute to a rapidly changing marketplace. Budget decisions are based on data that show how programs impact the bottom line. Institutions are expected to publish data for wide audiences regarding retention and graduation rates.

Writing center directors (WCDs) need assessments that speak to administrators who work daily within this context. We've heard on WCenter and at professional conferences about a number of writing centers facing serious administrative and budget cuts, merging with other units on campus, or closing up shop completely. Thus, we need assessments that allow us to communicate effectively and efficiently with administrators about the valuable work we do and why we do it, in ways our audience—who may be somewhat unfamiliar with or unsympathetic toward writing centers—can find convincing.

As the previous chapter has shown, when we connect writing center work to that of other programs on our campuses, we gain a much richer sense of writing center work and more clearly see for ourselves and communicate to others the uniqueness of the writing center's contributions. Likewise, by finding ways to connect our writing assessments to larger conversations about writing, we also make our work more accessible to others because those conversations happen in the media and across campus and are therefore less specialized and more familiar ground for all constituents. In linking our assessment work to these larger conversations with which administrators are already familiar, we are able to communicate more effectively for a variety of audiences. We have the opportunity to show how the writing center contributes to established values and best practices in higher education while also opening up ourselves to further collaborations with those on campus who now better understand the writing center's work. It is through this reciprocal relationship of articulating our values in a way others value, and reshaping our values to reflect others' values, that we can change the assessment dynamic from "us" *versus* "them" or "us" *and* "them" to a coherent, collegial, inclusive "us."

The rest of this chapter focuses on how you might devise assessment outcomes from professional resources such as the Council of Writing Program Administrators' (CWPA) *Outcomes Statement for First-Year Writing* and the Association of American Colleges and Universities' (AAC&U) Liberal Education and America's Promise (LEAP) goals. Doing so frames writing center work in ways that speak persuasively to the decision makers on campus who will read and act upon your assessment report. In my experience, data and analysis tying a single unit—such as the writing center—to the larger institutional context, and to larger conversations about national trends in the teaching of writing, student learning, and student support, tend to be more convincing to those readers than data and analysis focused only on locally determined outcomes. Additionally, as I'll illustrate later through some examples, finding the common ground between writing center values and outcomes published by professional organizations can help us understand writing center work in new and useful ways.

GETTING TO THE "WE": BRIDGING VALUES VIA THE CWPA'S OUTCOMES STATEMENT

In the financially challenged and rapidly shifting world of higher education, writing center assessments need to answer big questions: What is the writing center's role in helping the institution achieve what it aspires (and is expected) to be? How do we know that the writing center is responsive to the changing demographics of students on campus? What is the worth of our writing center to our campus culture? What is the writing center's role in contributing to a student's growth as a writer?

Because they connect the writing center to the larger picture of the institution's trajectory, these questions can seem daunting to answer. Additionally, the snapshot views of writers we can capture in the writing center are both limited and rather complexly constituted. Designing an assessment that investigates any one of these big-picture questions must also account for the fact that when students visit the writing center, they do so within an intricate web of student support services, writing instruction, curricular experiences, individualized writing practices, and previously formed attitudes about writing. Because of this complexity, and the intimate nature of our work with students as exemplified by the one-to-one conference, the writing center is able to glean a specific, unique perspective on students and their writing. Indeed, a theme running through writing center scholarship focuses on how special this writing-centered perspective really is, implying that there is no other situation quite like it on campus. Granted, what writing centers do is unique, but the work is not happening in a vacuum. A student who visits our writing center at Grand Valley State University has most likely experienced writing from a number of disciplinary perspectives, as taught by writing specialists and other faculty who may feel less confident about writing instruction. The student has most likely composed in a number of genres—from the essay exam to the lab report to the webpage—and has an understanding of writing shaped in part by using (or not) technology in composing texts for classes or in his or her personal life.

Given the rich array of experiences that constitute each student's visits to the writing center, it makes sense to place any assessment outcomes within this web of services, programming, and curricula that have at their heart students' academic success. We can do this by mapping our outcomes onto an institution's strategic plan, as the previous chapter explains and illustrates. Additionally, we can tie our outcomes to best practices in the teaching of writing, and in higher education more generally to the big-picture trends in higher education by which institutional strategic plans are informed and with which administrators are most familiar and comfortable.

Along these lines, it is useful to become familiar with the CWPA's widely used and respected *Outcomes Statement for First-Year Writing*, adopted in 2000 and available to read on the organization's website. This statement "describes the common knowledge, skills, and attitudes sought by first-year composition programs in American postsecondary education." Adopted at institutions around the United States by first-year writing and writing-across-the-curriculum (WAC) programs, it has become the basis of programmatic goals, grading criteria, and both student and program assessment. As such, the outcomes statement is perhaps the most explicit articulation of what directors of writing programs (including writing centers) believe students should learn in classroom-based writing instruction, and it is arguably the document that has had the most impact on writing programs' assessment outcomes.

Much has been written and debated about the outcomes statement, and a particular text of interest to WCDs is *The Outcomes Book: Debate and Consensus after the WPA Outcomes Statement*, published in 2005. In this collection of essays/articles, the outcomes statement is explored in a variety of ways, and a portion of the collection is dedicated to ways the outcomes can be adapted to various programmatic settings: for a technical communication program, for example, or as the foundation for a WAC program.

I see several good reasons to consult the CWPA outcomes statement in building assessable learning outcomes for a writing center. First, the CWPA exists to support the work of writing programs and administrators across the board: first-year writing, WAC, WC. As such, the organization speaks on WCDs' behalf. They're already doing some of the heavy lifting associated with helping faculty, staff, administrators, and the general public understand what college-level writing is all about. Because of this, if we build assessments that connect to the CWPA outcomes statement, we build assessments that automatically have connections to the big-picture messages that the CWPA communicates to legislators, administrators, and the general public. Additionally, we can show nonspecialists at our institutions that the values upon which we're drawing for our assessable outcomes are those that are endorsed by our professional organization and many institutions.

Second, the outcomes are specialized enough to reflect what we in writing centers value but are not so specific that we cannot adapt them to our local contexts. The outcomes have been adopted at various institutions across the United States in diverse ways; the CWPA's website and *The Outcomes Book* detail several institutions' adaptations of the outcomes to program and student learning assessment. The outcomes have provided a programmatic foundation for WAC/writing-in-the-disciplines and first-year composition (FYC) programs alike, and they have been adapted for assessment and curricular reform initiatives. As such, the outcomes represent a shared understanding about the state of writing at institutions across the country, and with that shared understanding comes a better opportunity for collaboration and comparison. For writing centers at institutions where the outcomes are already a part of the other writing programs on campus, adapting the outcomes for writing center assessment allows for more coordinated programming and assessment opportunities. For writing centers in contexts where the CWPA outcomes are not used by other programs, the opportunity to connect to a nationwide discussion of writing instruction and assessment and support remains an important possibility. And finally, the vast number of institutions that have adopted the outcomes to their local contexts give us models by which we can craft our own assessments. It is helpful, given that so many WCDs are the lone specialists on their campuses—or, at best, one of a few writing specialists—that there are so many models and examples of how to integrate the outcomes across a variety of institutions.

Third, and most importantly, the CWPA outcomes are based on research and theory about writing—the same scholarship out of which writing center theory and practice have come. They are learning-centered, process-focused, and discipline-sensitive goals that are applicable to writers across the university. As such, the outcomes are goals that WCDs can believe in and support. We would do well to demonstrate the writing center's role within writing instruction at American colleges and universities.

In sum, the CWPA outcomes offer WCDs and writing program administrators alike the opportunity to devise assessments that speak in harmony with the research and values of our field. It's rhetorically powerful to invoke our professional organizations in describing the writing center's values and purpose for existing as articulated in our assessment outcomes. And it's comforting to know that our assessments are on track with the rich scholarship related to literacy, that the outcomes we devise in our local writing centers are intimately tied to the values of writing professionals across the country.

BUILDING ASSESSABLE OUTCOMES FOR WRITING CENTERS FROM THE CWPA'S OUTCOMES STATEMENT

If you are new to writing center assessment, building learning outcomes and a methodology for addressing them is a daunting task. It's important to begin by taking stock of your writing center's values and concerns. Then, see which of those connect to any of the CWPA outcomes. Try building upon those outcomes for your assessment plan; doing so gives you the opportunity to connect to all that a professional statement and organization have to offer in terms of publicity, support, and legitimacy.

The outcomes statement groups the learning outcomes of FYC courses into several categories:

- Rhetorical Knowledge
- Critical Thinking, Reading, and Writing
- Processes
- Knowledge of Conventions
- Composing in Electronic Environments

Within each of these subsections is a bulleted list of learning outcomes that students should attain by the time they finish first-year writing courses. They are worded with enough specificity to be indicators for an assessment of student writing. For example, these are the (word-for-word) goals listed for students under "Processes":

- Be aware that it usually takes multiple drafts to create and complete a successful text
- Develop flexible strategies for generating, revising, editing, and proof-reading
- Understand writing as an open process that permits writers to use later invention and re-thinking to revise their work
- Understand the collaborative and social aspects of writing processes
- Learn to critique their own and others' works
- Learn to balance the advantages of relying on others with the responsibility of doing their part
- Use a variety of technologies to address a range of audiences

These learning outcomes are carefully crafted to lend themselves to many measures and data-gathering techniques that transcend campus location and program type. For example, "Be aware that it usually takes multiple drafts to create and complete a successful text" could be assessed indirectly, via a survey of students, or directly, via an examination of portfolios that include multiple drafts of each project. Further, the outcome could be made much more specific to the needs of a particular campus. It could become "explain why it takes multiple drafts to complete a successful text," or "show how multiple drafts played a role in the completion of a successful text," and could incorporate students' reflective writing about their processes or interviews/focus groups with writers talking through their projects. (Of course, you wouldn't choose all of these things to assess at once—or even over time; they are just suggested outcomes that could be explored via a writing center's assessment.)

Here is an example of how to turn one of the CWPA outcomes into an assessable learning outcome for a writing center. Let's continue with the extended example offered above: the outcomes related to processes, both within the first-year writing classroom and beyond. The first-year writing outcomes hint at (or perhaps echo) the "making better writers" aspect of writing center work. Below, I've again listed four of the bulleted outcomes under processes, but this time I have connected them to writing center goals that are listed in italics below each outcome:

- Understand the collaborative and social aspects of writing processes.

  - *Provide a forum for students and tutors to enact writing as a collaborative, social process.*

  - *Help students to manage writing as a social process that is an enactment of the "conversation of mankind."*

  - *Ensure tutors are well trained in understanding writing as a collaborative, social process—and in knowing how to engage with writers in productive ways.*

- Learn to critique their own and others' works.

  - *Help writers to identify their writing strengths and weaknesses.*

  - *Help writers to use teacher, peer, and writing tutor feedback to their work to devise plans for revision.*

  - *Help tutors to critique their own and others' works.*

- Learn to balance the advantages of relying on others with the responsibility of doing their part.

  - *Help writers to understand how to use the writing center as a consultation service at various stages of the writing process.*

  - *Help faculty to understand how they can prompt students to use the writing center as a consultation service at various stages of the writing process.*

  - *Train tutors to work collaboratively with writers while still respecting boundaries.*

- Use a variety of technologies to address a range of audiences.

  - *Help students to use technologies to realize their writing goals.*

  - *Help tutors to use technologies appropriately in their tutoring.*

  - *Train tutors to conduct online sessions appropriately.*

You've probably noticed many other writing center values, goals, or outcomes suggested by the CWPA outcomes focused on processes. The list here admittedly reflects my own interests, as influenced by my own local context. Let me walk you through my thinking about which outcomes to choose, how to adapt them to our writing center's context, and how to collect data focused on those outcomes. My point in sharing this example is to suggest that connections between writing center work and the outcomes statement are fruitful, but there are many other connections that might better suit your local context.

An Extended Example: Putting the CWPA Outcomes to Work for One Writing Center

One of my main concerns as a WCD has been helping faculty across the disciplines to understand that a writing center visit is only part of a student-writer's development. While we expect that students' writing and their conceptions of themselves as writers will improve based on their visits to the center, our real pedagogical focus is on helping student-writers to map plans for revisions, which they can follow through on after leaving the center.

Of all of those connections I noted early on between our writing center's values and the CWPA's statement, I was most intrigued with this CWPA outcome: *Learn to balance the advantages of relying on others with the responsibility of doing their part.* It resonates with me because it is at the heart of what writing centers do in helping students to learn to use feedback to achieve their own rhetorical purposes. Additionally, it addresses a concern that I have heard faculty articulate about the writing center: that if students use our services, they'll become dependent on tutors, not doing enough of their own work.

Under that outcome, I wrote a more specific outcome that is even more focused on our writing center's values; it reflects what many of us who direct writing centers understand—that the center is often the site where teacher feedback, writer's purposes, and peer/other responses converge, and that the writing consultant's role is often to help the writer describe his or her purpose, balancing that against the multitude of revision options offered by various readers' responses. Here is the outcome I wrote:

> *Helping writers to use teacher, peer, and writing tutor feedback to devise a plan for revision.*

To collect some data to help us determine whether we achieve this outcome, I decided to add a question upon logging out of the center that asked students about their plans for revision. The question, "What are your plans for revising your paper?" was displayed on the screen of our kiosk at the very end of the check-out process, when students were by themselves (i.e., not being "coached" by consultants). By asking this question, I was first testing whether students actually *had* revision plans upon leaving the center. By making it an open-answer question, I would learn how students describe the revision changes they planned to make. I was giving students the opportunity to articulate the roles of teacher, peer, and writing center feedback and (I hoped!) embrace a unique pedagogical feature of the writing center: writers must do the work of articulating their plans for revision. I hoped, too, to learn a bit about how students describe revision (what language/terms they use; what they seem most focused on) to help us devise later research or assessment questions.

We collected this data for a semester; it was coded by type of revision (local or global, or a mix) and patterns in terminology were noted. One finding, interestingly enough, was that students were focused on local concerns (grammar/mechanics/tweaking documentation) about half of the time; the other half of the time, students said they intended to focus on higher-order concerns such as developing content (most typically expressed as "expanding" or "adding to" the draft) or reorganizing the writing (most typically expressed as "moving" things around). I was excited to see that over 90 percent of students leaving the center answered this question—and indicated they did plan to make some revisions.

I like being able to share with faculty who doubt that we work on grammar/mechanics that students report we do indeed address those areas of their writing. Similarly, I like being able to share with faculty that there are just as many times when students come into the center and leave with ideas about how to revise in more major ways.

Finally, something I realized in talking with my staff about these findings is that we needed to be very explicit and clear with students at the end of sessions: What is your plan for revision? And we needed to ensure that all students left with something written down—a list, an outline, a session summary—to follow up on that plan. To ensure that all students coming into the writing center leave with a plan for revision, we added two brief questions to our computerized check-out system, which are answered by the consultant and tutor together: What did you work on (a closed set of questions), and what is the student's plan for revision? Students can auto-email to themselves the answers to these questions to use while revising their work.

We are currently engaged in devising focus group discussions to follow up with students about their plans for revision. We want to know whether students actually revised their work and how their revisions were received by faculty (or other intended audiences). If they didn't revise, why not? If they changed their revision plan, why? And so forth. I'm excited to see what we learn.

* * *

Another feature of the outcomes statement useful to writing centers is that it invites faculty and units other than those involved with first-year writing to see their connections to students' development as writers. After each section of outcomes is a caveat that faculty and units across campus can build upon those first-year writing outcomes in meaningful ways:

> These statements describe only what we expect to find at the end of first-year composition, at most schools a required general education course or sequence of courses. As writers move beyond first-year composition, their writing abilities do not merely improve. Rather, students' abilities not only

diversify along disciplinary and professional lines but also move into whole new levels where expected outcomes expand, multiply, and diverge. For this reason, each statement of outcomes for first-year composition is followed by suggestions for further work that builds on these outcomes. ("Outcomes")

The expectation is that first-year writing should provide a solid foundation in academic writing but that faculty in the disciplines throughout the university have a responsibility to help student-writers develop processes and rhetorical strategies that meet the disciplinary expectations of writing in the majors. Under "process," the statement includes these student learning outcomes to help faculty in the disciplines see their role in helping students develop as writers:

- To build final results in stages
- To review work-in-progress in collaborative peer groups for purposes other than editing
- To save extensive editing for later parts of the writing process
- To apply the technologies commonly used to research and communicate within their fields ("Outcomes")

Writing centers, which are typically not focused only on first-year writing students, implicitly or explicitly assist writers in these tasks. After all, "To review work-in-progress in collaborative peer groups for purposes other than editing" might as well be a mission statement for many campus writing centers! Perhaps your writing center emphasizes one of these areas in particular for students across the curriculum and at all levels. But let's focus for a moment on just one of these university-wide student learning outcomes: *To save extensive editing for later parts of the writing process.* This resonated with me for several reasons. First, it is tied to one of my goals for talking with faculty at our university, which is to help them view writing as a process and understand how the writing center can assist their students in that process. Second, it fits neatly with the other CWPA-focused goal I mentioned earlier: *Helping writers to use teacher, peer, and writing tutor feedback to devise plans for revision.* I am able to tie two assessment goals together, showing the relevance of revision plans—and the writing center's work in helping students to create them—to both first-year writers and the university's WAC program.

Once the value-laden goals of your writing center are identified within the CWPA outcomes, you can move into devising objectives—or indicators—that demonstrate those goals, and methodologies for assessing them. For example, if "helping students to build final results in stages" is the main learning goal I would like to focus on in a writing center assessment, I would need to identify ways that we can see the writing center's influence on student writers in this way. To put it another way, the outcome can be phrased as a question, with methodologies suggested by that question: *How does the writing center help writers to build results in stages?* Here is how our writing center has built data-gathering strategies around this outcome.

When do writers use our services? We capture this data when students check into the writing center by asking them why they are there. We also get a sense of this at check out when the tutor and student compose a summary of the session. These data help us to see whether students come to us very early in the process, before writing has even been completed, versus later in their processes. We can also get a sense of whether students come to us because they are stuck or because getting feedback is a natural part of their writing process. At what point in their processes do they use the center? Do they visit us multiple times on a single project?

What do they work on when they're in the center? When students log out of the center, the consultant and student compose a summary of their work together. Cumulatively, these visit notes can be coded to help us understand what students and tutors seem to spend their time on. (Our most recent assessment report shows that students and tutors mention global issues 50 percent of the time and proofreading/editing issues 50 percent of the time—a very balanced, and therefore interesting, finding.) Additionally, by tracking these visit notes over time, we can see whether sessions build on each other for students. What seems to happen to students from visit to visit? Is a consultation building upon where the last one left off?

What happens after students leave the center? By ensuring that students have a plan for revision upon leaving the center—and analyzing those plans—we can learn how students plan to incorporate what they learned and experienced in the center to their ongoing writing process. We can note trends across plans, or even explore what kinds of changes students most frequently say they are going to make: Will they make global revisions or editing/proofreading changes? Do they plan to meet with professors, return to the writing center, or consult resources? As mentioned earlier, a more recent assessment plan has been to talk with a group of students, see what kinds of changes they actually did make. Did they follow through on their revision plans? Why or why not? To connect all of this to another process-oriented extended outcome: Do students seem to leave editing issues for later in their processes? And to connect that to the writing center: Do students come back to the writing center to work on editing issues after a session that focuses on higher-order concerns?

As you can see, the kinds of questions I'm interested in answering are unique to writing centers; I have not adopted a professional organization's outcomes *instead* of developing an assessment plan rooted in the values and work that our center does. Rather, I have looked for the places in which the CWPA's outcomes statement highlights the kind of work our center is best poised to do, and doing so allows me to illuminate the writing center's unique role in the writing development of students across campus.

What is most exciting to me as a WCD, however, is that there are three ways to push our engagement with the outcomes statement further. First, if you work in a writing center on a campus with a first-year writing program or a WAC program, the CWPA outcomes statement provides an opportunity for collaboration among those programs. After all, the CWPA is one of our professional organizations—WCDs, WAC program directors, and first-year writing program directors are all welcomed members. For a writing center that is interested in growth and development, this is a community of professionals and colleagues with whom you want to be as connected as possible, because they are your best supporters on your campus. It is easy to imagine a rich, multidimensional assessment plan that is a collaboration among the writing programs and writing center at an institution and based on the CWPA's outcomes.

Second, the CWPA has partnered with the administrators of the National Study on Student Engagement (NSSE) to develop the Consortium for the Study of Writing in College (CSWC), which gives campuses the opportunity to add a sequence of writing-focused questions to their local versions of the survey of freshmen and seniors on their campuses. Overall, the NSSE is a well-respected and widely used instrument for measuring student engagement in the learning process—a marker of student success in college. Because it is administered in students' freshman and senior years, NSSE data offers to institutions a snapshot of how engagement changes during students' time at that college. Because it is cross-institutional, the NSSE offers institutions an opportunity to compare students' self-reported behaviors with those at other institutions.

A smart move for writing centers would be to adapt CWPA outcomes to our local contexts, then cross-check our assessment results against the data many of our institutions are already collecting via the NSSE more generally, but particularly from the twenty-seven NSSE-WPA consortium questions, which you can read about at the Consortium for the Study of Writing in College website. These questions ask students about the behaviors and habits that we know, via scholarship in the field, are indicators of successful writers—and they include questions about students' use of campus (or other) writing centers. We can learn much about our local writing centers from the cross-institutional data generated via the NSSE, and we stand to gain credibility with administrators by triangulating our own assessments with findings from the NSSE, an assessment instrument your administration might literally have already bought into.

And third, groupings of writing centers at like institutions can connect with one another, adapting specific CWPA outcomes to writing center work and using those outcomes to assess their individual programs, pooling knowledge that is cross-institutional. How many times have we seen people post on WCenter that they are looking for comparative data across writing centers? Adapting the outcomes statement to writing center work affords us an opportunity to build meaningful research and assessment projects that answer to big issues in our field, such as the role of writing center work in the retention of students at a college/university or the ways in which tutoring improves one's own writing.

CONSIDER YOUR FRAMEWORK: CONNECTING TO THE BEST PRACTICES ADMINISTRATORS KNOW

The CWPA outcomes statement is a natural place to look for assessable outcomes, because the organization is discipline-specific and therefore draws upon research, theory, and best practices in the teaching of writing. However, there are other organizations and educational trends worth examining for potential outcomes—and many will resonate more readily with the administrators to whom your assessment reports are addressed. At my institution, for example, the AAC&U's LEAP goals and the accompanying Essential Learning Outcomes and High-Impact Practices are highly valued.

In fact, the LEAP goals are a guiding philosophy for much of our programming. Given shrinking financial support from the state, our university—like many others—is engaged in determining the programs and curricula that will best help us achieve our university mission to provide a distinctive, high-quality undergraduate education. The LEAP goals collectively articulate the value of a liberal education within a global economy; they include things like ensuring students from all backgrounds have access to and demonstrate achievement of a breadth of disciplinary knowledge, integrative experiences within the curriculum, and civic engagement opportunities. More specifically, the stated LEAP outcomes, quoted below, expect that students demonstrate:

- Knowledge of human cultures and the physical and natural world.

- Intellectual and practical skills, including inquiry and analysis; critical and creative thinking; written and oral communication; quantitative and information literacy; teamwork and problem solving.

- Personal and social responsibility, including civic knowledge and engagement (local and global), intercultural knowledge and competence; ethical reasoning and action; foundations and skills for lifelong learning.

- Integrative and applied learning, including synthesis and advanced accomplishment across general and specialized studies. (LEAP)

The promise of delivering on these LEAP goals hinges upon a university providing students with many opportunities for high-impact practices: curricular and co-curricular opportunities that immerse students in rich, deep explorations and require them to integrate various kinds of knowledge and skills. Traditionally, high-impact practices have included internships, study abroad, *writing intensive courses, collaborative assignments,* common courses, first-year experience programs, service learning, global learning, *undergraduate research programs,* and capstone courses.

I have italicized several of these categories that immediately resonate with experiences sponsored by our writing center: we support writing-intensive courses with a fellows program; in addition to assisting writers with collaborative assignments, the work of a writing consultant might best be described as a collaborative assignment; we have offered a writing retreat to support a student undergraduate research program; and we have a long track record of sponsoring research/scholarship by tutors in the writing center via independent studies, honors college projects, and independent projects for presentation at state, regional, and international writing center conferences.

It is easy enough to count the number of ways the writing center supports these high-impact practices across campus or is a sponsor of them; likewise, we keep track of the number of students interacting with these support and sponsorship programs. Recently, we have been conducting surveys and focus groups to track the impact of these support programs and the writing center as a site of undergraduate scholarship and collaboration.

Our Writing Center's Values + LEAP Goals, Practices = Assessable Outcomes

Something I value most as a WCD is seeing consultants grow and change professionally during their time on staff. Our annual survey of outgoing consultants (who are graduating or leaving the center for other reasons) demonstrates in an overwhelming way the profound impact that working in the center has on them. Our center isn't alone in this finding, of course. The Peer Writing Tutor Alumni Research Project has found that tutors regularly credit a number of learning experiences to the writing center as well as their current success in a wide variety of professions. The project's website includes everything you need as a director to offer the survey to your alumni.

A section showing the impact of the writing center on the fifty-plus graduate and undergraduate students we employ annually has made a regular appearance on our assessment reports. However, an assignment by my dean that I admittedly chalked up to bureaucratic busywork recently encouraged me to create a much larger role for professional development in our center's ongoing assessment work.

The dean had created a chart that listed a number of high-impact experiences, as identified by the AAC&U, with spaces underneath for each unit head/program director to write out the unit's successes or activities in that area. Under "collaborative assignments," I listed that tutors regularly wrote resources for use in the writing center in teams, that they completed tutor training activities (such as interviews with faculty in the disciplines) in teams, and that they effectively worked "in teams" by facilitating peer response workshops in first-year writing classrooms via our fellows program. Under "undergraduate research programs," I cited the multitude of independent studies and honors college projects focused on writing center work by undergraduate tutors as well as the collaborative and individual independent research projects tutors have undertaken to present at state and regional writing center conferences.

These are all things that I had documented in the past but hadn't thought to link directly to the "high-impact practices" that are known to foster achievement of the LEAP goals. The more I investigated, the more I realized the broad and deep intersections among writing center work, LEAP goals, and high-impact practices. Here are just two:

1. Our writing center consultants regularly collaborate with one another to conduct mini-research projects or scholarly investigations to present at the Michigan Writing Centers Association and East Central Writing Centers Association conferences. Even if the project is rather small—such as devising a workshop on a particularly useful tutoring technique—they are engaged in collaboration with one another and with me, a faculty member. Many of the consultants want to use observations, surveys, focus groups, or interviews to investigate a writing center issue; in these cases, I help them navigate the process of securing approval of exempt status from the institutional review board, and I help them learn about sound interview/survey/focus group questions. We workshop their conference proposals; if accepted, the students practice their presentations ahead of the conference. Even a relatively simple project becomes a complex site of learning about the genres of conference proposals and conference presentations; learning how to navigate the institutional requirements to conduct field research; and determining how to collaborate with one's peers on an extracurricular research project.

2. The writing consultants' work is, at heart, a marriage between the curriculum and co-curriculum. Although part of their training is paid, the other part is curricular: enrollment in a one-credit tutor training seminar. The nature of their work is such that they are supporting classroom instruction and students' learning. But they are also developing professionally by learning how to handle a wide variety of situations, think on their feet, and become reflective practitioners.

Indeed, almost every aspect of the center's work with students and faculty, and opportunities for tutors' own development, touched on some aspect of the LEAP goals and either were fully-functioning high-impact practices or supported the university's offering of such opportunities throughout the university's curriculum and co-curriculum.

Measures, Findings, Reportage

Feeling that there are intersections between our writing center's work, the LEAP goals, and high-impact experiences is one thing; knowing it definitively and communicating it in a persuasive way is yet another. In all, there are four major areas described by the LEAP goals, and realized through high-impact experiences, that resonate with our writing center: successful written communication, both among students who use our services and the tutors themselves; interdisciplinary, integrative, and applied learning, as evidenced by the tutor training course, professional development program, and tutors' work in the center; teamwork and peer collaboration in our first-year writing courses via a well-established fellows program as well as through tutors' collaborative scholarly presentations at conferences; and intercultural knowledge and competence via our center's special focus on linguistic inclusiveness and intercultural exchange, both for the tutors and for the students who use our services.

In investigating all four cases, I was able to keep our assessment methods intact. For example, in showing the writing center's positive impact on "successful written communication," I simply reported on the assessment outlined earlier, which examined the role of the writing center in helping students devise revision plans. And in assessing the center's "applied learning" in the center, I continued to use an exit survey completed by tutors leaving the center, an alumni survey, a tally of presentations/honors projects/independent studies completed by students who work in the center, and a report on a staff meeting discussion about what they saw as the benefits and drawbacks to working in the center.

Linking our writing center's assessment outcomes to the LEAP goals has meant we've needed to tie our reports' introduction/background and analysis/discussion sections more explicitly to the AAC&U goals and best practices. Informally, I have been more intentional in linking the writing center's work to these well-respected movements in higher education—goals, outcomes, and practices that matter to people on my campus. For example, any budget requests show a direct connection between the funds requested and the kinds of curricular and cocurricular experiences the university fosters. I buttress these requests with assessment data. Additionally, in working with other units to develop collaborative programming, I have used the LEAP goals and high-impact experiences—and the writing center's support and sponsorship of those things—as a framework.

Showing the writing center's work with students across campus within this rich context of high-impact experiences for the consultants employed by the center places us in a good light. One of our university's strategic goals is to increase the number of students engaged in high-impact practices to 80 percent by 2015. By tying together the student learning outcomes related to our fellows program, tutor training, and support of intercultural communication, we demonstrate that the writing center is more than effective writing support for students across campus. The writing center is a site of exactly the kind of programming the university wants to develop over the next several years. And framing our work in this way has had a strong effect on our center in a very tangible way: this information was folded into a request for a new line—a full-time assistant director of our writing center—which we have been granted.

However, another tangible result of connecting what the writing center already values to the LEAP goals has been the rethinking of our professional development programming in the writing center to include yet another dimension: aside from the tutoring-related workshops that consultants' exit surveys indicate are invaluable to professional development, we have begun offering a strand of workshops toward helping tutors articulate in their resumes, cover letters, and interviews how their writing center experiences and skills connect to the jobs (and graduate schools) to which they apply. As you might imagine, the consultants have been extremely excited by the addition of merely optional development workshops, and as someone who finds great pleasure in working with the tutors, I find these workshops enhance my relationships with the staff.

The practices and aspirations of your institution may well be different than mine. Perhaps the LEAP goals don't have administrators fired up on your campus. And there is always the chance that the goals of your administration are not congruent with good pedagogy or best practices in writing center work. The point worth remembering is that creating your assessment outcomes within the frame of other campus assessment goals, best practices within writing pedagogy, and best practices in institutional programming and curricular development can only help your resulting assessment report to be on target to those who will read it. By tying your work to that of other units on campus and best practices in the nation, you rhetorically position your writing center in useful ways.

BRINGING IT LOCAL AGAIN—WITH A CAVEAT

Drawing on published outcomes endorsed by significant professional organizations to build assessable outcomes is a powerful way to connect the local work of your center to the larger, more public conversations about writing instruction. And it's a savvy rhetorical move for two reasons: it helps administrators to put your work within the larger framework of higher education that they may be somewhat more familiar with, and it keeps you from being a "lone voice" in articulating the values on which your center is built. Rhetorically, your assessment report can become something more than an explanation of the writing center's strengths and weaknesses; it can become a demonstration of how the center contributes to the overall mission of the institution. After all, your local outcomes are in line with a larger conversation about student writing and success.

Additionally, by connecting with something like the CWPA's outcomes statement, you increase the opportunities for collaborating with others on campus—directors of other writing-related programs, for example—in demonstrating the ways the various writing services and curricula on campus contribute to the development of better writers and writing. By connecting with conversations about best practices in higher education more generally, such as the LEAP goals, we have the opportunity to begin working with other groups on campus who have also shaped assessable outcomes around those values. At Grand Valley, the required composition course's grading criteria are based upon the outcomes statement, so drawing upon those same outcomes in writing center assessment ensures we stay in conversation, from an assessment standpoint, with the goals of our first-year writing program—one of our writing center's best partners. And the language of the LEAP goals has framed a number of initiatives on campus, such as undergraduate research opportunities and a revision of our general education program, that connect to the writing center's support of student-writers across the disciplines.

But here is the caveat: it can be easy to be carried away or even distracted by finding connections between your writing center's assessment and the assessments/values of others on campus. Collaboration at any cost sells out the important work of the writing center; it also won't allow for genuine, mutually beneficial partnerships between the writing center and other units. So it's imperative to find the conversations out there that link easily to your writing center's values.

I certainly understand—and value—the important, unique work that writing centers do on campuses and acknowledge that many of the things we do are not always explicitly valued by various professional organizations. After all, our work draws upon a rich history of writing center and writing instruction scholarship; there are established organizations, best practices, theories, and research findings that shape our policies, pedagogy, tutor training programs, and array of services. Therefore, we must be in the business of writing our own assessable outcomes based on our own values, critically examining the values that seem to be invoked or explicitly articulated by our institutions, and mapping the connections. In other words, we cannot simply adopt outcomes that others have written because doing so would not enable us to learn what we want to learn or share with others the story of what writing centers really do.

However, if we should be in the business of collaborating with others on campus—as exemplified by the collaborative work that happens in the writing center between tutors and students—we need to be willing to find points of agreement with professional organizations and other campus units that support our values and work. And doing that means being open to stretching our thinking just a bit, reconceiving of assessment as an opportunity to participate in a dialogue that is potentially larger than the field of writing center scholarship. Doing so not only helps us to communicate what we value with other audiences, it affords us opportunities to continue improving what we already value and strive to do well. Writing center professionals already value those basic concepts of collaboration and transformation—they're at the heart of what our centers do.

If writing centers make efforts to connect with other units and with the conversations happening in higher education, we stay relevant, responsive, integral. We learn how we can improve and grow and change based on how our assessments speak to the other bodies we answer to while still remaining true to what we value. Most importantly, we grow coalitions with others that position the center to benefit from collegiality and collaboration while we contribute our expertise in decision-making processes related to teaching and learning.

REFERENCES

Association of American Colleges & Universities. 2011. "Liberal Education and America's Promise (LEAP)."

Consortium for the Study of Writing in College. 2011. "Partnership for the Study of Writing in College."

Council of Writing Program Administrators. 2008. "CWPA Outcomes Statement for First-Year Writing." *Council of Writing Program Administrators.*

Harrington, Susanmarie, Keith Rhodes, Ruth Fischer, and Rita Malenczyk, eds. 2005. *The Outcomes Book: Debate and Consensus after the WPA Outcomes Statement.* Logan: Utah State University Press.

Huot, Brian. 2002. *(Re)Articulating Writing Assessment for Teaching and Learning.* Logan: Utah State University Press.

Kail, Harvey, Paula Gillespie, and Brad Hughes. 2011. *The Peer Writing Tutor Alumni Research Project.* University of Wisconsin–Madison.

INTERCHAPTER

Assessment is always rhetorical. We typically think of our annual and/or assessment reports as highly political, value-laden documents and therefore important rhetorical texts. But Peggy O'Neill, Cindy Moore, and Brian Huot show us in *A Guide to College Writing Assessment* (2009) that devising and implementing an assessment are also important rhetorical activities:

> Those who experience success with assessment understand it as a rhetorical act, involving consideration of exigency, purpose, and audience. From a rhetorical standpoint, it becomes important to ask questions such as "What is motivating assessment at a particular moment?" and "What is the ultimate purpose or purposes in terms of teaching and learning?" . . . Also, because upper-level administrators may need to be convinced of the value of a particular assessment and/or the relevance of the data, WPAs [writing program administrators] and faculty benefit from asking questions about this particular audience—questions about their disciplinary backgrounds, for example, their beliefs about teaching and learning, and their perceptions of assessment. Even understanding administrative preferences for how data should be analyzed and reported can be essential in ensuring the ultimate success of an assessment. (11)

Chapters 1–4 of this book were written with this rhetorical context of assessment in mind. Indeed, determining values, devising outcomes from them, and then determining appropriate methods for answering those outcomes, while integrating assessment into the life of your center, are at the heart of doing good assessment—and acknowledging that assessment is a powerful rhetorical act.

In what follows, respected researcher and assessment scholar Neal Lerner asks readers to consider an external audience's needs and values in determining the specific kinds of data to collect. Choosing to collect quantitative or qualitative data—or both—is a rhetorical strategy that can help you to communicate with external audiences who may have very different assessment needs (and understandings). Lerner's essay on choosing which kind of data to collect is framed within a rhetorical analysis of the assessment report audience. Chapter 5 continues this discussion by discussing the kinds of choices you might make about specific data collection strategies—as well as strategies for connecting assessment in meaningful ways to the other work within your center. Chapter 6 gives rhetorical strategies for maximizing the usefulness of assessment reports by communicating effectively with audience(s) who may have ideas about assessment that are different from your own, and who may not know much about the writing center's work.

OF NUMBERS AND STORIES
Quantitative and Qualitative Assessment Research in the Writing Center

Neal Lerner

Consider this scenario: A new dean has arrived on your campus from another institution, a dean with ultimate authority over your writing center budget. In your first meeting, she tells you that the writing center at her previous college did wonderful, terrific work. You feel yourself relax a bit, as much as might be possible in a first meeting with an academic administrator in a position of great power over you. Then the new dean follows up with how pleased she was that the writing center director (WCD) at her last institution had a firm grasp of the evidence for the effectiveness of that center, represented by a tidy annual report filled with an informative table and a neat bar chart that would always nicely summarize the year's work and offer direct evidence that the writing center was meeting its goals and justify continued—if not increased—funding. The new dean closes the conversation by expressing the wish and expectation that you, too, will offer such evidence that your writing center is a smashing success. Next year's budget numbers are due soon.

You make your way back to your office, situated in a corner of the writing center, which, as usual, is a hub of activity. Perhaps you can then make a few clicks of your mouse and call up the data—the numbers of students who visit your center and from where, the end-of-session surveys that students fill out, the comparison you've done between students' grades who visit the center versus the grades of students who do not. You, too, then, will create a tidy report for the new dean and offer a convincing argument for your slice of the budget pie.

Or perhaps, instead, you listen to the hubbub around you—the laughter as a student shares a draft of a personal essay, the hum of conversation as writers and tutors engage in the talk that is at the heart of the enterprise, the sound of a student practicing an oral presentation for a tutor in an adjacent room, the clack of keyboards as students use the bank of computers along one wall. You wonder how to capture these activities, this scene of the processes and social interactions of learning and teaching that are at the core of writing center work.

This is the dilemma that writing center assessment research embodies: How might we capture what we do and what we produce? Are numbers sufficient? Is "proof" even possible? And what kinds of assessment activities will produce the kinds of evidence that audiences such as the new dean will trust?

Writing centers are not unique or alone in trying to address these questions. Educational research as a whole has struggled to determine which approaches—namely, quantitative ones or qualitative ones—best capture the essence of teaching and learning and provide meaningful evidence to describe what we do as well as offer starting points for change. And this is not merely a conflict between numerical data versus qualitative data or numbers versus stories, but instead a conflict in the fundamentals of knowledge making.

In this interchapter, I explore this conflict, so that readers understand the research traditions and philosophies for the methods they choose in order to answer particular questions worth exploring. Such a foundation is essential, I believe, when we pursue assessment research not merely for funding but to advance what we know and offer that knowledge to others.

RESEARCH AS KNOWLEDGE MAKING

A common assumption is that quantitative assessment involves numbers or counting and qualitative assessment involves stories or narratives. While that distinction may be apt, the reality is more complex. Qualitative assessments might also have numbers; surveys are the most common example of methodological tools used to gather data that could be transformed into numbers but might still be part of a qualitative research project. And I could also imagine instances where narratives or stories might be elicited in quantitative research if the final analysis of those stories is to count up some reoccurrence of a feature or phrase that is seen as the effect of some previous action. The differences between these two approaches to educational research are much more fundamental, however, than numbers versus stories or the kinds of data or evidence or information they might elicit in the course of exploring a question.

Quantitative research—in its purest form—stems from the belief that the world works in predictable patterns, ones that might be isolated in terms of their causes and effects or the strengths of their relationships (i.e., correlation). According to educational researcher Frederick Erickson (1986), this belief comes from the research tradition in the natural sciences. As applied to educational research, this view is predicated on the belief that "animals and atoms can be said to *behave*, and do so fairly consistently in similar circumstances. Humans can be said to behave as well, and can be observed to be doing so quite consistently under similar circumstances" (126, emphasis in the original).

Also key to quantitative approaches to studying natural phenomena is that the researcher determines the meaning of events or acts, not the actors themselves (Erickson 126). In other words, a quantitative researcher comes to a research site with a predetermined hypothesis—in a sense, a predetermined assumption to describe the behaviors at the site—and methods are used to test the validity of that hypothesis. Thus, control groups or baseline data are needed to track change and isolate effects from their causes, or survey questions are finely crafted to offer a narrow range of responses, not allowing the open-ended responses that can endlessly complicate isolating of discrete factors. The noise of social reality and interaction is distracting in a sense (just as "noise" in a writing center might seem to outsiders to be unproductive—see Boquet 2002).

Now I do not mean to imply that quantitative researchers have an extremely narrow view of how the world works. Instead, studying phenomenon via controlled variables and experimental methods is more an acknowledgment of complexity and of the rigor of the scientific method in which conclusions can only be drawn if possibilities are controlled or eliminated. It's a complicated educational world out there, and controlling that complexity through scientific research methods and statistical analysis is one way to grasp and present our interpretation of its meaning. And it is a very persuasive way as the language of science holds great evidentiary power to many audiences Zerbe (2007).

Researchers in composition studies have used quantitative research methods to produce some landmark studies or reviews, including Braddock, Lloyd-Jones, and Schoer's 1963 review of empirical studies, Hillocks's 1986 meta-analysis of quantitative research, and the many attempts in the 1980s to understand and model cognitive processes involved in composition, perhaps most notably the work of Flower and Hayes (1981) and Bereiter and Scardamalia (1987). Closer to the writing center world, Cindy Johanek, who started her academic career as an undergraduate peer tutor, offers readers a strong justification and easy-to-follow models for doing quantitative research in her 2000 book, *Composing Research.*

Nevertheless, *qualitative research* has largely dominated knowledge making in composition studies, particularly in the last twenty years Johanek (2000, 11). Strongly influenced by work in sociology and anthropology, qualitative research in education is predicated on the desire to understand teaching and learning from the actions and perspectives of teachers and learners. In other words, it is not the researcher's explanation for what might be significant or meaningful (although it is key that researchers make clear to their readers what biases and filters they bring to the study); instead, the goal of qualitative research is to understand significance and meaning from the participants' perspectives and their social actions. A qualitative researcher is only an observer in some cases and in others is a "participant-observer," to better understand the perspective of participants. The written accounts of qualitative research are usually narrative in nature—the stories of those involved in teaching and learning—and like good stories, they focus on the personalities involved, the potential conflicts, and the attempts to resolve those conflicts. These accounts are often conducted over long periods of time, a condition that makes a great deal of sense when studying teaching and learning, as the results of a single class lesson or tutoring session would not be immediately apparent. In composition studies, such long-term or "longitudinal" qualitative accounts include those from Marilyn Sternglass (1997), Lee Ann Carroll (2002), Anne J. Herrington and Marcia Curtis (2000), and Anne Beaufort (2007).

So to which camp, then, will you declare your allegiance: quantitative or qualitative? Fortunately, unless you work in a particularly doctrinaire department, such declarations are unnecessary. WCDs quickly learn to be savvy campers or strategic readers of political maps. There is no reason why we cannot be equally savvy when it comes to writing center research. In other words, a quantitative study might offer the kind of evidence you need to secure funding from your new dean, but a qualitative study would offer the kind of evidence you need to understand *how* students are interacting with your center. The first set of evidence keeps you in business, and the second set of evidence contributes to improving what you do and adding to the larger body of knowledge in writing center studies (and will potentially lead to published scholarship, which may be necessary to get you tenured).

It is also important to note that qualitative and quantitative research need not be mutually exclusive (or hostile camps). As Bogdan and Biklen (1992) point out, good quantitative studies come from an understanding of the variables present in the context to be studied, and such understanding could come from an initial qualitative study. One common example of this approach is a multiple-choice survey that is built after an initial qualitative study to determine the questions to be asked and the possible responses to be offered. Or interesting qualitative work might come from an initial quantitative study demonstrating that the writing center made a contribution to student learning but could not reveal the essentials of *how* students learn or the processes and interactions that brought about an outcome.

Also, consider this example: Perhaps you would like to study if your tutors are offering "effective" tutoring. You could dive right in with your notion of what "effectiveness" might look like and conduct performance reviews based on those criteria, but another approach might be to conduct a qualitative study. You could conduct one-to-one interviews or distribute an open-ended survey to students, gathering their perspectives of "effectiveness." You could also ask your staff what they believe constitutes "effective tutoring." Finally, you could observe or record actual sessions and then conduct interviews with both tutor and student involved to review those sessions and determine what they felt were particularly effective aspects. From all of these efforts, you would have built a definition of "effectiveness" that comes from the perspective of those involved and is particular to your context. Then, perhaps, you might conduct those performance reviews.

While that example demonstrates a qualitative approach to "effectiveness" research, I also believe that quantitative approaches to understanding writing center work have great potential. Understanding the writing center's contribution (cause) to students' development as writers (effect) could well be explored through quasi-experimental means. Having engaged in this kind of research Lerner (1997), I can offer that once you try to control the many factors that might have an effect on what students learn, you are often left with a conclusion along the lines of "uh, maybe." However, many of us have colleagues in institutional research who are well equipped to extract meaning from "uh, maybe" and tie your assessment efforts to larger quantitative projects in which the institution itself might participate (e.g., the National Survey of Student Engagement; see http://nsse.iub.edu/). In these ways, the writing center has the opportunity to demonstrate its value among a broad array of students' academic experiences.

BUT WHAT ABOUT THE NEW DEAN?

New deans do not always demand bar charts and summary tables for you to demonstrate the value of your writing center. Some might be more persuaded by narrative accounts of how student writers learn or a description of the long-term value that your tutoring staff finds from their work (see, for example, Kail, Gillespie, and Hughes 2011). What is most important is that you recognize the audience, purpose, and context for your assessment efforts and that you know how best to appeal to a dean or administrator who favors quantitative or qualitative evidence.

In the world outside of our particular writing centers, we have much work to do to better understand the contribution our writing centers make and to communicate that contribution far and wide. We have long operated on a "felt sense" of our value or continue to exist at relatively low-resource levels because, well, many of us have offered our services for a very long time, and maintaining the status quo is always comfortable. However, we also have the opportunity via sustained research—whether qualitative or quantitative—to share our insights into teaching and learning in writing center settings. Those insights have the potential to transform a good deal of the educational landscape at our institutions and beyond. Writing center work embodies hands-on, individualistic approaches to instruction that have been trumpeted for well over a century but enacted far too rarely outside of the writing center. Whether represented by numbers or stories, the understanding of our work is vital to our immediate success; that understanding is also essential to the long-term vitality of our field.

REFERENCES

Beaufort, Anne. 2007. *College Writing and Beyond: A New Framework for University Writing Instruction.* Logan: Utah State University Press.

Bereiter, Carl, and Marlene Scardamalia. 1987. *The Psychology of Written Composition.* Mahwah, NJ: Lawrence Erlbaum.

Bogdan, Robert C., and Sari Knopp Biklen. 1992. *Qualitative Research in Education: An Introduction to Theory and Methods,* 2nd ed. Boston: Allyn & Bacon.

Boquet, Elizabeth H. 2002. *Noise from the Writing Center.* Logan: Utah State University Press.

Braddock, Richard, Richard Lloyd-Jones, and Lowell Schoer. 1963. *Research in Written Composition.* Champaign, IL: NCTE.

Carroll, Lee Ann. 2002. *Rehearsing New Roles: How College Students Develop as Writers.* Carbondale: Southern Illinois University Press.

Erickson, Frederick. 1986. "Qualitative Methods in Research on Teaching." In *The Handbook of Research on Teaching*, 3rd ed., edited by Merlyn C. Wittrock, 119–61. New York: Macmillan.

Flower, Linda, and John R. Hayes. 1981. "A Cognitive Process Theory of Writing." *College Composition and Communication* 32 (4): 365–87.

Herrington, Anne J., and Marcia Curtis. 2000. *Persons in Process: Four Stories of Writing and Personal Development in College*. Urbana, IL: NCTE.

Hillocks, George. 1986. *Research on Written Composition*. Urbana, IL: NCTE.

Johanek, Cindy. 2000. *Composing Research: A Contextualist Paradigm for Rhetoric and Composition*. Logan: Utah State University Press.

Kail, Harvey, Paula Gillespie, and Brad Hughes. 2011. *The Peer Writing Tutor Alumni Research Project*. University of Wisconsin–Madison.

Lerner, Neal. 1997. "Counting Beans and Making Beans Count." *Writing Lab Newsletter* 22 (1): 1–4.

Sternglass, Marilyn S. 1997. *Time to Know Them: A Longitudinal Study of Writing and Learning at the College Level*. Mahwah, NJ: Lawrence Erlbaum.

Zerbe, Michael J. 2007. *Composition and the Rhetoric of Science: Engaging the Dominant Discourse*. Carbondale: Southern Illinois University Press.

5

INTEGRATING ASSESSMENT INTO YOUR CENTER'S OTHER WORK
Not Your Typical Methods Chapter

Ellen Schendel

Writing centers are busy—at times, even chaotic—places. Many offer drop-in support; many directors manage multiple satellite locations; and writing centers may offer in-center as well as other kinds of support around campus, such as fellows programs, writing workshops, OWLs, synchronous and asynchronous tutoring programs, faculty/staff development workshops, and instructional support. There simply isn't time for a writing center director (WCD), even with a robust staff, to fit a completely new and ongoing activity into the daily work of the center. For that reason, assessment can only really work for writing centers when it's integrated into the other work of the center.

On the one hand, WCDs need to keep the writing center comfortable and non-bureaucratic, retain a democratic atmosphere where tutors are not "put upon" to do work that conflicts with assisting writers, and keep assessment from creating another layer of work for their centers to manage. On the other hand, directors have the desire—and perhaps the mandate—to increase assessment activities to better understand writing centers' work. How can we reconcile these seemingly different things? It's this kind of methodology—strategies for getting the work done effectively—that I would like to discuss further in this chapter, along with methods for gathering useful assessment data.

Many writing assessment scholars, such as Brian Huot in *(Re) Articulating Writing Assessment* (2002) and Linda Adler-Kassner and Peggy O'Neill in *Reframing Writing Assessment to Improve Teaching and Learning* (2010), have written about the need to change the discourse of assessment even as we use assessment to better understand teaching and learning. As suggested in chapter 2, by explicitly describing your values, devising outcomes and goals from them, and communicating your results in persuasive ways to your audience, you've done the most important work associated with assessment: you have based your assessment on foundational principles within the field of writing center scholarship and you have framed the discourse about assessment of writing centers with the values of your center and the field. Rather than shaping your writing center's work around the discourse of assessment on your campus, you've made your assessment goals and outcomes a statement of what your center values, believes, and does.

This is important work, but when directors think about doing assessment, we often focus on the actual gathering and writing up of information before we have a clear idea of our questions and interests, or before we think about what our assessment activities communicate to others about our values. And "doing assessment" is labor-intensive. In my own writing center work, collecting, analyzing, and interpreting the data feels like the most overwhelming work of the whole enterprise. It can be time consuming and feel chaotic, so it can end up feeling like the "heavy lifting" of assessment. Quite frankly, I enjoy planning assessments and reporting on them much more than actually gathering and analyzing the data; although I know it is creative, generative work, gathering and analyzing data fills me with self-doubt: Are the staff and I collecting the right information? Are we analyzing the data properly? Are the conclusions fair? Does this information really help the writing center to move forward? Are the methods sound, and will they stand up to scrutiny by external audiences? (At the end of this book, Bill and I grapple with yet another question: How do we manage the criticisms our assessments may receive from others?)

There are some obvious reasons for cutting to the core of these issues and collecting useful information in methodologically sound ways. You need the information to be reliable and useful, convincing enough to speak to what is going on in your center. And given the range and busyness of a WCD's daily professional life, doing assessment well requires creative ways of fitting it into your center's already busy atmosphere.

It can feel difficult to fit "gathering data" into the life of the center. If you're going to collect data about writers and writing, students and tutors are going to notice what is going on; you might feel resistant to letting assessment become an additional layer of bureaucracy that interferes with tutors and writers establishing rapport and efficiently turning their attention to writing. So you need to find space for assessment within your center's environment, and doing so likely means you will need to find points of synergy between assessment activities and those elements of the center that are already robust and functioning well. For example, if you have a stable group of experienced tutors, you might depend more upon their perspectives and assistance in generating assessment outcomes and gathering data. If you have a tutor training program in which the tutors do research, you might help them to do more localized research activities that feed into your larger assessment plans. If you have a well-functioning computerized log-in/log-out system that students and tutors use, you might start by analyzing data you can gather that way. Rather than taking time and attention away from writers and writing, assessment data collection methods can, and should, build on the activities and systems already in place, and do so in a way that enhances the work of the center and the people within it.

There are a number of strategies we WCDs can draw upon, from writing assessment literature and our own best practices within writing centers, in order to integrate the work of assessment into the life of our centers without it being "yet another thing we have to do." In fact, the argument I'm making in this chapter is that if assessment is another layer of work we're adding to our already jam-packed workloads, then it isn't good assessment—you won't learn much from it. And if it *interferes* with the good work of your writing center rather than enhances it, you shouldn't do it. It's that simple.

PART 1: FOUR STRATEGIES FOR GATHERING AND ANALYZING DATA EFFECTIVELY

The advice offered here is all about keeping your assessment processes simple: start with the data you already have; build small, more focused assessments around larger assessment questions; build assessment processes and procedures into the already-established processes of your center; and find ways to collaborate with others (particularly to make up for gaps in your own knowledge or expertise). This won't make assessment really easy, but it will keep the work associated with assessment from feeling too onerous while enhancing the overall meaningfulness of your assessment processes.

1. *Start with the info/data collection strategies and policies/procedures you already have.*

At the 2011 meeting of the East Central Writing Centers Association, I attended a smart session by WCDs Diane Boehm, Helen Racic-Klotz, (both at Saginaw Valley State University), Mary Ann Crawford (Central

Michigan University), Sherry Wynn Perdue (Oakland University), and Jacob Blumner (University of Michigan–Flint) titled "Writing Center Data: What Do We Need and How Should We Use It?" The purpose of the session was to discuss the kinds of information the presenters regularly collect and find new ways of using that information for assessment purposes. The presenters' advice was to think about the data that a center already collects in a fresh, generative way:

- What do you already know about your writing center, based on that data?

- What questions do these data prompt you to ask?

- What patterns do you see that need to be explained?

- What piques the curiosity of you and your staff and makes you feel energized to answer via more focused or different kinds of research?

- What questions and concerns do your data NOT speak to?

The first place to look for answers is within the data you already and routinely collect: numbers of visitors and visits, demographic profiles of visitors, answers to satisfaction surveys. If you've engaged in the process of generating values and outcomes that we've been working from in the first few chapters of this book, then you already know some of what you'd like to learn about your center. Then think about how you can build a layer on top of those data.

For example, perhaps there is a particular group of students about whom there is a higher level of concern, such as students in basic writing courses, students with low ACT/SAT scores, or non-native speakers. You could ask a colleague on campus to help you conduct a focus group with those particular students to find out why/how they use the writing center. Perhaps you could follow up with students to see whether their satisfaction levels changed between the consultation, when they fill out a satisfaction survey, and a few weeks later.

Here's an example of how the staff of my writing center moved from data and information we already had to a deeper assessment. One of the desired outcomes for the Grand Valley State University (GVSU) writing center is that students leave sessions with a plan for revision. Therefore, our electronic check-in/check-out system includes a prompt for consultants and students to write a plan for revision. To demonstrate the proportion of students who leave with a plan for revision, we look at the percentage of sessions that culminate in a revision plan as entered into that check-out system. But that revision plan, as typed, only tells part of the story. I wondered what kinds of revision plans students and consultants tended to work on most frequently. Were they of the sort (global) that demonstrate serious engagement with the revision process, as Nancy Sommers's 1980 research ("Revision Strategies of Student Writers and Experienced Adult Writers") shows can most benefit student writers? Did the staff engage in grammar/mechanics work with students? That is an important and time-consuming part of consultants' work, which my recent sabbatical research project indicated they didn't always feel empowered to do (forthcoming). The undergraduate and graduate writing consultants in my center also had questions about this data. Did students find the revision plans helpful? Did they actually make the revisions they said they were going to make? Why or why not?

Our first step in attempting to answer this question was to analyze the revision plans that students wrote about. We gathered a semester's worth of revision plans—over three thousand—and coded them as global or local, with further breakdowns within those categories. Chapter 6, which focuses on writing assessment reports, will tell you more about our findings, but the shorthand version is that 50 percent of our coding was related to grammar and mechanics, or local concerns, in writing, with the other 50 percent of the coding related to global revisions. Once we could characterize the kinds of revision plans students made upon leaving the center, we wanted to learn whether they actually made those revisions—and whether those revisions improved their writing and their senses of themselves as writers.

We later decided to engage in a qualitative research project in which we collected fifteen students' drafts (a manageable number of case studies for us that semester) when they first arrived at the center. We also collected the final drafts they submitted to their professors. And, we asked them to complete a survey about additional feedback they received from anyone else and what form that feedback took. We compared the revisions made in the papers with the session notes recorded in our system. When we analyzed just the nine cases where students did not seek additional writing support ahead of turning in their papers, we were able to see that students tended to make the local revisions to their texts rather than the more global ones. In all cases, one could argue that the revisions made the writing clearer or stronger or more effective.

However, we also compared the students' revisions to the revision plans captured in the session notes that the consultant and student composed at the end of the session. Among other findings, we noted a number of opportunities where the session notes mentioned a plan to make more global changes that could have resulted in a better organized or more clear paper—but the student did not make those changes. We wondered why, and decided to delve more deeply in a future assessment study.

We shared our findings with the staff and have redoubled our efforts to engage in more conversation and activities during tutor training about how to encourage and empower students to make more global revisions to their texts. We don't just want to make sure students leave with a clear plan for revision that they—at least in that moment—are convinced is a strong direction. We also want students to leave armed with the strategies they need to make those kinds of big revisions. This assessment led us to make some minor changes in our writing center procedures, too, so that we take advantage of the pedagogical moment when the tutor and student-writer craft the revision plan within our check-out system. Tutor training now includes a short activity where we examine example session notes to aid consultants in writing more robust revision plans—as these are sent via email to students and we need them to be clear and actionable.

What started as a quick calculation—the frequency with which students and consultants recorded revision plans in our system—turned into an opportunity for both textual analysis of those revision plans and some case study investigation into students' writing upon leaving the center. It resulted in modified tutor training activities to improve consultants' knowledge and experience with helping students make global, as well as local, revisions and a much stronger understanding of what effect the writing center has on student writers and writing.

You can see from the above example that we moved from "flat" data to collecting information that helped us better explain those data. But we have also done this work of fleshing out existing information through another means. Because one of our programming goals is to ensure the writing center is "a place welcoming of and encouraging to writers of diverse backgrounds," we wanted to know how our user profile compared to the university's demographics. We were able to ask the campus Office of Institutional Analysis for help in cross-tabulating our data against the university's student records database. We learned from this analysis that, although we see a larger proportion of ethnic minority students and our staff is more diverse than the general population at the university, we fell short in one area: the proportion of students coming to us who are nontraditional students (aged twenty-four and older) is lower than the proportion of nontraditional students among the general population at GVSU. In fact, in the writing center, the percentage of our clientele who are nontraditional students had fallen over a three-year period. Therefore, we were able to better understand what to focus on in realizing this goal of being welcoming and encouraging to diverse writers. We know, for example, that the "climate" of the writing center is likely respectful and empowering, but our available hours and locations missed the boat with nontraditional students. We are now engaged in a much more detailed "needs analysis" to understand what kinds of services nontraditional students need from service units like ours, and we plan to make changes to our programming that allow us to be more inclusive of that population.

2. *Don't assess everything all of the time. Some things warrant the collection of data over short periods; other data need to be collected on a regular basis.*

Find ways to break down your assessment questions into smaller chunks, which you can use to build a larger assessment study. This will not only make it easier for you to do assessments—fewer pots on the fire at one time—but will also allow you to reflect on and connect different assessment activities.

Here is an example of how we took a big project and broke it down into smaller, more manageable chunks. One big focus of our last three-year assessment plan was to collect revision plans. We changed our data collection at log in and log out because of it. More recently, we followed up to see if students actually follow through on their revision plans. Our timeline looked like this:

- Fall 2008: finished collecting revision plans

- Winter 2009: finished coding and analyzing revision plans; reported on revision plans

- Fall 2009: shared assessment findings with staff; generated new questions based on that data and interests of the staff

- Winter 2010: began new data-collection plan

- Fall 2010: held focus groups

- Winter 2011: collected case study data

- Fall 2011: reported on focus groups and case studies

We chose this particular series of events because each semester's "chunk" of work seemed possible for me, the sole administrator in the writing center at the time, to manage with the help of peer tutor assistants. And each step was connected to the one previous, providing us a sense of steady progress and coherence.

One thing we kept in mind is that we have "stock" assessments we're always investigating. We always track visitors and demographics; we always track satisfaction. We're always doing observations of consultants for developmental purposes, but we learn in the aggregate where the staff overall is strong or needs additional training.

In fact, we've started distinguishing in our center between "data we collect all the time" and "assessment studies"—the former meaning that information we gather to run the center and ensure it is on track, and the latter being longer, deeper inquiries into themes or features of that data. The metaphor we've used in talking about assessment in our center is an art gallery. We try to think of each semester as a single canvas surrounded by other paintings, each one of which details some aspect of our work discovered through assessment. Although the blank canvas is that semester's opportunity to invent again, it is also part of a larger series of thematically related paintings, giving us a wider view of the center's work, through multiple perspectives.

3.   *Assessment should fit with many other goals you have in your writing center: staff education, research projects, strategic planning, and tutor mentoring, to name just a few.*

In a recent conversation about writing center assessment, another WCD mentioned feeling like assessment could interfere with the work of the center. Collecting data could take time away from sessions or refocus the students' and tutors' energies away from the work at hand. I agree: assessment can do these things, and yet the best assessments are those that fit so seamlessly into the center that they are not noticeable, or they even enhance the work of the center.

In our case, the staff was interested in learning about the revision plans students made after their consultations; that prompted assessment processes that were somewhat obtrusively, deliberately integrated into our regular routines in the writing center. We added a question to our check-out system prompting students to write out those plans. A few minutes were required at the ends of sessions to complete this data-generating task. I realized, after gathering the data and seeing that students really did have those plans, that perhaps one strong reason they had plans at all was because they were being asked to write one out. Given the role that reflection and planning can play in writing, it seemed reasonable to make this question—"What is your plan for revision?"—a permanent fixture in our check-out system, and an important reflective moment at the end of every session.

In this case, assessment made us realize something important about our practice. Revision plans written out by the student with prompting from the consultant are now a part of our tutoring pedagogy (and assessment data collection). These revision plans can be sent to faculty as part of the session report notes (upon the student's request), and to the student-writers themselves; we train our consultants in how to help students write useful revision plans. Indeed, following up on what happens to students' revision plans when they leave the center and write their texts has prompted a whole series of assessment/inquiry projects in our center.

A much larger realization I've come to is the importance of assessment in shaping an intellectual community within our center that is serious about the study of writing. Assessment, quite simply, is a very easy way for undergraduate peer consultants, who may not have strong backgrounds in research methodology, to engage with an organized research project (see Olson, Moyer, and Falda 2002 for more discussion of this point). In our center, one of our ongoing programmatic goals is to get tutors involved with research; from there, we generate research projects by discussing our last assessment findings and building research questions and lines of inquiry. In mentoring students to conduct research, they are "giving back" to the center; we are often able to fold those projects into the ongoing assessment of the center. In other words, and to extend the metaphor above, the peer writing consultants' research projects become some of those completed paintings within our larger gallery, within our growing series of assessments.

I'm particularly interested in this tactic and have written before that assessment is a form of research that writing program administrators, like WCDs, can engage in (see O'Neill, Schendel, and Huot 2002). In fact, in my own life as a WCD and a faculty member responsible for research in composition studies, assessment becomes a primary means of unifying my scholarly and administrative lives—an important survival strategy. I don't think of assessment as "capital-*R* research" as defined by our campus' institutional review board but rather as systemic inquiry that uses various methods common within the academy—focus groups, observations, surveys, interviews, textual analysis—to better understand the tutoring, teaching, and learning that happens in the writing center.

4. *Ask for assistance from folks who have more expertise than you do.*

I cannot stress this enough: there is a very slim chance that a single WCD has the expertise to conduct the variety of assessments he or she can dream up. This is sometimes complicated because of the isolation many WCDs experience; they are not up to speed on institutional assessment values because they are not included in those conversations. It often becomes necessary to bring in a colleague from the social sciences to help you build/pilot a survey or facilitate a focus group. You may want to examine the observation or check-in/check-out forms used by other writing centers and posted on the internet before creating your own. And if you're like me, you'll need to get in touch with the institutional analysis office on your campus, which exists to gather information and help other units crunch the numbers related to anything from demographics to retention/persistence. On our campus of 27,000 students, institutional analysis typically sends me data within a few days of my asking for it—and they are the only ones who can do this work because I simply have neither the access to information they have nor the statistical background to guarantee the information I generate on my own is accurate. I need the assistance of our experts on campus.

Our most recent assessment, which built on our analysis of revision plans, required us to call in experts for a variety of purposes:

a. To facilitate focus groups, we had to get a professor from the writing department who is experienced in conducting such discussions and usability testing.

b. To help us build a process for soliciting survey and focus group participation, I consulted with the assessment administrator on our campus, who was able to show me models of participant solicitation letters, help me to weigh the advantages and disadvantages of different kinds of survey-building software, and point me in the direction of the right person in information technology when I was ready to e-mail two thousand student survey invitations.

c. To help us build data-coding strategies and troubleshoot processes for gathering information related to assessments of student texts, I worked with writing program administrators at my university who had done writing-based assessments in the past.

d. To understand what our huge database of information meant for the diversity of our clientele, we turned to institutional analysis to cross-tabulate our user records with those of the general student population, so that we might understand the demographics of writing center users as well as whether writing center visits are an indicator of student success.

Additionally, don't do assessment alone. Find out what other units on campus are assessing and consider building on that. To use the art gallery metaphor one more time, consider the writing center just one room of a much larger gallery that is the university. The importance of that single room, filled with vivid artwork, cannot be denied; but how much more impressive is the gallery's collection—how much more meaningful the artwork—when it resonates with the other rooms filled with the work of other artists?

At Grand Valley, our very strong first-year writing program builds on the *Outcomes Statement for First-Year Writing* from the Council for Writing Program Administrators (CWPA). The faculty collaboratively grade final portfolios based on a grading rubric strongly echoing the CWPA outcomes. So I try to focus assessment of our fellows program, which supports the first-year writing courses, on those outcomes and goals too. You can read much more about developing writing center assessment plans from the *Outcomes Statement* in chapter 4.

However, though certain collaborations are typical in our writing center's assessment—we seem to always need data from institutional analysis, and we generate assessment outcomes that speak to the outcomes of the other writing programs on campus—other collaborations are ever-evolving. Right now, our writing center is in the midst of some major changes. Beginning in 2013, our writing consultants will occupy an additional space in a new library building—a space we will share with undergraduate speech consultants from the School of Communications and peer research coaches trained by the library. This Knowledge Market, as it is called, will require a whole new approach to assessment, one that is sensitive, flexible, and intricately tied to the other units' goals and outcomes. We won't set our ongoing assessment questions aside; rather, they're likely to shift and evolve as we better understand the collaborations with these other Knowledge Market partners and as we learn from those programs how assessment helps them with their work. To learn whether our collaborative venture is working, we will need to share assessment of the work that happens within the Knowledge Market space. The Knowledge Market partners have begun discussions already by talking about the data we each already collect and why we collect it. From there, we are sharing assessment strategies and brainstorming what kind of collaborative assessment program will work for that space.

These are the principles I try to keep in mind when assessment work seems like it is looming large, threatening to take over the other really important work of our center. In those moments, talking to others on campus about what they'd like to learn about the center helps me to focus my own thinking and find synergies between information that is already out there that can help me to contextualize the writing center's work. I also find great energy in the consultants, who like learning more about our work and students' experiences as writers who grow and change because of the center. They are an endless source of inspiration and energy for determining what we might assess—and how.

PART 2: METHODS FOR COLLECTING ASSESSMENT DATA

When Bill and I first envisioned writing this book, we wanted to avoid a laundry list of assessment methods because a) there are simply too many options; b) as you've seen from Bill's literature review, there are many other wonderful resources on the web and in print that describe particular methods in great detail; and c) we believe strongly that good assessments are built with a particular context in mind. We want readers to develop your own knowledge and options, without choosing methods for you or interfering unnecessarily with your decisions (see the annotated bibliography of sources we think are worth examining further as you devise writing center assessments). We believe that the most important thing a WCD can do in developing an assessment method or plan is to be clear in articulating your values as outcomes that you really care about. There are people on your campus who can help you get to the data you need to explore those values and outcomes. You also might want to consult with others on campus about assessment orientations or methods that may be valued more highly than others on your campus.

But we also think this book wouldn't be complete if it didn't provide a way of thinking about how different data help us to learn important aspects of our work and answer different questions about our centers' effects on writers. In his interchapter, Neal Lerner made a persuasive argument about why we need different kinds of data—qualitative and quantitative—as part of our assessment methods and reportage. What

I want to do here is share with you, in list format, the ways I have collected assessment data over the years and who I turned to for help in getting that information collected and analyzed. You'll see that there are so many ways to collect data that it's impossible to even list them all. But we do want to suggest options.

Data Collected All the Time:

- *Counts.* Number of one-to-one sessions, tours, presentations, online consultations, grammar hotline calls, and workshops given. This can be expressed by time spent doing these activities, number of students (and faculty) "touched" by these programs, and budget percentage used for each kind of activity.

- *Curricular and demographic data about visitors to the writing center,* such as which courses the students were coming from, who referred them, what they arrived at the center to work on, and age/gender/major/etc. This information is useful for generating questions to ask about your clientele, making decisions about promotional materials, and determining with which units we need to forge new relationships.

- *Satisfaction surveys.* Filled out immediately upon check out, e-mailed to students completing online consultations, and/or solicited after a period of time post-visit; they may also be distributed after workshops and other special programming. They can help you to gauge whether the people with whom you come into contact find the writing center open, helpful, and professional; whether the services you offer suit their needs; and, whether consultations result in a self-perceived change in one's writing or one's writing development. Evaluations given a period of time after the consultation or program has passed help to gauge what lasting effects writers might have gained from their writing center experiences. Like the demographic information collected by your center, these satisfaction surveys can help you generate more specific questions for further investigation.

- *User statistics ("hits") at various places on the writing center's website.* If you use a university content management system, this data is likely generated automatically for you. Otherwise, you may need to embed coding onto your pages to count hits. Analyzing this information can give you a sense of what resources seem to be most useful to writers and which pages you might move to the front of your website, as they contain the information visitors are most likely to use.

- *Formative peer observations of tutorials.* We use a standard form for these observations, which include a number of "yes/no" prompts and plenty of space for notes and questions. Because the goal of these observations is the consultants' reflection on their work through colleagues' eyes, we are not too worried about consistent scoring or standardization of the evaluation scale. For assessment purposes, we are happy enough to say that this is part of the consultants' work life—to be observed by their colleagues—and to read the forms quickly and to notice the general issues that rise to the surface consultants study each other's work.

- *Exit surveys of graduating writing consultants about their experiences at the center.* We use a free, web-based survey service to send about-to-graduate consultants open and closed questions about their experiences working in the center. (Did they find the center supportive? Did they get the training they needed?) as well as an educational and personal growth perspective (Did they learn something about themselves by working in the center?). This information can help you to assess the experiences of the tutors working in your center—another group of students who are likely benefiting from having a writing center on campus.

- *Time card records.* Collecting the number of hours tutors spend working in the writing center conducting appointments and drop-in hours, facilitating peer review groups or other work-shops in classroom settings, managing online consultations, par-ticipating in staff development or training programs, and other administrative or writing center tasks. This kind of information can illustrate where writing center resources are being used. You might realize that aspects of your programming are under- or overfunded, or that shifting resources can help you to begin a new service that the center needs.

Data Collected Occasionally or on a One-Time Basis

These data typically help us to answer questions generated by our careful analysis and study of the routine data we collect. These data tend to be collected occasionally because they are more time intensive than we can manage on a regular basis, because they require a bit of a commitment (time or effort) by visitors to the writing center (which can require compensation of some sort), or because the methods get us the answers we need so that we needn't ask the question again.

- *Surveys of "regular," one-time, and non-users of the writing center* to learn about their impressions of our services. These surveys have helped us to answer questions like "Why do some students come once and never return?" and "What makes someone on campus *not* seek out our services?" and "What is the buzz about the writing center on campus?" They've also helped us to conduct a needs survey regarding whether to establish a satellite center as well as collect suggestions from students about what new services to develop. We worked with institutional analysis on multiple features of this assessment effort: to determine the right number of students to contact in each category—"regular" users, one-time users, and non-users—as well as to cross-tabulate our list of users with the university's student population to find the e-mail addresses of students who had never visited the writing center. To lure students into completing the surveys, we offered a $25 dining card to one lucky, randomly drawn winner in each category.

- *Surveys of faculty who do—or don't—refer their students to the writing center.* Again, these surveys have helped us to answer questions like "What compels faculty to refer students to the center?" and "What is the buzz about the writing center among faculty?" and "What kinds of services might we develop to meet the needs of writers across the disciplines?"

- *Focus groups of writing center users.* Conducted by a faculty member experienced with focus group methodologies, this activity allowed us to glean information from a group of students via a sustained conversation of about an hour regarding their experiences in the center and what they learned about themselves as writers. For our purposes, we were interested in seeing what students who visited us only once, as well as students who had visited us multiple times, had to say about the effect of the center on themselves as writers, so we invited a variety of students to participate in the focus groups. To compensate them for their time, we fed them a pizza lunch during the focus group session, gave the participants "I *heart* writing" T-shirts, and raffled off bookstore and campus dining gift certificates. This activity took a significant amount of time to organize: contacting a faculty member and grad student to facilitate and take notes during the focus group; devising a consent form to be read to/signed by participants; determining what technology to use in recording the sessions; devising a strong set of questions; writing a convincing enough letter/e-mail to entice students to participate; reserving spots for student participants; booking appropriate rooms; acquiring prizes; and having the focus group notes transcribed. Additionally, the focus groups required funding to purchase food and door prizes and pay the student wages required for the note taker and transcription of those notes.

- *Analysis of student writing collected in the writing center.* The assessment I described earlier in this chapter focused on examining the changes students made from draft to final submitted paper. In this case, it was easy enough to highlight/note the differences from one draft to another and then code whether those changes were higher-order or later-order concerns. Then we were able to write a paragraph for each paper that described the frequency, type, and "quality" of the changes. After each of the nine case studies were completed, the center's assistant director studied the commonalities and differences among the case studies and wrote a brief about the trends we saw across the group.

- *Interviews/focus groups with faculty.* These might be opportunities to generate new assessment questions, learn what faculty think or know about the center, or test certain perceptions or understandings of the center that you wonder whether faculty have.

- *Peer and supervisor observations of tutorials.* These may be formative (opportunities for reflection and learning) or summative (a means of evaluating the consultant). They may involve closed questions/prompts or lots of latitude in what the observer notices and the consultant wants to discuss. Individually, they are opportunities for individual reflection and learning. Together, they can provide a picture of what the staff's work looks like.

- *Pre- and post-tutorial surveys.* This is a way to capture the students' feelings about their writing, the writing center, and the tutoring process before and after a tutorial.

- *Collection/analysis of session notes.* All that data you collect when students check in and check out of the center . . . how can you mine it? Can you cross-tabulate it with data from your campus's institutional analysis office?

- *Collection/analysis of student writing to the check-out prompt, "What is your plan for revision?"* In our case, this is data we collect all the time because we see the pedagogical benefits of requiring everyone to answer this prompt upon check out. Being able to say that everyone leaves with a plan for revision is as important to us as collecting data to study further—about what students seem to learn in their sessions or choose to focus on for revision after having worked with our consultants. But we have also asked different kinds of revision questions at check out for different assessment purposes. For example, when we shifted from one kind of appointment-making software to another, we asked students about their experiences with the new system.

- *Writing center staff alumni surveys.* It can be a laborious process to locate and survey your alumni, and this is an example of a group of people you do not want to pester too frequently. Additionally, surveying your alumni once every so often gives you a better sense of how people view their work in the center as their lives and careers progress. The Peer Writing Tutor Alumni Research Project provides an excellent template for the kind of survey instrument you might build for your own staff.

PUTTING THE PIECES TOGETHER

There are likely many more methods for gathering information about your writing center than I listed above—and the number of options can feel overwhelming. But by starting with your own center's values and objectives, you've narrowed the options a bit. By determining how to scaffold smaller assessments to create deeper or broader looks at larger questions, you'll build a plan that is manageable and, by being cumulative, meaningful. By drilling down via qualitative measures to understand some of your quantitative data, you flesh out for yourself and your staff a particular picture of the center's work. By remembering that you *mustn't* assess everything all of the time, it's manageable—even exhilarating—work.

For example, you likely collect visit data every semester so that you can chart your center's growth. And you likely collect data that help you to study the budgetary efficiencies of your center just so you don't run out of money halfway through the year. Those kinds of numbers are key to simply running the center, for anticipating what kinds of changes might be happening on your campus that increase or decrease the number and kinds of programming your center offers.

However, while you collect this data all the time because it is useful in one sense, you have probably felt it doesn't do much to help you answer other kinds of assessment questions. For example, what is the impact of those visits on the writer? What difference does having a writing center make on your campus? Answering these questions takes more focused time and energy, and once you find an answer, it might prompt more questions for which you can pursue answers and you stop assessing that original issue and move onto another. You might find that there are different questions and concerns that join your symphonic assessment and go away again. In moving through a six-year cycle of writing center assessment, I found it very important to define the outcomes we were looking for but also to study those outcomes in different ways, semester by semester. We studied student writing one semester to learn what writers did with their papers upon leaving the center, and the very next semester we moved on to study students' self-efficacy and whether it is changed by working with writing consultants. One small, defined, focused assessment project gave way to the next, and, by the end of a couple years, we had a much richer picture of the work our writing center does. And many new questions too.

By sitting down and examining the data we already had, and the answers we'd already generated in previous assessments, we were able to generate a detailed and extensive set of goals, outcomes, and methods. We asked ourselves why our writing center is important to student writers. We examined our mission statement, vision and values statement, and the CWPA's *Outcomes Statement*. And by engaging in conversation about these documents and following the processes outlined in this book, we articulated these goals and outcomes:

Goal 1: Students will receive services to help them become better writers and achieve their writing goals.
Objective 1: Students' consultations help them to develop as writers. By working with writing consultants, students develop a better understanding of themselves as writers, and they apply what they learn in their consultations to other writing contexts.

Objective 2: Students will become more confident in their ability to successfully complete a writing assignment after working with a consultant.

> *Method 1:* Pre- and Post-Consultation Survey. As part of our case study approach to assessment, we administered pre- and post-consultation surveys to learn what change might have occurred in students regarding:
>
>> • Their confidence level in completing the assignment.
>>
>> • Their confidence level in sharing their writing with others.
>>
>> • Whether they felt they learned a lesson that could be applied to future writing projects. (Self-perceptions immediately upon checking out of the center.)
>
> *Method 2:* Focus Groups. Two (2) one-hour focus group discussions were facilitated by a faculty member not associated with the writing center but trained to facilitate focus groups. Notes were taken and transcribed by a student assistant not affiliated with the writing center. Notes were discussed and analyzed by the faculty member and the WCD.
>
> *Method 3:* Data gathered from all students at check out via our custom-built appointment scheduler and database, ScheduleIT. Upon using the writing center, users log in and log out, and we capture various data through ScheduleIT. We ask specifically about students' ability to complete the assignment upon checking out of the center.

Objective 3: Students will make global and local revisions to their writing. As a result of visiting the writing center and working with a trained peer writing consultant, students will make strong revisions to their writing ahead of turning it in to their professors. Doing so suggests that students find the consultations useful and the insights gained about their writing and themselves, as writers, to be persuasive.

> *Method 4:* Analysis of draft and final assignment (Case Study Part I). We collected copies of the drafts students brought with them to writing center consultations and final drafts submitted to professors by those students and did a textual analysis/comparison of the two.
>
> *Method 5:* Comparison of revisions made to session notes and observation notes (Case Study Part II). Consultants trained to conduct

observations did so for the fifteen students from whom we collected drafts and final papers. These observation notes were compared to the session notes recorded by the student and consultant at the end of the consultation, which detail the student's revision plan. We conducted this investigation to better understand what "drops out" of the session notes versus what is included—and to learn more about the relationship between the session itself, the session notes, and students' revisions.

Goal 2: Writers of diverse backgrounds will find the center a welcoming, inclusive environment. The writing center will be inclusive and welcoming to the populations we serve. This means that we will serve faculty and staff as well as students, that people of different ethnic origins and disciplinary backgrounds will find us responsive to their needs, and that we will advocate for the needs of writers who have particularly dire needs when it comes to being successful writers—for example, students with writing-related learning disabilities, international/English as a Second Language writers, and those who are completing high-stakes projects (theses, dissertations, publications).

Method 6: Demographic information about writing center users compared to campus population at large, broken down by:

- Ethnicity
- Gender
- Age
- Year in school
- GPA

Method 7: Focus Groups. Two (2) one-hour focus group discussions were facilitated by a faculty member not associated with the writing center who is trained to facilitate focus groups. Notes were taken and transcribed by a student assistant not affiliated with the writing center. Notes were discussed and analyzed by the faculty member and the WCD. (Gauges self-perceptions quite some time after a visit.)

The answers we generated were shared with the staff at a fall start-up meeting, and new assessment questions were raised and professional development workshops held, to help us continue to improve in the areas where we noticed we could be doing better work. This case study approach, which was much too time intensive to do all the time, was of great use to us. It generated:

- A better understanding of students' experiences in the center.

- A better understanding of how students use their consultation notes in their revisions, which:

  - *Helps us talk to faculty and others about the work of the writing center and its role in students' writing development.*

  - *Helps us to think about what we can do to enhance our effectiveness as tutors.*

- Strong opportunities for tutor research; consultants involved in collecting and analyzing data were able to make presentations at conferences based on this local, site-based inquiry. (We seek internal review board approval before conducting and presenting assessment that we may want to discuss at conferences or in publications.)

- Material to share with the staff as part of tutor training and ongoing professional development activities, as well as topics for professional development workshops that our consultants can facilitate, to enhance our practices based on what we discovered during the assessment.

- Questions for further study—a jump-start on the next assessment project, which we hope will enhance the work we just completed.

In the end, through this process, I came to understand that assessment can be time-intensive masterpieces and quick sketches, tied together by common themes. It is a mix of long- and short-term strategies and an opportunity to build both quantitative and qualitative measures that enhance one another. And it is an opportunity to thread important activities in the life of the center together: inquiry, assessment, student research, and professional development. As director, my tasks were to:

- Get goals and outcomes and methods squared away and submitted to the dean and the university's assessment committee.

- Find experts from around campus who could help us with various aspects of our assessment: facilitate focus groups, help us crosstabulate data, etc.

- Train consultants in data collection and get their help in analyzing what we learn and generating the next set of questions.

- Facilitate the sharing of results with the staff.

- Mentor students who are using assessment as opportunities for research.

Although this list is quite a bit of heavy lifting to initiate assessment processes and manage the timeline and to-do list, the most important thing to remember is that one framed masterpiece doesn't reveal everything that can be understood about the writing center. There are many facets to writing center work worth studying. You have a sensibility as a WCD that is key to making assessment work: instincts about what information is worth pursuing; skills and experiences as a writer that allow you to reflect upon and integrate information even as you are composing the overall assessment plan; a felt understanding of what collaboration can offer. Trust these instincts, even as you open conversations with others around your campus to get the ball rolling on an assessment plan.

REFERENCES

Adler-Kassner, Linda, and O'Neill, Peggy. 2010. *Reframing Writing Assessment to Improve Teaching and Learning.* Logan: Utah State University Press.

Boehm, Diane, Helen Racic-Klotz, Mary Ann Crawford, Sherry Wynn Perdue, and Jacob Blumner. 2011. "Writing Center Data: What Do We Need and How Should We Use It?" East Central Writing Centers Association Conference. Kalamazoo: Western Michigan University.

Council of Writing Program Administrators. 2008. "CWPA Outcomes Statement for First-Year Writing." *Council of Writing Program Administrators.* http://wpacouncil.org/positions/outcomes.html.

Huot, Brian. 2002. *(Re)Articulating Writing Assessment for Teaching and Learning.* Logan: Utah State University Press.

Olson, Jon, Dawn J. Moyer, and Adelia Falda. 2002. "Student-Centered Assessment Research in the Writing Center." In *Writing Center Research: Extending the Conversation,* edited by Paula Gillespie, Alice Gillam, Lady Falls Brown, and Byron Stay, 111–31. Mahwah, NJ: Lawrence Erlbaum.

O'Neill, Peggy, Ellen Schendel, and Brian Huot. 2002. "Defining Assessment as Research: Moving from Obligations to Opportunities." *Writing Program Administration.* 26 (1/2): 10–26.

Schendel, Ellen. Forthcoming. *Writing Lab Newsletter.*

Sommers, Nancy. 1980. "Revision Strategies of Student Writers and Experienced Adult Writers." *College Composition and Communication* 31 (4): 378–88.

6

WRITING IT UP AND USING IT

Ellen Schendel

The greatest challenge we face in writing assessment reports is the schizo-phrenic task of communicating with an audience that we aren't sure is really listening and yet holds quite a bit of power in terms of how our future is supported with resources. We sometimes feel (or know) that the reports we write aren't being read or used by anyone. At other times, the reports feel like high-stakes documents with enormous consequences for our writing centers' futures, and the power lies in our audience, who may know little about writing centers. In either case, our best option is to make an assessment report meaningful and useful to us, viewing the document as an opportunity to tell the story we want others to hear about the writing center. As such, an assessment report can be extremely helpful, both to ourselves and others, as we determine what persuasive stories to tell about the writing center to administrators, faculty, staff, and students, and as we determine where the writing center might go next.

But to balance making the assessment report truly useful to us as directors with meeting the needs of our audience, we need to use our skills as experienced writers and rhetoricians:

- Carefully presenting "good news" and "bad news" in the report, discussing each fairly and ethically in describing what our assessment findings mean.

- Articulating what we do in ways that nonexperts will understand while using what we do and value to frame the interpretation/discussion of data.

- Creating a story about the writing center that is supported by the data and that is told clearly in the report.

- Planning and articulating trajectories for our work and using the assessment reports to collaborate with others on individual, as well as shared, visions of where things have been and where to go next.

- Using the report to inform our public communications about the writing center, such as publicity materials, writing center tours, conversations with faculty/staff around campus, and staff orientation/education.

Linda Adler-Kassner and Peggy O'Neill (2010) describe in more detail—and with many useful strategies—how conducting and reporting on assessment helps us to devise frames that can change the larger discourse on assessment in our culture. After all,

> story-changing is more than just window dressing through language . . . it requires simultaneously conceptualizing, acting upon, and representing work thoughtfully grounded in research, method, and practices. . . . [that] must be designed and built collaboratively, with careful attention to the values and passions of all involved, through a process that provides access to all. (183)

In other words, for our assessment reports to be truly meaningful and useful to us, they must be persuasive; the only way for them to be persuasive is to ensure they speak to—and shape—the conversation on assessment.

Throughout this book, we have pointed to ways in which you can find points of engagement with your audience: by echoing strategic plans and mission statements in your writing center's own documents; by building assessment plans collaboratively with the other units on your campus and in cooperation with the outcomes or identified best practices offered by professional organizations. It's in the assessment report where your audience must be shown these connections you've built so carefully into your assessment plans and processes.

One of the articles that has been influential in my thinking about how to speak effectively to assessment report audiences is Richard Haswell and Susan McLeod's "WAC Assessment and Internal Audiences: A Dialogue" (1997), which is written for writing-across-the-curriculum (WAC) program directors engaged in assessment. At the time they wrote this article, Haswell was a WAC director and McLeod was an associate dean, and the advice they offer draws on these two very different perspectives of assessment report writer and assessment report reader. In fact, the article includes a dialogue in which they talk about the upcoming report that Haswell is authoring. (This dialogue is worth reading if you anticipate a resistant reader for your report and would like to think about how you might sidestep land mines.) They point out a series of clashes that can happen over an assessment report, a few of which include:

1. "The clash between a vision of a part and a vision of the whole"; that is, what your writing center as an independent unit might aspire to be versus how an administrator, with an institution-wide gaze, might see it.

2. "The clash between description and action"; that is, the interest-ing-ness of the data you collect versus how you plan to act upon it.

3. "The clash between expert and public understanding"; or the need for you, the writing center director (WCD), to be a strong translator of writing center work for the administrator. (232–34)

Haswell and McLeod recommend, therefore, that you get to know your audience as much as possible ahead of devising the assessment and writing the report; that you examine model reports; that you find an administrator with whom you can share your findings as your report unfolds, just to test the way you think and write about them; that the report be action-focused; and that you have a strong understanding of how the assessment will affect resource allocation (234–35). Although the assessment report of a writing center might be a very different animal than the WAC program's evaluation report, the advice Haswell and McLeod offer about the process of analyzing your audience and thinking through the rhetorical nature of your report is applicable to any WCD engaged in assessment.

What I would add to Haswell and McLeod's useful points is that aligning your center with an administrative view of the institution's work is more than savvy report writing; it is opening your center up to dialogue with yet another constituency—the administrators who are increasingly making tough financial decisions on our campuses. As Bill and I have said in multiple ways throughout this book, adding an institutional view of the writing center to your layered understanding of its work by connecting your center's assessment outcomes to the institution's mission statement is integral to your center's success. Taking an open, collaborative stance toward even the writing of an assessment report is to open yourself up to the possibility that your center was doing even more than you realized it was.

In the rest of this chapter, I'll outline strategies for writing successful assessment reports and share more specifically how such documents can become useful strategic planning and collaborative programming documents, informing—and even helping us do—the many kinds of work directors must manage. In addition to drawing upon my own experience as a writer of such reports in both the writing center and in our Department of Writing, I'm sharing some perspectives drawn from serving as the University Assessment Committee chair several years back, where the committee's role was to be a peer responder to the unit's report, and my more recent service on our university's reaccreditation steering committee, which viewed assessment reportage as one piece of a much larger network of institutional information. These faculty governance and administrative experiences have played large parts in how I think about how to balance three different goals: making assessments readable, making them useful to the WCD, and keeping true to the story that needs to be told in the report.

BUILD A CONNECTION: UNDERSTAND YOUR AUDIENCE

Although all writing center assessments must begin with your values and questions, the writing up of your assessment data must connect successfully with your audience too. The best way to understand who your audience is and what they need from your report is to talk with the people who will read (and perhaps act upon) your report: the dean to whom you immediately report as well as any faculty/staff/administrators who collect and synthesize assessment information from across the university.

A brief, fifteen- to thirty-minute meeting with each of the key people in your audience can help you to answer important questions such as:

- What seem to be the trends in assessment at our institution?

- What are your goals for assessment in your purview (or at the institution)?

- What advice do you have to offer as I write about our writing center's assessment efforts?

- Will I receive a response to the report? If so, from whom?

Knowing this information was key as I wrote our last assessment report in 2008. At Grand Valley State University (GVSU), we underwent a major restructuring in terms of assessment reportage. A faculty governance committee was created; a new officer was hired to report to the provost on accreditation and assessment across the institution; a new position was created in the campus Faculty Teaching and Learning Center to facilitate student learning assessment within individual classrooms and across programs; new forms and procedures were set up to guide people through the assessment process. It probably won't surprise you to learn that this push for assessment came a few years before our university's ten-year reaccreditation visit. However, this focus on assessment has continued—most likely, because the campus community bought into assessment as a way to learn how we're meeting our institutional mission and strategic planning initiatives, as well as the administration wanting to stay ahead of what legislators require as they demand more accountability and transparency.

In the process of learning more about the university's new assessment reporting requirements, I was able to glean what mattered to administrators and the faculty governance committee who would be reading the reports I submitted every three years:

1. A strong connection between the writing center's assessment and strategic planning;

2. A genuine commitment toward continuous improvement;

3. As much of a connection to student learning goals as is possible for a service unit like the writing center (which is not technically classified as an academic unit).

After learning what my audience was after in this process—and, more specifically, in the reports they read—I sought assessment reports submitted by similar units on my campus. As I read, I asked myself: How did these report writers successfully meet the needs of their audiences? What kinds of responses (if any) had they received? How did those report writers balance the needs of their unit with the expectations of their audience? How did those reports tell coherent, persuasive stories about the unit?

Examining other assessment reports is my second main recommendation for learning all you can about your audience's needs. After all, your writing center's assessment report is being read within the context of many others submitted by units across the university; your report won't be read in isolation, so it is going to be to your benefit to follow the conventions of the genre as they are expressed at your institution while also finding ways to distinguish your unit among those reports.

And finally, it's important to do your own audience analysis. Ask yourself these questions:

- How knowledgeable about the writing center are the readers of your report? Do they have any personal experience with the writing center, or are they completely new to reading about your center?

- What are your readers' specific areas of responsibility? Student services? Teaching? Administration?

- How is your report likely to be used by readers? Will it be used to justify resource allocation, or will it be simply "checked off" as a completed requirement?

After you have a firm grasp on your audience's values and purposes for reading the report, you are ready to start writing.

BUILD A REPORT: TELL THE WRITING CENTER'S STORY IN A PERSUASIVE WAY

At many institutions, assessment reports must be written in a prescribed format. At some institutions—and mine is no exception—online systems such as WEAVE and Chalk & Wire dictate the exact organizational structure of the report (and even, as horrible as it seems, which blank lines should be filled in with what information). From the perspective of administrators and assessment committees, clear and strict formatting requirements make sense: consistent formatting requirements, word limits, and structures make a large body of reports easy to read, compare, and act upon. From the perspective of a report writer, however, the constraints of a mandated report structure can be smothering, even tedious.

What's most important, regardless of the structure in which you're required to fit your assessment information, is that you think of the report as a narrative about your center's work. It begins with the most important elements of your writing center's philosophy, then it zooms in to examine a few features in depth. Finally, your report wraps up by pulling back to put the close-up into a larger context. The suggestions below are drawn from my experience as a reader and writer of such reports, from the flexibly formatted to the highly constrained format spat out by WEAVE.

The Background Section as Story: Giving Readers the Narrative Thread

Typically, an assessment report can begin with some background information about the writing center: its history, mission, vision, values, and perhaps a summary of its strategic plan. Choosing which details to include in this background section is essential to your audience's understanding of the rest of the report; it must, therefore, articulate the values that are most important to your writing center and that are reflected in the outcomes and methods you articulated in your assessment plan. Hopefully those values connect or echo the values of the institution, the discipline of writing studies, and perhaps the other units with whom your center collaborates.

One way to think about how to write the background section is to focus on what you want to be the dominant narrative about your center. Have you grown enormously in recent years? Has your mission changed? Have you gotten smaller but more focused? Have you experienced some recent successes that need to be highlighted? Have you faced serious challenges but still provide a much-valued service to students and faculty?

Below is the text of the background section with which I began the writing center's 2008 assessment report. I wanted readers to glean two major themes from our report: we're a large, complex operation, and we provide an array of services to support teaching and learning about writing. Additionally, I wanted to educate readers about what our writing center does, and how that fits into the world of writing centers beyond GVSU. Finally, I wanted to preview the rest of the report a bit, giving readers a sense of how our ongoing writing assessment was building on this year's results. This last rhetorical strategy—emphasizing the snapshot nature of this particular report—is one I thought would resonate with the faculty governance committee that would read and respond to the report, and with administrators, all of whom wanted to grow a culture of assessment at the university that the writing center had already accepted:

> The Fred Meijer Center for Writing and Michigan Authors, with locations at GVSU's Allendale, Pew/Downtown, Holland, and CHS campuses, provides students, faculty, and staff the support and resources necessary to improve as writers. The hallmark of our work is the one-to-one tutorial (consultation), in which undergraduate and graduate student tutors (writing consultants) sit down face-to-face to work with writers on any paper for any class at the university. In addition to providing students with one-to-one tutoring in the

writing center itself, the writing center sends consultants into all WRT 098 and WRT 150 classrooms, and into select WRT 305 and SWS [writing intensive] (by request of the instructors) to work in small groups and one-to-one with students.

Within the writing center itself, we conducted 7759 consultations in the fall and winter terms of the 2007–2008 academic year. Writing consultants also provided approximately 7254 hours of support in WRT 098, WRT 150, and select WRT 305 and SWS classrooms over the 2007–2008 academic year.

According to the Writing Centers Research Project data collected by the University of Louisville, the average number of consultations per year in the writing centers of institutions like GVSU (comprehensive universities with masters programs) is 1661. The GVSU writing center conducts 367% more than that average number of consultations. In addition, it is rare for a writing center to provide in-classroom support for writing instruction across the university, and rarer still for a writing center to provide consultants in every section of first-year writing (WRT 098 and WRT 150).

Our staff of approximately 55 tutors ("writing consultants"), most of whom are undergraduate students and a few of whom are grad students, are trained via a two-day orientation and by completing a one-credit academic course called WRT 306: Seminar for New Writing Consultants.

Assessment data is gathered in part by TutorTrac software, which is stored on the computers students use to log into and out of the center. Upon logging in, data are collected about the students' reasons for visiting. Upon logging out of the center, students report on their satisfaction with our services, their plans for revising their work, and what they worked on with the writing consultants. We also collect assessment data from students in the WRT 098, WRT 150, and WRT 305 classrooms in which the consultants work on a weekly basis. Students report on end-of-semester evaluations (conducted via Blackboard, much like course evaluations) their confidence level, comfort, and overall satisfaction in working with the writing consultants. Faculty teaching WRT 098, WRT 150, and WRT 305 classes, as well as those hosting consultants in their SWS classes, fill out evaluation forms on the consultants' work, too. These forms prompt faculty to write about whether and how they believe their students' writing has improved because of the consultants' work, as well as overall evaluation of the consultants' professionalism and engagement with students. When we conduct workshops in SWS classes across the university, we collect assessment data via evaluation forms filled out by the students who worked with consultants.

This assessment cycle, we have focused our efforts on finding out about students' experiences in the writing center: what they work on the most with consultants, what revisions they plan to make to their papers upon leaving the center, whether they are comfortable and satisfied in working with the writing consultants, or why they don't visit us at all (or very frequently). Our next assessment report will focus on the changes that occur to students' writing as a result of their work with consultants: an examination of pre-tutoring and post-tutoring drafts, whether grades improved as a result of working with the writing consultants, and whether writers who worked with the writing consultants were able to transfer what they learned in their session to future writing projects.

As I read over this background section now, I wish I had made three additional rhetorical moves. First, I wish I had emphasized the writing center's mission statement. Although the assessment report's cover sheet includes a copy of our unit's mission, vision, and values statements, I should have tied those more concretely to both what we assessed and how we assessed it. Second, I wish I had more clearly tied our mission and services to the writing programs we support through our fellows program and workshops. Doing so would more clearly emphasize the way in which our writing center is an integral team player in writing instruction across the university.

And third, I wish I had included some less assessable facts or understandings about the writing center. I recently read Jim Collins's *Good to Great and the Social Sectors: A Monograph to Accompany Good to Great* (2005), which points out the many and varied limitations to applying business models to nonprofit organizations. Chief among these limitations, of course, is that inputs and outputs of a corporation are money but the inputs and outputs of nonprofits (such as educational institutions, and even more specifically, writing centers) are often value-laden—the sort of products that are not served by purely quantitative data. This is fairly obvious to any of us working in educational settings; what I found so useful about Collins's text is the way he frames the discussion of how to assess the impact of a nonprofit entity on our culture.

By way of offering an example of an important outcome that is not data-driven, Collins tells the story of Tom Morris, the executive director of the Cleveland Orchestra in the late 1980s, and how they tracked "great results":

> Are we getting more standing ovations? Are we expanding the range of what we can play with perfection—from clean classical pieces to complex modern pieces? Are we invited to the most prestigious festivals in Europe? Are tickets

in greater demand, not just in Cleveland, but when we play in New York? Do people increasingly mimic the Cleveland style of programming? Do composers increasingly seek to have their work debuted at Cleveland? . . . It doesn't really matter whether you can quantify your results. What matters is that you rigorously assemble *evidence*—quantitative or qualitative—to track your progress. (7)

Of course, I think that particularly in the educational sector, given the culture of assessment and accountability in which we're working, we *will* need to quantify some things for some audiences (see Neal Lerner's interchapter in this volume). But it's important not to forget, as we provide a framework for our assessment reports and tell the stories of our writing centers, to describe the kinds of everyday—and extraordinary—accolades and validations that come our way, such as: more faculty referrals to the writing center; better student "buzz" on campus, as seen in campus newspaper articles or increased usage statistics or a more competitive pool of applicants for open tutoring positions; the adoption by other writing centers of a program or strategy you've devised; the participation of tutoring staff in state, regional, or national conferences, and the reception of those presentations/workshops by other conference attendees. It's this kind of suggestive evidence that our writing center is on the right track, or is viewed as valuable by others, that we should use to frame our assessment reports.

Despite my inevitable "what I'd do differently next time" feelings about this background section, I still very much like it. My own experience as the director is that there is always something going on in the center—we're an energetic, busy, sometimes chaotic place. As you'll see later in this chapter, I have tried to capture that same feeling of "big and busy" on our promotional materials, website, and faculty talks. It was in the writing of this background section that I had the hard numbers and "wow, we do a lot!" moment that convinced me of the power of this big-and-busy message.

Goals, Objectives, and Methods

My experience as a reader of assessment reports is that it's best when the goals, objectives, and methods sections are clear, concise, and free of editorializing. The framework or narrative thread provided in your background section should connect to the goals you've articulated, the assessable outcomes you've devised, and the reasonable methods you've chosen to gauge the writing center's achievement of those outcomes. Clear and concise ensures readers will see the direct links you intend them to see between your goals, objectives, and methods.

Moreover, your goals and objectives should be so strong that they stand on their own; if you've done the work Bill recommends in chapter 2 to devise goals and objectives that are articulations of your writing center's values, there really isn't much more you need to say in this section of the report.

Finally, by clearly and concisely stating your goals, objectives, and methods, you allow the weight of the report to be on your discussion/action items. You keep the report action-focused, as Haswell and McLeod advise. And you keep yourself, as the report writer, on track with what is most important about assessment: using the information to help your writing center continue to do good work.

Findings, Discussion, and Actions

In the assessment report structure I'm prompted to follow in WEAVE Online, our university's chosen online system for management of assessment data, *discussion* of findings is left up to the writer to insert wherever it is most appropriate. My general rule was to put commentary about specific findings into "Findings," and larger commentary about the overall assessment into the "Action Plans" section. I wanted readers to easily find the results of our assessment, and I wanted them to see how ongoing assessment would play a role in our actionable work as a result of the current findings.

You may be prompted to break these sections up so that findings (or results), discussion, and actions are distinct from one another. If I were in this position, I would still find a way to frame the findings section, and for two important reasons.

First, it's more helpful to readers—and for you in staying focused on the story you want to tell in your assessment report—to include some commentary about what your assessment results mean. Doing so ensures you're using the occasion of the report to present a careful narrative about your writing center. This does not mean that you hide negative results or overinflate the good news you discovered in the assessment; rather, help readers to notice the story that your writing center needs to tell, which is informed by the data of the assessment and other information to which you are privy.

Second, you should ensure that readers have some sense of what you think is most important about the results—good or bad. In the flat consistency of WEAVE's report builder, all goals are equal; all objectives are equal; all methods are equal; all results are equal. However, in my real-life experience as the person conducting the assessment, all elements under each section are *not* equal. Some goals and objectives are simply more essential to our writing center's identity than others; likewise, some findings are clearly more important for us to act upon than others—or more possible, given our resources, mission, or institutional context.

For example, an important context for our writing center has been its explosive growth since moving into a new space and its concurrent branching out to provide writing support for students beyond the freshman and sophomore years. Our fastest-growing populations in the two years leading up to this assessment report were graduate students and international students; our fastest-growing location was at GVSU's downtown Grand Rapids campus, which serves students with professional majors such as business, criminal justice, education, nursing, and the health sciences. Therefore, when writing about the center's work, I focused our data gathering on our very diverse population of writing center users rather than students served by our center's freshman composition program. Of course, that very important aspect of the writing center's work was assessed, but the bulk of our assessment goals and methods were focused on that larger drop-in/appointment contingent, because the profound amount of growth we experienced in the center and our commitment to serving students across the entire university—not just in the first two years of college—was an important strategy in achieving our stated mission of helping any writer on campus.

When I give results in assessment reports, I frame them within a brief editorial that indicates their relative importance and meaning for our center. For example, one of our 2008 assessment report's goals was "Students who work with consultants improve as writers." Under this goal, one of our objectives was "Students will become more confident in their ability to successfully complete a writing assignment after working with a consultant." We assessed this objective through several methods, including post-session surveys that students filled out upon checking out of the writing center. In describing our survey findings, I began with this paragraph:

> Research has shown that students' writing success is affected by their self-confidence (self-efficacy). We would like to know whether working with writing consultants affects students' self-efficacy, which might then affect their success as writers.

The intent of this paragraph was to help readers see the logic of using students' self-assessment of confidence levels, and of investigating confidence in the first place. Further, it serves a rhetorical purpose, tying our writing center assessment to best practices and research in the teaching of writing.

At another point in the report, I needed to present some very basic data about student perceptions of our services. In addition to surveying students leaving the center, we surveyed students who never visited the writing center (to find out why), students who visited us only once (to see why they never came back—was it because they got what they needed or because they had a bad experience?), and students with whom our consultants worked in class as part of our first-year composition fellows program. Student satisfaction with our services is not as important as learning outcomes to readers of this report, but the overwhelming good vibe our center has with students across campus was something I wanted to document in this report. Here is how I framed that data:

> A high level of comfort among students is very important to the success of our tutoring program; it stands to reason that students who are more comfortable working with the tutors are perhaps more engaged with the tutoring and therefore learning more.

And here is one last example, which I include because it illustrates some of the work I argued for in chapter 4: evoking research and best practices (such as the Council of Writing Program Administrators' *Outcomes Statement*) in a writing center assessment report. In this case, the editorializing I included in the (partial) results section included below was geared toward something I wanted to discuss more in the actionable items section: how the writing center fits with students' discipline-specific writing needs and whether the revision plans they determine in the writing center align with writing instruction in the disciplines:

Goal 2: Students who work with consultants improve as writers.
Objective 1: After working with consultants, students articulate a plan for revision.

Measure: Analysis of survey data.

Findings: Upon checking out of the center, students were prompted to write brief descriptions of their plans for revision. The first 300 discursive responses that were specific—not vague, such as "revise" or "make changes" or "take into account what we discussed today while revising"—were coded as follows:

1. E=editing/proofreading corrections

2. GR=global revision, such as "rewriting the paper with my new thesis in mind," or "rethinking" the topic, or reorganizing whole paragraphs/sections

3. LR=local revision, such as "rewriting the conclusion" or "reworking part of my methodology section"

4. F=finishing a draft of the full paper; drafting a paper from scratch from an outline/notes

5. C=clarifying the assignment (with the professor); doing more research before going further; deciding on an angle to approach the topic—"stopping" the writing for a bit to get a better handle on the writing task

6. T=Transitions, or "flow" between paragraphs

Although this is a rather quick-and-dirty coding scheme that oversimplifies a writer's revision plans, it does allow us to see what kinds of revisions students plan to make post-consultation, and whether those planned revisions are substantial in nature.

Following this coding procedure for the first 300 (of approximately 3000) answers to these questions, we found:

- 99 references to editing/proofreading changes

- 91 references to more global revisions

- 57 references to local revisions

- 30 references to smoothing out transitions between ideas/paragraphs

- 13 references to needing to better define a topic, speak with a professor, or do more research
    10 references to writing a rough draft or finishing the paper via an outline

- 4 references to making no changes to the writing or simply turning it in "as is"

What I was thinking when I wrote the passage above was how important it is for the writing center's assessment to demonstrate alignment with a consistent goal of all our campus writing programs. Research as old as Nancy Sommers's "Revision Strategies of Student Writers and Experienced Adult Writers" (1980) tells us that part of one's growth as a writer is viewing writing as a process of discovery that necessarily implies substantial revision when necessary. And that is tied specifically to something I think our writing center should be doing: empowering writers, particularly when the writing task seems especially onerous or stressful. Of course, all of that discursiveness doesn't belong in the results section, but it can appear in the discussion section. My intent in the findings section was merely to suggest some themes that are important within our writing center's assessment.

It stands to reason that even as your goals, objectives, and methods must align in a logical fashion, so should your findings, discussion/analysis, and action plan. It's in these latter sections that you, as the report writer, will get to return to the narrative thread begun in your background section and show the readers how you interpret the results of the assessment for the future of your writing center.

In our assessment plan from 2008, from which the above examples are drawn, I wrote:

It is clear from the data collected that students work on a wide range of writing issues within the center (and in the classrooms, with the consultants). They often work on grammar and mechanics issues—surface-level concerns or later-order concerns—but they are just as apt to work on global, higher-order concerns such as their writing processes (brainstorming, development, and strategies for editing), the organization of their writing, and content development. Of the 300 student responses we analyzed, very few (only 4) indicated the student planned to do nothing with their drafts.

What we know from research on the composing/revision process is that students (particularly incoming freshmen and other inexperienced writers) tend not to make global revisions to their writing, even when prompted to do so by instructors. It is encouraging to see that so many students acknowledged they need to do more than change a word here and there for their writing to improve. However, we now need to track what students actually do when they leave the writing center. Students seem to find consultants' suggestions and the revision plans they devised while in the center convincing enough to note while logging out of the writing center, but do students internalize this feedback and actually make the changes to their writing? Are they given the writerly tools—the process knowledge—to make major (as well as minor) changes to their papers? After all, it is one thing for a writing consultant and student to realize that a draft needs a better sense of focus, but it's an entirely different thing for the consultant to give students the tools to make that complex kind of revision upon leaving the center. . . .

A future assessment of the center's services must attempt to answer those questions. . . . Additionally, more work must be done to ensure GVSU faculty have given the writing center information about the writing in their classes, and that the writing center is effective in adapting to the individualized needs of students in the various disciplines across the university.

As you can see, my focus in this write-up was to educate readers a bit about why the writing center does what it does, and about how we can use the data we gathered in that assessment round to lead us to future assessment questions. It also sets some goals: conduct more focused research into students' experiences with the center as well as connect more with faculty across the disciplines to ensure that our work with students connects to curricula in the majors.

Haswell and McLeod show that it's imperative for any assessment report submitted to an administrator to be action-focused. In the end, the whole reason for the report, typically, is so that someone (you, your dean, a campus committee) can make decisions. But keep in mind that your job in this report is to present the action plan *you* expect the writing center will follow. If it's clear and compelling and tied to your assessment data, it's likely to be the only action necessary.

Action plans can be categorized into three areas:

- Things our data show we should start or stop doing to be more effective.

- Things we should change slightly or radically to be more effective.

- Things we need to follow up on, either because we aren't sure what the data mean or because we learned we need additional information to determine an action plan.

An additional fourth area—depending on your institution's assessment report cycle and whether it is tied to budget requests—might be a request for the resources necessary to carry out your action plan.

Typically, it's a good idea to determine future actions on items that multiple methods have demonstrated need attention; that way, you're prioritizing the most important actionable items and not allowing fuzzy data to drive your planning. However, it's important to be alert for the action items that are relatively easy and inexpensive to address that can improve the center's effectiveness. And there is the potential to discover a particularly interesting direction for your writing center.

In the case of our assessment plan from 2008, from which the examples in this chapter are drawn, we included action items that illustrate all of these principles. Here is a brief list of what we did after the assessment:

- Based on multiple methods, we learned from students and tutors that we needed to stop being a drop-in only center and also start offering appointments to students. To make this work, we realized we needed an online appointment system—a function TutorTrac would allow but our information technology office would not, citing security reasons. We therefore worked with Institutional Marketing—where the university's web services are housed—to devise a new all-in-one online appointment and data collection system to replace TutorTrac. This customized system has served us—and the students who visit us—quite well.

- We needed to revise our assessment goals, objectives, and methods for next time. This assessment cycle yielded a good baseline, snapshot view of who uses our services and what happens in our center. Later assessments would need to focus on what happens when students leave the center. Do they complete the revision plans they make in the center? Why or why not? And to what ends? What do faculty think of the plans students make for their texts? These kinds of questions were taken up in our next assessment report, and were discussed briefly in chapter 5.

- Our assessment results demonstrated extremely rapid growth and that we had outgrown our current administrative structure. One action item made clear that restructuring the administration of the center was a priority; since then, our center has lobbied for—and secured—a full-time assistant director position, based largely on assessment data, but also on researching what writing centers at benchmark institutions have in place.

- Based on our analysis of students' revision plans, we needed to connect with more faculty in the disciplines to ensure our consultations are sensitive to the very different disciplinary needs of writers coming into our center. This was the interesting direction where we decided to make a highly resourced, time-intensive effort.

It's this last item—connecting with faculty—that has proven to be the most important outcome of our 2008 assessment report and subsequent strategic plan. That year, I applied for and secured a Presidential Teaching Initiatives Grant from the Pew Faculty Teaching & Learning Center on our campus. The goal of the grant project was to work with eleven faculty in eight disciplines across the university to create disciplinary genre guides to inform tutor training and consultations with students in those majors. I'll let a portion of our grant project proposal describe the rest:

> Our assessments indicate that the writing center achieves our mission of helping writers help themselves. During the 2007–2008 academic year, 99.5% of students asked whether "today's consultation was helpful to you and your writing" answered that the sessions were "very helpful" (86.5%) or "somewhat helpful" (13%). Yet these same students sometimes indicated in their discursive comments that they wish they'd gotten more discipline-specific help with their writing.
>
> A survey of students who visited the writing center only one time, never to return, indicated that the bulk of those students were satisfied with our services and simply didn't come back; only 4% indicated that the reason they didn't return to the center was because "I didn't receive the help I needed, so I chose not to return." A few of these students pointed to a lack of assistance they received with the disciplinary features of their writing as the reason they didn't return.
>
> A challenge for any writing center staffed by peer consultants is to provide effective support to writers from upper-level courses in disciplines outside the consultants' own areas of expertise. While some scholars have pointed out that in these circumstances the consulting is more "pure"—the writer is the expert, and the writing consultant is there to ask questions and describe how the writing seems to be organized and functioning—others have argued that some students arrive in the writing center with vague directives from their instructor, or very little experience in writing for that particular disciplinary audience. These students need more direction from the writing center;

nondirective methods of tutoring seem to leave the writer—and the tutor—dissatisfied with the consultation and longing for more substance.

One way we have addressed this issue in our writing center is to recruit our staff of 50+ undergraduate tutors from a wide range of majors. Additionally, we educate tutors about the disciplinary features of writing across the university so that their feedback to writers can be rhetorically sensitive. However, there is more we can do.

We in the writing center think it would be helpful to partner with faculty from across the university to devise "consulting guides" for the common genres (or forms of writing) within each discipline—guides that can be used as agendas for consultations in which the consultant is not majoring in the same discipline as the student. These guides, made available in the writing center's various locations and on our website, would be important writing resources for students and also would serve as training resources for tutors. Importantly, because the guides will be constructed in collaboration with faculty in the disciplines and vetted with the faculty in those units, they will function as officially sanctioned descriptions of faculty expectations for writing.

In other words, in addition to serving as educational guides for students and writing consultants alike, the genre guides will ensure that the writing center and the departments who send students our way will have a "meeting of the minds" about how writing consultants and student-writers might best spend their time together. These guides will be one way for the writing center to achieve an important strategic planning goal: to provide better, more effective support to students writing in the disciplines.

A year of using the guides in our writing center has yielded several tangible, though not always quantifiable, successes: more students from across the disciplines are coming into the center because faculty better understand what we do and have invested themselves in helping shape our work. In one year, we experienced a 23 percent overall increase in student usage of the writing center; however, we experienced a 61 percent increase within the disciplines for which we have these disciplinary genre guides. "More" certainly does not indicate "better," it does indicate more opportunity for students to use our services and suggests that disciplines in which faculty participated in the project bought into the idea of the writing center and referred more students to us.

There are other indicators of this project's success as well:

- Unexpectedly, faculty have incorporated the guides into their own teaching, posting the PDFs to their Blackboard sites and using the guides as the basis of assignment descriptions and peer review sessions. In one case, faculty discussed the disciplinary guides at a departmental meeting and officially "endorsed" them. We've created strong allies among the faculty we worked with last summer; they're referring strong tutor candidates when we hire and spreading the word that students in any discipline can get help in our writing center.

- Our writing consultants feel much more comfortable working with writers outside their own disciplines. We've formally surveyed the staff about their experiences using the guides and have honed the way we introduce new tutors to the guides and encourage the use of the guides based on this survey data. Twice, we've reported on these guides at conferences, getting useful feedback from interested colleagues who have come to our talks.

- A number of colleagues from other writing centers and writing programs have contacted our center, asking if they might use the documents in their contexts or link to them.

And finally, the project's success is indicated by the fact that it continues; after the first time-intensive, grant-funded push to create fourteen documents, we've been able to work with a department each semester to develop additional guides and other materials.

This is a project borne of assessment, and it has inspired our upcoming assessment, which is more focused on disciplinary writing and upper-level students' experiences in the writing center. We're rethinking who we are as a writing center in healthy, exciting ways because of assessment, and because we needed to write up our results for others.

STARTING OVER AGAIN: USING YOUR ASSESSMENT REPORT TO REFRESH YOUR STRATEGIC PLAN

And finally, a key, forward-thinking role of your center's assessment report is to prompt fresh strategic planning. If your writing center already functions from a formal strategic plan, your assessment report should prompt you to review and, if necessary, refresh it: sharpen it; determine new directions; or simply stay the course. In the case of our writing center's 2008 assessment report, our strategic plan both widened and narrowed: we added the disciplinary genre guides project; we began, with the help of Institutional Marketing, the development of a much better record keeping/appointment management database for the writing center. In examining the demographic makeup of our writing center staff, we determined we should continue to become more diverse in various ways, hiring students with differing disciplinary expertise and from a variety of cultural backgrounds while also ensuring that our hiring practices and workplace policies encourage nontraditional and international students to apply for positions.

We realized we needed to make trade-offs, letting go of programming we liked that wasn't doing particularly well or that was not used much by students (such as graduate student writing groups). In doing so, we were able to narrow and intensify our focus on obtaining better resources to serve the many graduate students needing one-to-one writing support and better serving larger populations of students across campus. In other words, we realized it wasn't time to diversify our services, but rather devise more effective and efficient one-to-one tutoring support.

With new strategic goals come new outcomes and assessment strategies. After our 2008 assessment report was submitted and our strategic plan refreshed, we had articulated the following goals, outcomes, and methods in a strategic planning document sent to our dean and shared with the rest of our college:

Goal 1: The center will meet the writing needs of faculty, staff, and students across campus
Objective 1: Ensure that the writing support we provide squares with faculty expectations for writing across the disciplines.
> *Strategy 1:* Make contact with faculty across campus in department meetings, in small groups, and individually to find out their views of the center and what the center can do to better meet their students' needs.
> *Strategy 2:* Focus group discussions with faculty about the handouts, materials, and tutoring strategies used in consultations, to ensure that consultants communicate the right message to students about writing in various disciplines.
> *Strategy 3:* Partner with faculty across the disciplines to create "writing guides" to form the basis of consultations in various fields.
>> *Measure 1:* Statistics regarding the number of students we saw in the center and from which disciplines.
>> *Measure 2:* Focus group notes.

Methods 3–5: Student, faculty, and writing consultant feedback to the use of guides in consultations.

Objective 2: Ensure that consultants are providing effective writing support that is sensitive to disciplinary context for students across majors.

Measure 1: Examination of pre- and post-consultation drafts of student writing, to find out what changes (if any) are made by students because of their conversations with consultants.

Measure 2: Discussion of Measure 1 findings with disciplinary faculty.

Goal 2: The center will recruit more diverse consultant applicant pools and retain a diverse staff of consultants.

Strategy 1: Seek advice from Inclusion & Equity and the Office of Multicultural Affairs about recruitment strategies.

Strategy 2: Seek out nominations of international students through the Padnos International Center.

Strategy 3: Foster relationships with faculty in under-represented disciplines to nominate students to be consultants.

Strategy 4: Foster a working environment that is inclusive and provides opportunities for intercultural exchange so that consultants and potential consultants feel comfortable and view as important their contributions to the center's work.

Strategy 5: Make diversity/intercultural awareness a component of consultant orientation and training.

Measure: Demographic profile of staff.

I have only included those goals and strategies that are new or refreshed initiatives for our center. There are, of course, other goals that we want to meet as part of our daily work, such as ensuring that tutors are appropriately trained, certain data are collected regularly and accurately, our budget isn't exceeded, and our services to students are of excellent quality. Our regularly assessed outcomes and regularly collected data are still in play. What is outlined above are the special initiatives we are working toward.

And I should note an important part of our process in moving from an assessment report to a strategic plan: sharing the assessment outcomes with the staff and learning what they thought it all meant. Those reactions and responses helped me to write the assessment report on the data we'd collected; additionally, it ensured the full staff was involved in determining the direction of our strategic plan.

DOUBLE-DIPPING: USING ASSESSMENT REPORTS AS SHORTCUTS FOR OTHER WORK

The action plan your assessment report ends with, or the resulting refreshed strategic plan, needn't increase the amount of work your center does or that you, the director, must take responsibility for. In fact, the process of writing your assessment report will clarify the talking points you can share with administrators, faculty, staff, and students at your institution; it clarifies what you know about the writing center and where it's going. When you spend the time writing an assessment report that tells the story you want others to understand about the writing center's work, you can use that story to do other kinds of work for you too:

- Cite your report as evidence for resource requests/reallocations—getting what your center needs. If assessment data show you need more graduate assistants (and our usage statistics from 2008 suggested as much) link your assessment findings to your graduate assistant requests. Although the grant I described above is not a permanent resource for the writing center, it did enable me to get some important work done for the center with the help of faculty. The grant application itself draws on information from our assessment report—some of it almost directly copied and pasted.

- Share the report with staff to orient tutors to your local context and to brainstorm about what the center does well and needs to continue working on. What do they think the data mean? What questions do they raise for them? In our case, I shared the findings about students' revision plans with the staff. It led to a rich discussion about how we can better help students leave the center with concrete revision plans, which may include "talk to my professor to clarify the assignment" and "seek help from a librarian in finding sources about X." It was the writing consultants who saw many possibilities for what "leaving the center with a revision plan" might mean. Also, we determined that making the librarians a resource we turned to for training would be helpful, so that we could really help students determine a plan of action involving research and library support. This was an outcome of our assessment that I never could have imagined on my own.

- Use information from the report in promotional materials, including a "Fast Facts" page on your website, to which you can point faculty, staff, and students who want (or need) to know more about your writing center's work. We've found such a page helpful in numerous instances—from a writing consultant simply wanting to know more about our center's usage to a talk I gave about our services with faculty in the business college. Passages of text on our website are culled from our assessment report.

- Approach collaborations with other units around campus. Share what you learned in your report that might touch on what they do, and find ways to help each other. In our case, we've been investigating how to better collaborate with the library and other tutoring services in a shared learning commons that will be a part of our new library building, under construction at the writing of this book. We've learned a lot about the kinds of services students say they need—such as topical writing workshops and more late-night tutoring hours—that we can really only provide, given limited resources, with the help of the librarians and other tutoring services on campus.

GETTING DOWN TO BUSINESS

In the end, a useful way for our writing center to think about its work is as a Venn diagram, with the university's strategic plan in one circle and the writing center's strategic plan in another. The two circles overlap in the middle, where the writing center plays a special role in realizing and pushing forward the institution's goals, and where the institution can most clearly see its strategic plan in the work of the writing center.

The entire writing center circle is within my interest and view. We must assess various aspects of our work—tutor training, student learning outcomes, disciplinary writing support, fellows program, faculty-as-writers programming—and yet I feel committed to having a robust assessment that tests, pushes, and informs the part of our circle that overlaps with the university's strategic plan. The overlapping section represents the assessment information that I must include in each and every assessment report, because it keeps the writing center at the table when it comes to the university's goal-setting and resource allocation. It's attention to the overlap that ensures the writing center takes some cues from the university and is responsive to the needs and goals articulated in the university's strategic plan. After all, our writing center wants to be useful and a service; we have specialized, disciplinary expertise that informs how we can realize that role, but as Jeanne Simpson reminds us in "Whose Idea of a Writing Center Is This, Anyway?" (2010), we must also be open to hearing how others think about our work too:

> Perceptions matter. Clinging to a fixed idea of a writing center, whatever each of us thinks that idea is, shuts off opportunities. This inflexibility causes writing center folks to be unnecessarily defensive about our work and to be offensive to others when we tell them their ideas are wrong. We need to understand that we can only influence, not control, the way others see our missions, goals, and methods. We need to be open to having our own visions adjusted in surprising ways. The boundaries between what "should" happen in a writing center and what does happen and what might happen are porous to say the least. "We don't" is a dangerous phrase. Maybe we do. Maybe we could. (4)

It's this reciprocity, this dialogue between writing center and the larger institution, that I think should permeate our assessment processes and, importantly, our assessment reports. Such documents are, after all, an opportunity to educate readers about the center's work, shape our future work, and importantly, shape the institution's work. Your center's assessment documents should be written with the expectation of response from others at the institution. The right rhetorical strategy for your campus is whichever one helps you to be heard but also keeps others welcoming you to the table for your center's perspective, advice, and leadership.

REFERENCES

Adler-Kassner, Linda, and Peggy O'Neill. 2010. *Reframing Writing Assessment to Improve Teaching and Learning.* Logan: Utah State University Press.

Collins, Jim. 2005. *Good to Great and the Social Sectors A Monograph to Accompany Good to Great.* New York: HarperCollins.

Haswell, Richard, and Susan McLeod. 1997. "WAC Assessment and Internal Audiences: A Dialogue. In *Assessing Writing Across the Curriculum: Diverse Approaches and Practices,* edited by Kathleen Yancey and Brian Huot, 217–36. Greenwich, CT: Ablex.

Simpson, Jeanne. 2010. "Whose Idea of a Writing Center Is This, Anyway?" *Writing Lab Newsletter.* 35 (1): 1–4.

Sommers, Nancy. 1980. "Revision Strategies of Student Writers and Experienced Adult Writers." *College Composition and Communication* 31 (4): 378–88.

AFTERWORD

Translating Assessment

Brian Huot and Nicole Caswell

While Ellen and Bill graciously asked us to read and respond to this volume, we must confess that our response does not attempt to evaluate or improve upon the volume. One strong set of impressions throughout the reading of the volume and the drafting of the response revolves around the crucial role assessment plays for an institution and the identities of the people who make the writing center one of the most effective places for learning on a college campus. The status and position of most writing centers make their assessment a scary process for writing center staff and administrators. Often lacking the generation of FTEs or stable revenue streams like those reserved for tenure-track lines, writing centers appear vulnerable during a time of economic woe and turmoil. On the other hand, as this book demonstrates throughout, assessment can also provide writing center professionals with a voice in the conversations where decisions are made from assessment evidence to argue and secure more resources and institutional commitment. This promising aspect for assessment as a powerful discourse that can promote, document, and protect writing centers drives much of the work we do with writing teachers and program administrators (including writing centers), focusing on understanding how to read, write, and talk with authority and expertise about writing and writing program assessment.

It seems to us that what we have been attempting to do in teaching a usable assessment process is to translate assessment discourse for teachers and administrators to use for their own purposes. This volume might be seen as an assessment-translation discourse for writing center professionals. Our role here, at the conclusion of this particular translation, is to help readers understand the connections we see between what writing centers assessment can become and the work of assessment for practitioners and administrators in academic programs—seeing these chapters as translation discourse or seeing translation as a metaphor for writing about program assessment to an audience of writing center professionals.

Translation implies two distinct languages, and any substantive understanding of language includes some deliberate effort toward understanding the contrasts between the cultures those languages represent; this is why just memorizing the dictionary, grammar, mechanics, and usage of a new language won't mean someone can actually communicate in that language. Likewise, learning the words and definitions associated with assessment is necessary but not sufficient to a full discursive membership in assessment. One of the enduring issues for many people trying to write this kind of translation discourse is to make sure that an audience of non-assessment people can understand assessment-related ideas, terms, and concepts with which they might not be very familiar. Perhaps even more importantly, the translation of assessment principles should also ensure that writing center administrators can actually use new assessment information to create effective assessments, which in turn helps them to make the most of their centers. This might seem pretty straightforward, though we have found the task to be more complicated and potentially more important than just tailoring assessment concepts for professionals in a particular field or area of composition studies.

For example, during the coauthoring of a translation-type text for nonspecialists in writing assessment, we remember an e-mail conversation in which one of our coauthors argued for extended attention to examples and definitions of rubrics. Our coauthor maintained that it might be hard or impossible for us to understand that some folks did not know what a rubric was. Of course, this was not really accurate since in our work with colleagues in program administration we often explain such rudimentary concepts; further, it became apparent to us that we were as knowledgeable about our audience as our coauthor. The real issue was the kind of conversation we and our coauthor envisioned having in the essay we were writing together. Our coauthor wanted us to focus more on explaining and giving examples of rubrics, and we resisted this focus because we believe it only reinscribes a mistaken assumption by those just learning about assessment: that making and using rubrics (or mastering any assessment technology like statistics or interrater reliability, etc.) should be a primary concern. After all, knowing a single assessment instrument in great detail doesn't mean someone understands how to use assessment to her writing center's advantage.

In helping faculty design assessments, we often argue against the use of rubrics altogether, since there are many effective assessments that do not use rubrics at all (Hester et al. 2000; Isaacs and Molloy; Smith; and many others). We're not against the use of rubrics per se, but we are aware of the effort they require and only use or recommend their use when necessary. This unnecessarily narrow focus on rubrics and other assessment artifacts and procedures, like outcome statements or norming sessions, is often available in listserv discussions, and we believe that such discussion can impede any real understanding and control of assessment for improving writing centers and other instructional programs because folks are focusing on the "stuff" of assessment without understanding its origins, uses, strengths, etc.

A parallel example closer to most writing center professionals' experience is the student who shows up in the writing center believing that she needs to work on grammar exercises; any good tutor initiates a conversation toward other issues and activities and returns in later sessions to work on proofreading and editing if necessary. The tutor's knowledge of writing process, tutoring pedagogy, and student needs tells her that grammar is usually not the place to start because it will not lead to the rich and deep thinking possible from insightful writing. The writing center tutor understands that even though the student wants to talk about grammar or other language conventions, having this conversation now will not help the student proofread and edit, not to mention address communicative features in her text. We've come to think of our effort to translate assessment in terms of productive-or-not conversations. To return to our student visiting the writing center wanting help with grammar, it's not that grammar isn't important or that the tutor doesn't have grammatical information that the student lacks, but rather that a grammar-based conversation during initial attention to revision will probably not be helpful to the student in the long run because even if the grammar is perfect, grammar will not ensure that the content, organization, development, tone, etc., are what they should be. The same can be said for focusing on rubrics as a way of understanding assessment—it can be a useful step, but starting an assessment project focused on rubrics is problematic because of the potential limitations it puts on how assessment might be understood. Just as repairing grammar is not understanding writing, neither is developing rubrics understanding assessment.

CREATING A CULTURE FOR WRITING CENTER ASSESSMENT

Of all the issues facing writing center professionals beginning to work in assessment, none is more important or more crucial than helping to change the culture of the writing center to include assessment. In the *College Composition and Communication* essay "Creating a Culture of Assessment in Writing Programs and Beyond" (2009), Cindy Moore, Peggy O'Neill, and Brian Huot provide some rationale for writing program administrators, and by extension writing center directors (WCDs), thinking about assessment as a culture-changing activity:

> We use the phrase *culture of assessment,* instead of something more prosaic such as *writing assessment program,* deliberately, to evoke the dynamic approach to assessment that is supported by research and theory. A culture is not static, or finite; it is ever-evolving and web-like, encompassing many interconnected values, practices, and people. Because the best assessments are ongoing and necessarily involve every component of a program, including students, faculty, administrators, curriculum, and resources, and because they both reflect and are affected by individual and institutional values and beliefs, culture is, we believe, a fitting metaphor for the approach that we endorse. (W125)

When we refer to assessment as culture-changing for writing centers, it's important to remember that this culture-changing goes both ways. Local, public conversations at specific institutions about assessing writing cannot help but be different when writing center administrators have a voice. Chapter 4 in this volume extends the ability for writing centers to use assessment to effect important changes in institutional culture by illustrating how connecting local, institutional values and goals with publicly recognized statements about assessment can provide a mandate for moving a specific institution toward current, recognizable theory and practice for the teaching and learning of writing. In other words, answering an outside mandate for assessment provides an opportunity for writing centers to use the valued, even privileged, discourse of assessment to demonstrate how important and valuable writing centers are and how writing centers are already connected to the most widely recognized approaches for ensuring students' acquisition of academic literacy. Additionally, assessment furnishes an opportunity for writing centers to translate their stories and values into an assessment discourse with heightened status and for a wider audience. Being a vocal and informed participant in campus conversations and decisions with administrators and colleagues from other fields ensures that local assessment will not only be aligned with a writing center's culture and values but will actually promote writing centers' importance to other and new audiences across campus.

Writing center professionals can become aware of how their participation in assessment can make visible the role the writing center plays in supporting student learning and connecting the teaching and learning of writing to prevailing professionally sponsored principles; it is also understandable for writing center professionals to be concerned by how assessment will change the culture of the writing center. Certainly, educational assessment has been responsible for restricting curricula to what can be measured in ways insensitive to the contexts in which students learn to read and write. Chapter 2 in this volume argues, though, that there is no need to fear that writing centers will become marginalized by writing assessment; in fact, this book contends (and we agree) that writing centers should embrace assessment as a chance to showcase the positive, wide-ranging influence they have on campus.

So what more specific kinds of changes in writing center culture might assessment bring? For one thing, the isolated position of a writing center would certainly be subject to change. Writing centers' visibility and contribution to the overall pedagogical mission of the institution may bring writing centers more attention and more resources. They might also bring more scrutiny. It might be less and less possible for writing center professionals to make important decisions on their own based upon unarticulated principles or lore. On the other hand, the commitment to assessment from WCDs is a commitment to collecting and analyzing data that support the role of the center itself. So while assessment brings additional scrutiny, it also gives WCDs arguments that not only answer such scrutiny but assume an important leadership role on campus for the teaching and learning of writing.

While writing center assessment can be utilized as an opportunity, there are good reasons that writing centers should see assessment as part of their ongoing work. Soliciting information about the ways a center is serving students, faculty, and/or specific programs across campus can be used to make informed decisions about extending writing center outreach programs, providing evidence for writing center calls for more resources, and documenting the use of available resources. There are various reasons why writing center assessments need to occur, but most of those reasons seem to deal with mandates from those outside of the writing center (at least as evident in so many WCenter discussions of these issues as well as much of writing center scholarship). While those are of importance and necessity, it is also important to make sure that the resulting data help to further the mission of the writing center and help improve localized writing center practices. Even if the call for assessment is coming from the outside, the assessment can, and should, lead to productive writing center work. The assessments need to be shaped to answer the call of those requesting the data and meet the local center's values and concerns. Early collaboration with other stakeholders helps pinpoint what our research questions are, what we want to find out, and how we plan to use that information. Writing assessment research within the writing center community can help further shape the field of writing center research by helping WCDs negotiate and navigate these collaborations.

Writing centers are in a unique position to engage in writing assessment because (1) directors are already members of campus assessment communities; (2) writing assessment can help further the mission of the writing center; (3) writing assessment can help support colleagues at other colleges/universities who fear imposed writing assessments that conflict with local values; and (4) writing assessment can help build productive relationships. A necessary relationship WCDs should cultivate is with the institutional research office. The goal of most offices for institutional research is to collect and analyze information that can be used in designing, implementing, and analyzing projects that affect the university community. In addition to having access to information about students, like retention and/or attrition rates, many such offices will also collect information a writing center might find helpful. Of course, every writing center can also be its own valuable source of data, collecting information from students not only about their use of the writing center but also about what departments and programs they represent and about how helpful the writing center has been.

In reframing writing centers as sites of assessment and research, we recommend that every writing center client be asked to complete a consent form so that the center can aggregate individual information into data that can be used to support the center's mission. For example, if the average GPA of writing center clients goes up the semester after the client's use of the writing center, administrators might find such information helpful, not to mention how they might use such information to make an argument for the continued if not increased support for writing center activities.

Extending a writing center's collaboration can also involve seeking and securing help for data collection and analyses that may be beyond what writing center professionals usually know. For example, working with university statisticians can help centers make statistically based arguments that are often very persuasive to powerful stakeholders in an institution's upper administration or with powerful stakeholders outside the institution itself. In "WAC Assessment and Internal Audiences: A Dialogue" (1997), Richard Haswell and Susan McLeod demonstrate how different audiences for assessment require different kinds of arguments and texts. Once a writing center expands its circle of collaborators, it can also expand its sphere of influence and the sphere of audiences who are willing to hear such arguments.

In their introduction to *Assessment of Writing* (2009), an edited collection that does not contain a chapter on writing center assessment, Marie C. Paretti and Katrina M. Powell contend that collaboration between colleagues in different fields is "essential to the successful implementation of any writing assessment program" (2). Echoing this more general principle, Bill and Ellen posit that "writing center assessment can—and should—become a site of collaboration and convergence, a means of connecting what *we* (writing centers) do with what *we* (institutions/professional communities) collectively can do." In addition to extending writing center conversations about collaboration into assessment, Bill and Ellen highlight the positive outcomes that writing center assessment can have for writing center work generally, and for the position of writing centers in the university and their mission of best supporting student writing.

CONCLUDING TRANSLATIONS

Although we have talked about the opportunities available to writing centers that become active in assessment, it seems to us that we have missed our own opportunity to talk about one of the core activities of assessment—the asking and answering of meaningful questions. Seeing assessment as research is not a new or novel concept (O'Neill, Schendel, and Huot 2002), but such a focus for a "translation" text for writing center assessment implies some concepts and principles that are not immediately apparent. First of all, seeing assessment as research emphasizes that writing center professionals who formulate research/assessment questions are in charge of the assessment/research process. Writing center professionals are not just tutors or mentors, they are also researchers.

Additionally, using assessment as an opportunity for research positions writing center professionals to be knowledge-givers and professionals who not only take part in professional conversations, but assume the role of setting research agendas and furthering the knowledge base for writing centers and other programs devoted to improving the teaching and learning of writing. This kind of translation discourse gives WCDs a means with which to become more active in shaping assessments and discourse about assessment on their campuses:

> For the most part, writing assessment has been developed, constructed and privatized by the measurement community as a technological apparatus whose inner workings are known only to those with specialized knowledge. Consequently English professionals have been made to feel inadequate and naïve by considerations of technical concepts like validity and reliability. (Huot 81)

This book, it seems to us, creates ways of talking about and knowing how to do assessment that deprivatizes and demythologizes it. In chapter 2, Bill describes a process through which faculty were able to design and own an assessment that not only satisfied an outside mandate but also helped to change the culture of both the institution and the writing center. While chapter 3 details the ways in which faculty can translate their values for the role of a writing center in a small college into a formal assessment process, chapter 4 provides an equally detailed account of "how to turn one of the CWPA [Council of Writing Program Administrators] outcomes into an assessable learning outcome for a writing center" (90). These two chapters, in particular, embody what we have come to understand as important guidelines for effective translation discourse. Both chapters talk about the "stuff" of assessment within a relevant context and detail a process that is dynamic enough to have value but transparent enough to make sense beyond the context in which it occurred. It's clear that Bill and Ellen view assessment as a positive force on their campuses not only to promote the values writing centers embody for the teaching and learning of writing but also to ensure that writing centers are sustainable. Articulating research questions and conducting assessment scholarship within individual writing centers takes time and energy to be done well, as evident in Bill and Ellen's examples within this book; but the value of writing assessment work proves to be more fruitful than responding to a mandate. The practice of writing assessment provides the opportunity for WCDs to demonstrate their engagement with the local institution, and to advocate for more localized writing assessments while carving out new, more important roles as writing professionals.

REFERENCES

Hester, Vicki, Peggy O'Neill, Michael Neal, Anthony Edgington, and Brian Huot. 2007. "Adding Portfolios to the Placement Process: A Longitudinal Perspective." In *Blurring the Boundaries: Developing Writers, Researchers and Teachers,* edited by Peggy O'Neill. 61–90. Kresskill, NJ: Hampton Press.

Haswell, Richard, and Susan McLeod. 1997. "WAC Assessment and Internal Audiences: A Dialogue." In *Assessing Writing Across the Curriculum: Diverse Approaches and Practices,* edited by Kathleen Yancey and Brian Huot, 217–36. Greenwich, CT: Ablex.

Huot, Brian. 2002. *(Re)Articulating Writing Assessment for Teaching and Learning.* Logan: Utah State University Press.

Isaacs, Emily and Sean A. Molloy. "Texts of Our Institutional Lives: SATs for Writing Placement?" *College English* 72 (5): 518–538.

Moore, Cindy, Peggy O'Neill, and Brian Huot. 2009. "Creating a Culture of Assessment in Writing Programs and Beyond." *College Composition and Communication* 61 (1): W107–32.

O'Neill, Peggy, Ellen Schendel, and Brian Huot. 2002. "Defining Assessment as Research: Moving from Obligations to Opportunities." *Writing Program Administration* 26 (1/2): 10–26.

Paretti, Marie C., and Katrina M. Powell, eds. 2009. *Assessment of Writing (Assessment in the Disciplines).* Tallahassee, FL: Association for Institutional Research.

Smith, William L. 1993. "Assessing the Reliability and Adequacy of Using Holistic Scoring of Essays as a College Composition Placement Program Technique." In *Validating Holistic Scoring for Writing Assessment: Theoretical and Empirical Foundations,* edited by Michael M. Williamson and Brian Huot. 142–205. Cresskill, NJ: Hampton.

CODA

William J. Macauley, Jr. and Ellen Schendel

Our book focuses on the writing center assessment process as a journey that we've both taken, and which we've largely enjoyed and found important—even interesting and fun. But what we would like to muse upon for a few pages, here at the end of this book, is the very real experience you're likely to have multiple times (at least, we did): that terrible feeling that you got it all wrong, that you made a mistake. Sometimes you will be correct in thinking that, and it's a potentially paralyzing fear. But we want you to know that we've been there; every writing center director (WCD) has. Doubts and mistakes are par for the course in assessment—and in leadership. But they are also an important part of our development. The question is how we will handle mistakes as they arise.

Alina Tugend, a columnist with *The New York Times*, recently published *Better by Mistake: The Unexpected Benefits of Being Wrong* (2011), and her work provides a great deal of information that we can use in writing center assessment. Tugend writes:

> defining mistakes and acknowledging that we all make them is only the beginning. It doesn't do us much good unless we also try to change our approach—when we and others make mistakes—in ways that will benefit us and those around us. (40)

In other words, we will make mistakes. We'll learn about mistakes in our assessment processes when we don't get the information we want or need; we'll learn about mistakes in our centers' programming when we discover through assessment what isn't working so well. Both are scary prospects, in part because WCDs are often the only people on their campuses clearly dedicated to the center's program. As a result, we can often personalize our work in the center. This is one of the places where our marginalization is most problematic. As Tugend contends, the best we can do is learn from those mistakes and allow others to learn from them, too.

But Tugend does more than simply announce that mistakes are a normal part of success; she also writes about a number of studies focused on error that have resulted in useful concepts we can apply to our roles as directors who manage assessments for our centers. First, Tugend relies heavily on the work of Carol S. Dweck (2008), a professor of psychology at Stanford University, whose research uncovered two distinct mindsets related to how people process and even use mistakes: the fixed mindset and the growth mindset. Of the fixed mindset, Tugend writes:

> Those who see their abilities as fixed, as innate and inflexible . . . think they are simply not smart or talented enough to do the task required and they learn to be defensive and foist blame on anything or anyone but themselves. (46)

By contrast, those who have a growth mindset

> see ability as a malleable quality and therefore believe that with enough effort they can overcome obstacles. They may not embrace mistakes, but they tend to see them more as part of the process of learning than as a reflection of their intelligence or abilities. (46–47)

Nobody likes to make mistakes, especially where others can see them. Meanwhile, neither can any of us deny that we make them. The question really boils down to what we do with the mistakes we make: are they growth opportunities or recriminations? Are they signs of progress or limitations? How would we answer these questions if we were discussing a student's writing rather than our own writing center's programming, or our own assessment efforts?

Tugend also makes good use of the research conducted by Chris Argyris (1992), professor emeritus at Harvard Business School. Of primary interest here is Argyris's differentiation between single-loop learning and double-loop learning. Single-loop learning happens "when a mistake is detected and corrected without questioning the underlying values of the system" (76). Argyris provides an alternative, though:

> Double-loop learning, on the other hand, means to question the underlying factors themselves and subject them to critical scrutiny—in effect, it turns the question back on the questioner and asks not only about objective facts, but also about the reasons and motives behind those facts. (76)

In other words, "single-loopers" solve immediate problems. For a WCD conducting assessment, this might mean switching to another rubric, dropping a data collection method, or stopping an assessment altogether. If that same WCD were approaching the problem from a double-loop perspective, there would be another question: Why did the mistake happen? Doing so requires a depth of understanding and a strong sense of agency. And this becomes an essential opportunity for further inquiry. For example, why did we assume that students made global changes in their writing after a tutorial? Why have we assumed that nondirective tutoring is always better? Whose agency is really being enacted in our writing tutorials?

Because so much of the scholarship on writing center assessment can so easily be read as "I do this or I did that," it is easy to take a single-loop approach to writing center assessment. However, part of the reason that our colleagues' assessments have worked is because they could become double-loop learners: they could ask why as well as what. That is not to suggest that a writing center assessor cannot find in the scholarship the methods that will work well for his center. It does suggest that her thinking about *why* is just as important as what to assess and how to do an assessment.

This perspective requires something more than know-how, determination, or grit (true or otherwise). It requires what Tugend refers to as "resiliency." As adults and researchers/scholars, we know that mistakes and missteps are inevitable. Tugend refers to the research of Brooks and Goldstein (2003) when she writes that resiliency requires the ability to "attribute mistakes, particularly if a task is achievable, to things [we] can change" (57). Resilient people look for others who can help them. The resilient "have the 'insight and courage' to recognize when a task may just be beyond their abilities. While they may be temporarily cast down, they don't see themselves as failures." (57). Tugend quotes Brooks and Goldstein directly when she writes that the resilient possess "the belief that adversity can lead to growth. They view difficult situations as challenges rather than as stresses to avoid" (57). In short, assessment is work that takes time and expertise. Giving it plenty of the former allows for the latter. Take your time, ask for help when you need it, and don't let mistakes discourage you. And most importantly, learn to roll with the punches. The rewards are well worth it.

So, embracing mistakes is part of doing writing center assessment work effectively. Mining those mistakes for what we can learn, toward moving forward, is key. However, an important second component is to think deliberately about what we are modeling for the neophytes in our classes, centers, and professional organizations. It is necessary that we become able to accept mistakes and doubts for ourselves; yet it is not sufficient. We have a responsibility to others, as well, especially those for whom we are connections with the field, representatives of how our field works, leaders in our local centers, regional writing center communities, and beyond. Acknowledging this leadership role is inherent in conducting assessment because we have to make the decisions about what we assess, how we assess it, and what we do with the information those assessments reveal. After all, we're going to find things we want to continue doing, things we want to stop doing, and things we want to improve—all of which will require some changes in our writing center culture, and that is change that we must lead. But the role of the WCD and the assessments she makes of her center carry greater significance than simply answering a local question.

How to step into that leadership role to lead the kinds of changes suggested in a writing center assessment—which often have implications for changes in the institutional structure or community beyond the center itself—is another challenge for directors. In his 1994 book, *Leadership Without Easy Answers*, Ronald A. Heifetz, who directed the Leadership Education Project at the John F. Kennedy School of Government, argues that the primary responsibilities of leadership are in bringing organizations to the threshold of change, creating an appropriate context for change, and deliberately shaping the direction and outcomes of that change. However, one of the key concepts preceding change and enabling the leadership that can bring it about, for Heifetz, is a leader's understanding of what kind of change is necessary. For Heifetz, two specific forms of change are most prominent: technical problem-solving and adaptive change. Technical problem solving focuses on solving familiar problems, using familiar solutions and/or minimally disturbing the status quo. Adaptive change, on the other hand, involves unfamiliar problems that cannot be solved with familiar methods; adaptive change is disruptive to the status quo.

Both of us have encountered the need to step into technical problem solving and adaptive change roles. For Ellen, when faced with growing concerns on campus about international students' writing abilities, it meant devising ways to ensure that international students were aware of the center's services to help them but also retraining tutors to better work with that population. Although it took some time, energy, and modest resources, those problem-solving activities were pretty easy to implement. Much more difficult, and still in process, are the adaptive changes Ellen is a part of on her campus. This involves reaching out to faculty in whose programs many international students are enrolled and talking with them about responding to and grading English-as-a-second-language writing. It has meant joining a couple of university-wide committees to investigate the various issues related to teaching and learning and support services on campus unique to international students, and proposing new programs, services, processes, and policies to meet those students' needs. That work requires the input and expertise of a wide variety of people, among whom the WCD is one person well informed from a particular perspective. And, in this case, that perspective and the writing center's programming become one piece of a larger institutional assessment and strategic planning process.

For Bill, the challenge was that departments were beginning to use peer tutors of their own to work with student writers within their majors. The writing center was increasingly perceived as serving only English majors, employing only English majors, and advocating writing that was only meaningful within the English major. Bill had to resist the temptation to react and understand that there were many others involved, others who wanted support for their student writers. Bill also doubted that they would willingly take on the added responsibility of running their own separate tutoring services. The technical solution was relatively easy: hire peer tutors from majors other than English. Analysis of the writing center's usage revealed that the natural sciences were served least by the writing center, so another technical solution was to build up the resources in support of writing in the sciences and make sure that the natural sciences faculty knew they were available.

However, there were adaptive changes that needed to happen because the culture of the college was such that the writing center had to fight for a different perception of its intentions and services. Faculty from the natural sciences, as well as the other major divisions (arts, humanities, and social sciences), were invited to participate in small discussion groups, looking at the writing they were teaching and wanted their students to learn. The writing center learned a great deal from those lunches. One of the departments that had been most successful in providing writing support for their majors suddenly contacted Bill to see if a productive collaboration could develop. In three short years, the writing center's collaboration with the chemistry department went from two dedicated chemistry writing tutors to shared training of these tutors, to training chemistry faculty in working with student writers and training writing center staff in writing the lab reports specific to the chemistry major. Curiously, once the chemistry department had this kind of working relationship with the writing center, other departments that had been reluctant in the past became interested in similar collaborations. The results were not simply greater demand for the services of the writing center—a technical solution—but a much more developed relationship between the college community and the writing center and a richer range of learning and tutoring for the writing center staff and the writers with whom they worked, a significant, adaptive change.

These experiences are like the phenomena discussed in Jim Collins's *Good to Great and the Social Sectors: A Monograph to Accompany Good to Great* (2005), a good read, if you're interested in pushing further your thinking about how writing center assessment connects to larger institutional assessments and strategic planning initiatives. What is perhaps most useful about the book is the way Collins describes how to use an assessment as the beginning of a culture change that moves your program from being "good" to being "excellent." His strategy is to first get "the right people on the bus" with you, people with whom you can share your assessment results and action plans; in the case of WCDs, these "right people" are tutors, other program directors around campus, writing program administrators, and other academic service units. We need to ask ourselves whose input is most valuable when it comes to what we want to do? Whose expertise is useful? Who among our writing center staff can help us to communicate vision about the changes we see as possible and necessary to achieving excellence in our center? What are the units or committees with which we need to build collaborations to achieve our assessment goals?

After those people have been identified—not just as impactful or knowledgeable people but as those who have a vested interest in helping you to achieve your objective—you need to understand and represent yourself as an experienced, expert change agent who can get the "flywheel" turning. What small (technical) changes can you make—with the right people on board—that will lead to additional changes, which will compound until you have made progress on the cultural or institutional (adaptive) changes that need to be made? You have to focus on identifying the most important thing that you and your center can do really well. You have to have a mindset that allows you to see how changes within that one part of your program will help to shape the whole program and overlap into institutional culture in useful ways. Then you have to make your ideas and goals important for others.

Chip Heath and Dan Heath's *Made to Stick: Why Some Ideas Survive and Others Die* (2007) discusses "sticky ideas." They describe sticky ideas as those that "are understood and remembered, and have a lasting impact—they change your audience's opinions or behavior" (8). But it is not simply about "curb appeal";

> Sticky ideas have to carry their own credentials. We need ways to help people test our ideas for themselves—a "try before you buy" philosophy for the world of ideas. When we're trying to build a case for something, most of us instinctively grasp for hard numbers. But in many cases this is exactly the wrong approach. (17)

In short, what makes an idea credible is its ability to stand on its own and demonstrate both the efficacy of the choices that were made in building it and the appropriateness of the methods and data selected. And those data need not be numbers alone, especially when we are talking about writing centers that operate so much within the realm of human behavior and relationships. In no small measure, the ability to do so is both a result and demonstration of the idea's credibility (as well as the thinker/researcher/assessor who developed it)—and that credibility is not dependent specifically on quantitative data but on the interpretation and understanding of a variety of information arrived at, over time, in assessing the writing center. Meaningful assessment is likely recursive and cumulative and helps us to find the center of gravity in what we do well. Those sticky ideas become the legacies with which we can lead change in our centers and on our campuses.

Or, to say it another way à la Heifetz, writing center assessments can point to the need for either technical problem solving or adaptive change. Being aware of and thoughtful about the kind of change an assessment is intended to provoke can make a big difference in the success of that assessment and the sense of satisfaction one might take away from it. And small successes in technical problem solving can make a big difference when it is time for real, adaptive change.

This may seem a strange send-off—a focus on mistakes giving way to leading change, not just in our centers but around campus. However, leaders understand that mistakes will be made, and they are nimble enough to build from them, even while they strive to minimize them. We believe that creating writing center assessments based on writing center research, informed by the unique work of the writing centers on all of our campuses, and reflective of our own expertise as WCDs, can be developed within this context. Each of these elements is necessary, and none are sufficient on their own. We must also be sensitive to our centers' unique institutional cultures instead of carrying out assessments imposed or dictated by others without the kind of expertise we have to offer. While we are recognizing our expertise, we have to acknowledge the responsibility that comes with our expert work, which can feel quite daunting at times. However, when we embrace our roles as experts, as problem solvers, as leaders, we free ourselves from many of the fears that have so hampered writing center assessment, as well as the expectation that we must respond to some distant and unknown assessment authority.

It's us. It's our work. It's time to get busy with moving our centers and our field ahead.

REFERENCES

Argyris, Chris. 1992. *On Organizational Learning.* Cambridge, MA: Blackwell Publishers, Inc.

Brooks, Robert, and Sam Goldstein. 2003. *Nurturing Resilience in Our Children.* Chicago, IL: Contemporary Books.

Collins, Jim. 2005. *Good to Great and the Social Sectors: A Monograph to Accompany Good to Great.* New York: HarperCollins.

Dweck, Carol S. 2008. *Mindset: The New Psychology of Success.* New York: Ballantine Books.

Heath, Chip, and Dan Heath. 2007. *Made to Stick: Why Some Ideas Survive and Others Die.* New York: Random House.

Heifetz, Ronald A. 1994. *Leadership Without Easy Answers.* Cambridge, MA: Belknap Press.

Tugend, Alina. 2011. *Better by Mistake: the Unexpected Benefits of Being Wrong.* New York: Riverhead Books.

APPENDIX

Annotated Bibliography for Writing Center Assessment

William J. Macauley, Jr.

Included here are sources that we have found useful in understanding writing center assessment and in developing this book. These sources come from our own research and reading, from selected bibliographies, and from references made in scholarship we have found pertinent to writing center assessment. Many of these sources are discussed further in chapter 1.

Although the majority of these sources are focused specifically on writing center assessment, many are included here because of their relevance to contextualizing writing center assessment theory or methods within the larger bodies of scholarship focused on writing program assessment and writing assessment. In addition, the line between writing center research and assessment is often blurred; in our opinion, this is acceptable because all good assessment is also good research—though oftentimes localized inquiry rather than research writ large.

Overall, our goal is to provide the widest possible range of resources that might be of use to those who are developing writing center assessments.

Adler-Kassner, Linda, and Susanmarie Harrington. 2010. "Responsibility and Composition's Future in the Twenty-first Century: Reframing 'Accountability.'" *College Composition and Communication* 62 (1): 73–99.

This article provides a useful context for current practices in writing assessment. It then goes on to argue for a reframing of writing assessment as responsibility rather than accountability because it shifts the emphasis from justification to others to our own responsibilities. Good ideological piece for writing centers and their agency in writing center assessment.

Adler-Kassner, Linda, and Peggy O'Neill. 2010. *Reframing Writing Assessment to Improve Teaching and Learning*. Logan: Utah State University Press.

This book provides detailed discussion of the larger implications and ramifications of writing assessment. Although this might be daunting for neophytes to writing center assessment, for those who are looking for larger arguments for writing and writing center assessment, Adler-Kassner and O'Neill make a compelling case for recontextualizing writing assessment as a social responsibility.

Ady, Paul. 1988. "Fear and Trembling at the Center." *Writing Lab Newsletter* 12 (8): 11–12.

This article is a good, early example of pre- and post-testing as a means of assessing the impact of writing centers. Current readers may notice the localized nature of assumptions and the strong presence of the author in the results and interpretation. Nonetheless, the piece is an example of what is (and could) be done with pre-/post-testing.

Barnett, Robert W. 1997. "Redefining our Existence: An Argument for Short- and Long-term Goals and Objectives." *Writing Center Journal* 17 (2): 123–33.

This article argues that goals/objectives statements can work reflexively to both demonstrate commonality with the rest of the campus and develop shared missions/objectives.

Beal, Phillip E., and Lee Noel. 1980. *What Works In Student Retention: The Report of a Joint Project of the American College Testing Program and the National Center for Higher Education Management Systems*. Iowa City: American College Testing Program and National Center for Higher Education Management Systems.

This study could be very useful in helping a writing center to assess its relation to retention or to the design assessments of retention-related issues.

Beebe, James. 1995. "Basic Concepts and Techniques of Rapid Appraisal." *Human Organization* 54 (1): 42–51.

This article is a nice complement to the work cited elsewhere in the book and bibliography by James Bell, Johanek, and Donelli and Garrison. It provides specifics on how to do a rapid appraisal, which calls for multiple small-scale research tools, complementary data, and appraisal team interaction.

Bell, Elizabeth. 1982. "A Comparison of Attitudes Toward Writing." *Writing Lab Newsletter* 7 (2): 7–9.

This study will seem very familiar, and it does a nice job of comparing tutor and first-year composition (FYC) student writer attitudes/perceptions of writing and of themselves as writers. There is a nice turn-around later that reveals the tutors seeing themselves as continuing to improve while the FYC students tended to see themselves more often as lacking or unsuccessful. The study reports positive change over the semester.

Bell, James H. 2000. "When Hard Questions Are Asked: Evaluating Writing Centers." *Writing Center Journal* 21 (1): 7–28.

This is one of the most frequently cited pieces in recent writing center assessment literature. The article connects writing center assessment with educational program assessment and provides six broad categories of assessment. The article discusses the strengths and weaknesses of each category of assessment for writing centers, and then makes the case for multiple small-scale assessments and provides an example or two. The article includes a good taxonomy for broad writing center assessment decisions.

Broad, Bob. 2003. *What We Really Value: Beyond Rubrics in Teaching and Assessing Writing.* Logan: Utah State University Press.

This book advocates DCM, or dynamic criteria mapping, which allows users to not only develop meaningful outcomes/values but continue doing so through constant comparison/emergent design practices. Because writing centers focus so much on collaboration, this is a meaningful model for writing center assessment. DCM also provides multiple opportunities for engaging writing center staff in ongoing research and assessment.

Brown, Robert. 2010. "Representing Audiences in Writing Center Consultation: A Discourse Analysis." *Writing Center Journal* 30 (2): 72–99.

This research is unique in that it provides a taxonomy of ways that audiences can be represented and then uses discourse analysis to explore how tutors use these representations through discourse analysis.

Carino, Peter, and Doug Enders. 2001. "Does Frequency of Visits to the Writing Center Increase Student Satisfaction? A Statistical Correlation Study—or Story." *Writing Center Journal* 22 (1): 83–103.

This is a great example of a quantitative survey study. More importantly, maybe, it is also a terrific tutorial in demystifying quantitative methods and tools. The accommodating tone makes this a good read, despite the authors' worries about numbers and statistics equaling boredom.

Charles, Jim, and Brenda Davenport. 2000. "English Education Majors as Unpaid Tutors in the University Writing Center: A Service/Research Project." *Writing Lab Newsletter* 24 (5): 6–10.

This is not an assessment article. The argument is that prospective teachers learn a lot more about the actual writing process by participating in action research with student writers in the writing center. The methods here could be useful in assessing the development of tutors' learning about writing as well as their development as tutors and/or writers.

Clark, Irene. 1988. "Preparing Future Composition Teachers in the Writing Center." *College Composition and Communication* 39 (4): 347–50.

This piece argues for the writing center as a part of teacher training that can enable a deeper understanding of real writers at work. Teacher education programs can benefit by using writing centers as part of teacher training because the work contributes to teachers' ability to assess student writing, develop responses to student writing, and understand teacher roles. This piece could be useful in grounding assessments of professional development.

Cogie, Jane. 2006. "ESL Student Participation in Writing Center Sessions." *Writing Center Journal* 26 (2): 48–66.

This article is a great example of case study methods. It provides a discussion of research on working with English-as-a-Second-Language (ESL) students in writing center sessions. It identifies an omission in the research, which is the role played by the ESL student. The article then analyzes the roles played by ESL students within selected tutorials. The article emphasizes tutor reflection on the conflict between the desire for brevity and a need for cultural information.

Connolly, Colleen, et al. 2003. "Erika and the Fish Lamps." In *Weaving Knowledge Together: Writing Centers and Collaboration*, edited by Carol Peterson Haviland, Maria Notarangelo, Lene Whitley-Putz, and Thia Wolf, 14–27. London: Routledge.

This piece is an interesting discussion of writing center atmosphere as a reflection/rejection of larger institutional context, linking tutor images of themselves with the ways they decorate the writing center and questioning the utility and deep meaning of atmosphere tropes. This chapter can be used as a way of thinking through the assessment of writing center spaces and social environments.

Cosgrove, Cornelius. 2010. "What Our Graduates Write: Making Program Assessment Both Authentic and Persuasive." *College Composition and Communication* 62 (2): 311–35.

This article argues for assessment that answers questions most important to the assessors. It also argues that the reports on those assessments should be written in a way that is understandable and persuasive for outside audiences. For a writing center director (WCD) who is choosing to follow her own interests rather than others', this may be an important argument.

Cox, Bené Scanlon. 1984. "Priorities and Guidelines for the Development of Writing Centers: A Delphi Study." In *Writing Centers: Theory and Administration*, edited by Gary Olson, 77–84. Urbana, IL: NCTE.

This article provides a great model for survey-based assessment/research as well as discussing the priorities of WCDs in 1984. The Delphi survey method—a series of increasingly focused surveys sent to experts in the field—was used to achieve ranked priorities for establishing/developing writing centers.

Cushman, Tara, et al. 1995. "Using Focus Groups to Assess Writing Center Effectiveness." *Writing Lab Newsletter* 29 (7): 1–5.

This article includes a useful discussion of focus groups as a potential writing center assessment tool, good advice, and a thorough explanation of why these methods make sense for writing centers. However, neither results nor a discussion of their application is included.

David, Carol, and Thomas Bubolz. 1985. "Evaluating Students' Achieve-
     ment in a Writing Center." *Writing Lab Newsletter* 9 (8): 10–14.

This is an interesting study of a writing center's impact on error control.
Results indicate that the writing center not only contributed to improvement in error control but enabled students to avoid constructions that
may have led them to error and helped students to recognize constructions that were more prone to error.

Davis, Kevin. 1988. "Improving Students' Writing Attitudes." *Writing Lab
     Newsletter* 12 (10): 3–6.

This is a good example of quantitative methods being used effectively to
assess the impact of the writing center. The study used numerical analyses to confirm what other writing center research has claimed: the writing center has a positive impact on student writing.

Davis, Kevin, et al. 2010. "The Function of Talk in the Writing Confer-
     ence: A Study of Tutorial Conversation." *Writing Center Journal* 30
     (1): 45–51.

This study uses discourse analysis to explore/describe tutor dialogue.
The study found that most the effective sessions were a mix of directive
and nondirective discourses.

Denny, Harry, and Lori Salem. 2009. "A Tutor-Led Assessment Project at
     St. John's University: Discussion with Harry Denny and Lori Salem."
     University of Wisconsin–Madison Writing Center.

In this podcast, Denny and Salem discuss moving beyond satisfaction
surveys and putting more focus on assessment growing out of tutor
experiences and using focus groups to understand perceptions of the
writing process.

———. 2009. "Assessing What We Really Value in Writing Centers: A
     Conversation with Harry Denny and Lori Salem." University of Wis-
     consin–Madison Writing Center.

This podcast discusses assessment more generally. It argues that good
assessment starts with clear goals, purposes, and audiences. Writing center assessment should reflect writing center values and is often more useful when it is exploratory rather than reactive. The speakers recommend
using external sources, and getting tutors involved. Finally, the speakers
say get different audiences involved ASAP.

DiPardo, Anne. 1992. "'Whispers of Comings and Goings': Lessons from Fannie." *Writing Center Journal* 12 (7): 125–45.

This article is a great example of a case study used to explore a writing center question: How does a non-Anglo tutor work with a non-Anglo student to negotiate questions of academic discourse when underlying issues of invisibility are not addressed?

Donnelli, Emily, and Kristen Garrison. 2003. "Tapping Multiple Voices in Writing Center Assessment." *Academic Exchange Quarterly* 7 (4).

This piece builds from Lerner's argument that numbers aren't enough, Bell's taxonomy of assessments, and Johanek's contextualist paradigm to argue for conducting multiple small-scale assessments of various kinds to holistically answer a writing center research question. The article presents a great idea and discussion, but it doesn't avoid the familiar problem of hyper-localization.

Elliott, Norbert. 2005. *On a Scale: A Social History of Writing Assessment in America.* New York: Peter Lang Publishing.

Elliott provides a deep historical discussion of where writing assessment came from and where it has ended up. Particularly interesting here is the story of educational assessment as an American industry.

Enders, Doug. 2005. "Assessing the Writing Center: A Qualitative Tale of a Quantitative Study." *Writing Lab Newsletter* 29 (10): 6–9.

This is a cautionary tale of a WCD giving up too much control of writing center assessment (for nothing but good reasons). But it also discusses and exemplifies reasons and opportunities for conducting our own meaningful writing center assessments.

———. 2009. "What We Talk About: A Longitudinal Study of Writing Tasks Students and Writing Center Tutors Discuss." *Writing Lab Newsletter* 33(9): 6–10.

This is a great example of a longitudinal study that focuses on the writing tasks discussed within tutorials, rather than on the discourse itself.

Field-Pickering, Janet. 1993. "The Burden of Proof: Demonstrating the Effectiveness of a Computer Writing Center Program." *Writing Lab Newsletter* 18 (2): 1–3.

This article advocates reviewing and annotating successive word-processed drafts as an assessment, as demonstration of the writing center's impact on student writing.

Franklin, John T., et al. 2000. "English Education Within and Beyond the Writing Center: Expectations, Examples, and Realizations." *Writing Lab Newsletter* 24 (8): 10–13.

This article uses case study methodology to examine the success of a writing center in meeting the needs of secondary education majors who work there.

Gallagher, Chris W. 2009. "What Do WPAs Need to Know about Writing Assessment? An Immodest Proposal." *WPA: Writing Program Administration* 33 (1–2): 29–45.

This article lists eleven propositions about what WPAs should know re: assessment. It also provides guidance for WCDs and our professional organizations. The article also provides a useful, broad context for writing assessment.

———. 2010. "Assess Locally, Validate Globally: Heuristics for Validating Local Writing Assessments." *WPA: Writing Center Administration* 34(1):10–32.

This article presents a heuristic for writing assessment that encourages a full, rich discussion of not only what assessment is but why methods are chosen. The heuristic also connects these choices with the primary bodies of literature that are currently shaping and guiding assessment. Good tool for planning writing center assessment.

———. 2011. "Being There: (Re)Making the Assessment Scene." *College Composition and Communication* 62(3): 450–476.

Gallagher uses Burkean theory to argue against the kind of defensive positioning writing assessment has too frequently chosen. Several ideas are included for substantiating our expertise in assessing our own work. Similar arguments can and should be made by writing center directors.

Gardner, John N., Betsy O. Barefoot, and Randy L. Swing. 2001. *Guidelines for Evaluating The First-Year Experience at Four-Year Colleges*, 2nd ed. Columbia, SC: The National Resource for the First-Year Experience and Students in Transition.

These guidelines provide a series of questions about the first-year experience that can be used to develop writing center assessment ideas and questions as well as define the writing center in relation to the first year.

Granovetter, Mark. 1976. "Network Sampling: Some First Steps." *American Journal of Sociology* 81 (6): 1287–1303.

This piece argues that network sampling techniques have been used for small-scale samples and local communities, but they can be developed to deal with larger communities. These methods can be used by writing center assessors on multiple scales.

Grimm, Nancy. 2003. "In the Spirit of Service: Making Writing Center Research a 'Featured Character.'" In *The Center Will Hold: Critical Perspectives on Writing Center Scholarship*, edited by Michael A. Pemberton and Joyce Kinkead, 41–57. Urbana, IL: NCTE.

This chapter not only makes a case for writing center research as a central component of writing centers but explains why and how that can be accomplished.

Griswold, Gary. 2003. "Writing Centers: The Student Retention Connection." *AEQ* 7 (4).

This article assesses the values and activities of writing centers in relation to retention scholarship/research findings and positive factors in retention. The article reveals a great deal of common ground. If a WCD were interested in connecting with retention efforts, this is a great place to start.

Harrison, Michael I., and Arie Shirom. 1999. *Organizational Diagnosis and Assessment: Bridging Theory and Practice.* Thousand Oaks, CA: Sage.

This resource offers an unusual perspective on assessment for writing centers because it focuses on the assessment of organizations. Writing centers working to improve their performance, services, or actual organization could make good use of this comprehensive resource.

Hawthorne, Joan. 2006. "Approaching Assessment as if It Matters." In *The Writing Center Director's Resource Book*, edited by Christina Murphy and Byron Stay, 237–45. Mahwah, NJ: Lawrence Erlbaum.

Hawthorne does a nice job of walking readers from understanding what writing center assessment is to how to do it, moving back and forth between assessment and research.

Hayward, Malcolm. 1983. "Assessing Attitudes Towards The Writing Center." *Writing Center Journal* 3 (2): 1–10.

This article is an interesting permutation of using surveys to ascertain differing perspectives on teaching and tutoring writing. The comparison of writing faculty and tutor responses revealed that their primary goals were the same, though faculty later tended toward correctness and tutors tended more toward personal development. In reviewing referral practices, the same patterns emerged.

Henson, Roberta, and Sharon Stephenson. 2009. "Writing Consultations Can Effect Quantifiable Change: One Institution's Assessment." *Writing Lab Newsletter* 33 (9): 1–5.

This article is a good example of a productive quantitative assessment that speaks to administration, assessment, and accreditation audiences. The study found that students from different levels of writing courses improved in different ways with writing center intervention.

Hodgdon, David G. 1990. "Assessing a High School Writing Center: A Trek into the Frontiers of Program Evaluation." *Writing Lab Newsletter* 14 (8): 13–16.

This piece applies Stufflebeam's CIPP assessment protocol (see annotated entry below) to writing center assessment. In some ways, this approach is very similar to Walvoord because it identifies specific goals, measures, outcomes, and feedback loops, but it is unique as well because it is always about relationships between the writing center and other campus constituencies.

Huot, Brian. 2002. *(Re)Articulating Writing Assessment for Teaching and Learning*. Logan: Utah State University Press.

Along with a rich discussion of writing assessment, this book provides five principles for a new writing assessment paradigm that aligns easily and smoothly with writing center theory, pedagogy, and writing centers' habit of building from the local.

Hylton, Jaime. 1990. "Evaluating the Writing Lab: How Do We Know That We Are Helping?" *Writing Lab Newsletter* 15 (3): 5–8.

This article lays out an accessible, general process for developing writing center assessment plans. It also provides some insights and specifics about the assessment development process and how to maneuver through it.

Inoue, Asao B. 2010. "Engaging with Assessment Technologies: Responding to Valuing Diversity as a WPA." *WPA: Writing Program Administration* 33 (3): 134–38.

This is a very thoughtful response piece that encourages a more applied view of diversity as it impacts writing assessment. More specifically, Inoue argues that assessment tools must be scrutinized as active vehicles for biases and prejudices inherent in the systems from which they evolve. Although more theoretical than many of the pieces included here, this piece helps us to think very deliberately about how inclusive or exclusive our assessment "technologies" might be—not a cautionary tale but a call for further development.

Johanek, Cindy. 2000. *Composing Research: A Contextualist Paradigm for Composition and Rhetoric.* Logan: Utah State University Press.

Johanek argues that composition studies should move away from the oppositional dualism of qualitative versus quantitative methods, focus more attention on where (epistemologically) our research questions are coming from, and choose methods based on the questions we are asking and the kinds of answers we seek.

Jones, Casey. 2001. "The Relationship Between Writing Centers and Improvement in Writing Ability: An Assessment of the Literature." *Education* 122 (1): 3–20.

This article is a meta-analysis of scholarship related to the impact of writing centers on student writing improvement, which can be read both as disheartening and an opportunity.

Kail, Harvey. 1983. "Evaluating Our Own Peer Tutoring Programs: A Few
    Leading Questions." *Writing Lab Newsletter* 7 (10): 2–4.

This article argues that WCDs should do assessment for their centers
first, asking questions that are pertinent initially to the writing centers
themselves. The article provides great questions that one might use to
contextualize assessment. It is thorough and provides both examples
and engaging discussion of why those questions might be useful.

———, and Kay Allen. 1982. "Conducting Research in the Writing Lab."
    In *Tutoring Writing: A Sourcebook for Writing Labs*, edited by Muriel
    Harris, 233–45. Glenview, IL: Scott, Foresman.

This piece is a terrific walk-through of the important ideas in starting
writing center research or assessment. First, it differentiates between
exploratory and experimental research, then it goes into detail about
case studies and survey-based research. Afterward, the chapter provides
a useful discussion of how others can/should help and how to engage
the writing center staff in the research. Finally, the piece describes the
process of investigating the differences between the impact of silent editing practices versus oral editing practices, as an example of the ideas discussed earlier in the chapter.

———, Paula Gillespie, and Brad Hughes. 2011. *The Peer Writing Tutor
    Alumni Research Project*. University of Wisconsin–Madison.

This project is a wonderful assessment tool because it provides a great
set of resources for pursuing this kind of assessment, and it brings your
data into contact with the data of so many other participants. Beyond
that, the basic question is one that writing centers have speculated about
for years: the long-term impact of working as a peer writing tutor.

Kalikoff, Beth. 2001. "From Coercion to Collaboration: A Mosaic Ap-
    proach to Writing Center Assessment." *Writing Lab Newsletter* 26 (1):
    5–7.

This piece argues for the kind of small scale, multi-pronged assessment
advocated by Jim Bell and activated in Donnelli and Garrison.

Lamb, Mary. 1981. "Evaluation Procedures for Writing Centers: Defining Ourselves Through Accountability." In *New Directions for College Learning Assistance: Improving Writing Skills*, edited by Thom Hawkins and Phyllis Brooks, 69–82. San Francisco, CA: Jossey-Bass.

This chapter begins with a survey of writing centers and their assessment practices (120 at that time) and the differentiation between formative and summative assessment. The survey found that most centers used basic counting, questionnaires, pre-/post-tests, external evaluation, and publications/professional staff activities as indicators of their work and values. There are lots of examples of the tools used 30+ years ago (they will seem quite familiar).

Law, Joe, and Christina Murphy. 1997. "Formative Assessment and the Paradigms of Writing Center Practice." *Clearing House* 71 (2): 106–8.

This article starts with a very bold statement about the lack of research that pairs writing center assessment with formative assessment. The article also makes a case for tutoring writing as part of the formative assessment tradition. The article then works to tie writing center theory/practice with formative assessment.

Leaker, Cathy, and Heather Ostman. 2010. "Composing Knowledge: Writing, Rhetoric, and Reflection in Prior Learning Assessment." *College Composition and Communication* 61 (4): 691–717.

This article isn't about writing center assessment, but the methodology used in this study—prior learning assessment (PLA)—could be very useful for writing center assessment.

Leff, Linda Ringer. 1997. "Authentic Assessment in the Writing Center: Too Open to Interpretation?" *Writing Lab Newsletter* 21 (5): 12–14.

The results of a questionnaire were too consistent from one year to the next and too positive, both taken as indicators of weakness in the survey instrument. This piece walks through not only why but how to revise a questionnaire.

Lerner, Neal. 1997. "Counting Beans and Making Beans Count." *Writing Lab Newsletter* 22 (1): 1–4.

This article nicely balances accessibility and audience. The piece argues for using the most accessible data to make the kinds of arguments that administrators will value.

————. 2001. Choosing Beans Wisely. *Writing Lab Newsletter* 26(1): 1–4.

This article provides insights into assessment assumptions and how they can distort/call into question the assessment results. The article discusses preliminary research questions as well. This is one of the very few examples of follow-up publications that show the development of thinking and/or methodology in writing center assessment.

————. 2003. "Writing Center Assessment: Searching for the 'Proof' of Our Effectiveness." In *The Center Will Hold: Critical Perspectives on Writing Center Scholarship*, eds. Michael A. Pemberton and Joyce Kinkead, 58–73. Urbana: NCTE.

This chapter provides historical context, critiques the few published studies of writing center effects on student writing, argues for writing centers in relation to first-year writing assessments, and provides a number of local examples

————, and Harvey Kail. 2004. *A Heuristic for Writing Center Assessment*. MIT.

This is a great tool for developing assessment questions and exploring methods.

Lynne, Patricia. 2004. *Coming to Terms: A Theory of Writing Assessment*. Logan: Utah State University Press.

Lynne focuses her work on ferreting out the implicit and explicit impacts of the positivist paradigm on writing assessment. She then argues for a rethinking of writing assessment, based in literacy scholarship, that she claims would be more appropriate to writing assessment theory and practice.

Macklin, Nicole, Cynthia K. Marshall, and Joe Law. "Expanding Writing Center Assessment." *Writing Lab Newsletter* 27 (1): 12–16.

This article argues that the learning that tutors experience within a writing center should be included in writing center assessment.

MacNealy, Mary Sue. *Strategies for Empirical Research in Writing*. New York: Longman.

This book contextualizes research differently from others in this bibliography, by arguing that empirical methods are appropriate for the humanities and social sciences, and then also thoroughly discussing multiple methodologies that are both quantitative and qualitative. The discussion and methods here break through that idea that empirical research methods have to be quantitative by providing discussion of the full range of research methodologies.

McCracken, Nancy. 1979. "Evaluation/Accountability for the Writing
    Lab." *Writing Lab Newsletter* 3 (6): 1–2.

This study focuses on error analysis and the use of pre-/post-tutorial writing samples. The article includes useful assessment design questions and discussion. McCracken also provides a productive discussion of process and outcomes, particularly outcomes for student writers.

Moneyhun, Clyde. 2009. "Performance Evaluation as Faculty Develop-
    ment." *WPA: Writing Program Administration* 34 (1): 161–65.

This article describes the process of collaboratively building and then operating a faculty assessment program—readily adaptable to any role in the writing center and very much reflective of the communal nature of writing centers.

Morrison, Julie Bauer, and Jean-Paul Nadeau. 2003. "How Was Your
    Session at the Writing Center? Pre- and Post-Grade Student Evalua-
    tions." *Writing Center Journal* 23 (2): 25–42.

This piece is a useful companion to Carino and Enders, looking at the effects of grades on student satisfaction with tutorials over time. This is a good example of pre-/post-tutorial model and outcomes-based assessment.

Murphy, Christina, Joe Law, and Steve Sherwood. 1996. *Writing Centers:
    An Annotated Bibliography.* Westport, CT: Greenwood Press.

This comprehensive writing center resource includes more than 1,400 entries and is organized into topical chapters that provide a wide range of resources. Because this resource is now twenty-five years old, it is an excellent catalog of scholarship that may have been forgotten or lost.

Neulieb, Janice. 1982. "Evaluating a Writing Lab." In *Tutoring Writing: A Sourcebook for Writing Labs*, edited by Muriel Harris, 227–32. Glenview: Scott Foresman.

This piece is a very broad overview of writing center assessment foci, methods, and reporting. One most interesting feature of this chapter is that writing center assessment seems to have retained a good deal of what Neulieb describes in terms of what a writing center is and does.

Newman, Stephen. 1999. "Demonstrating Effectiveness." *Writing Lab Newsletter* 23 (8): 8–9.

This article works to correlate grades, writing center use, and SAT scores to demonstrate the impact of the writing center on student writing.

Niiler, Luke. 2003. "The Numbers Speak: A Pre-Test of Writing Center Outcomes Using Statistical Analysis." *Writing Lab Newsletter* 27 (7): 6–9.

This study collected qualitative data and analyzed it using quantitative methods. The study found a positive writing center impact on student writing.

———. 2005. "The Numbers Speak Again: A Continued Statistical Analysis of Writing Center Outcomes." *Writing Lab Newsletter* 29 (5): 13–15.

Like the Lerner "Bean" articles, Niiler follows up his first study with a revised and improved reconsideration. This article demonstrates continuing development of quantitative assessment methods when read along with Niiler's 2003 piece.

North, Stephen. 1984. "Writing Center Research: Testing Our Assumptions." In *Writing Centers: Theory and Administration*, edited by Gary Olson, 24–35. Urbana, IL: NCTE.

North continues to challenge the status quo by pushing WCDs to test their assumptions about discourse theory. North also argues that one commonality between all writing centers is that the tutorial is the ideal space for the teaching of writing.

Olson, Jon, Dawn J. Moyer, and Adelia Falda. 2002. "Student-Centered Assessment Research in the Writing Center." In *Writing Center Research: Extending the Conversation*, edited by Paula Gillespie, Alice Gillam, Lady Falls Brown, and Byron Stay, 111–31. Mahwah, NJ: Lawrence Erlbaum.

This is a particularly useful article for writing center assessment. It engages students as researchers, demonstrates the value of interdisciplinary research, and provides discussion of rapid assessment, a research strategy that aligns nicely with Johanek and Jim Bell's work.

O'Neill, Peggy, Cindy Moore, and Brian Huot. 2009. *A Guide to College Writing Assessment*. Logan: Utah State University Press.

This book is somewhat unique in this bibliography in that it focuses on the kinds of assessments that writing program administrators make. This book is useful to writing center assessment because it can help a WCD to align her assessment work with the assessment work of a writing program. It can also be useful in helping WCDs to think broadly about the variety of questions and methods available. Along with a number of useful forms and documents, the contents of this book can be readily used in/adapted to writing center assessment.

Ortoleva, Matthew, and Jeremiah Dyehouse. 2008. "SWOT Analysis: An Instrument for Writing Center Strategic Planning." *Writing Lab Newsletter* 32 (10): 1–4.

SWOT analysis is discussed as a foundation for strategic planning, an essential tool for articulating objectives, and a useful tool for setting up assessable goals. SWOT is a great tool for both goal setting and assessing outcomes—be sure to use and respond to all four quadrants.

Paretti, Marie C., and Katrina M. Powell, eds. 2009. *Assessment of Writing (Assessment in the Disciplines)*. Tallahassee, FL: Association for Institutional Research.

This book focuses more on theoretical discussions and local examples of writing assessment contexts, purposes, and outcomes. The book includes a thorough representation of ideas and options in writing assessment, much of which is applicable to writing center assessment.

Pennington, Jill, Neal Lerner, and Jason Mayland. 2008. "Two Experts Talk Writing Center Assessment: A Conversation with Neal Lerner and Jason Mayland."

This podcast covers broad ideas of meaningful assessment from institutional research (IR) and writing center assessment perspectives, going into some detail about the important differentiation between correlation versus causation. Participants in this podcast encourage interaction with IR offices early on and throughout the writing center assessment process. IR offices and personnel have a lot to offer and can be real assets in both writing center assessment development and analysis.

Picciotto, Madeleine. 2010. "Writing Assessment and Writing Center Assessment: Collision, Collusion, Conversation." *Praxis* 8 (1).

Picciotto struggles to develop writing center support for a writing exit exam, required by the writing curriculum, and works to understand appropriate ways of using the exit exam as part of the assessment of her writing center.

Roberts, David H. 1988. "A Study of Writing Center Effectiveness." *Writing Center Journal* 9 (1): 53–60.

This is an interesting study and set of assessment methods because it works to compare group and individualized instruction by testing null hypotheses. The article presents a methodology that could be useful in the writing center.

Rodis, Karen. 1990. "Mending the Damaged Path: How to Avoid Conflict of Expectation When Setting up a Writing Center." *Writing Center Journal* 10 (2): 45–57.

This article is useful to assessment design because it helps us to think about whether we want our assessments to confirm or counter the expectations of others, particularly those of stakeholders on campus. It is also a good model for a simple assessment of perception related to the purpose, work, and resources of the writing center within the context of the writing being done elsewhere on campus.

Salem, Lori, and Harry Denny. 2009. "A New Approach to Student Surveys at Temple University with Harry Denny and Lori Salem." University of Wisconsin–Madison Writing Center.

The participants in this podcast argue for a more nuanced approach to student surveys that focuses on attitudes, which can later be used for training and professional development.

Severino, Carol. 1994. "The Writing Center as Site for Cross-Language Research." *Writing Center Journal* 15 (1): 51–61.

This article makes a compelling argument that the writing center is a vital site for L1 (English as a first language) researchers and L2 (English as a second language) researchers to collaborate and benefit from one another's disciplinary and methodological practices.

———, Jeffrey Swenson, and Jia Zhu. 2009. "A Comparison of Online Feedback requests by Non-Native English-Speaking and Native English-Speaking Writers." *Writing Center Journal* 29 (1): 106–29.

This is a strong study of non-native English speakers' and native English speakers' requests for help with writing. The focus of the study is a comparison of these requests in face-to-face and online contexts. The focus is clearly on the non-native versus native speakers in those environments, rather than face-to-face versus online learning.

Shea, Kelly A. 2011. "Through the Eyes of the OWL: Assessing Faculty vs. Peer Tutoring in an Online Setting." *Writing Lab Newsletter* 35 (7/8): 6–9.

This study focused on comparing face-to-face tutorials with online tutorials as well as peer versus faculty tutoring. The findings do not readily align with current writing center assumptions, and they lead the author to think about more formal training for tutoring staff as well as training for writing center users.

Sherwood, Steve. 1993. "How to Survive the Hard Times." *Writing Lab Newsletter* 17 (10): 4–8.

This piece argues for demonstrating effectiveness as one of several strategies for defense against budget cuts. Just beneath the surface of all the strategies, though, is the argument for meaningful, varied, and ongoing writing center assessment.

Steward, Joyce S., and Mary K. Croft. 1982. "Evaluating the Lab Program."
    In *The Writing Laboratory: Organization, Management, and Methods*,
    92–94. Glenview, IL: Scott Foresman.

This piece is very, very brief. It lists a small selection of writing center assessment options that can be useful now and provides some historical insight into writing center assessment.

Stufflebeam, Daniel L. 1968. *Evaluation as Enlightenment for Decision-Making*.
    Address delivered at the Working Conference on Assessment Theory,
    Sarasota, FL. Retrieved from ERIC database (ED048333).

This paper, though dated, provides a useful context for the development of educational evaluation and decision making. It provides an explanation of what is missing and then argues that there are four kinds of decisions (planning, performance, implementation, and recycling) and four kinds of evaluations (context, input, process, and product). It goes into further detail about design. This piece is useful not only because it provides a discussion of methods but because it also argues for differentiations between categories of assessment.

Tashakkori, Abbas, and Charles Teddlie. 1998. *Mixed Methodology: Combining Qualitative and Quantitative Approaches*. Thousand Oaks, CA: Sage.

A number of the resources included here and in the literature review in chapter 1 encouraged multiple, small assessments. Several others argue for a more diverse set of research methods. This book helps a writing center assessor/researcher to think more broadly about research/assessment options and to combine methodologies in deliberate ways that allow for more rich and multifaceted projects.

———, eds. 2003. *Handbook of Mixed Methods in Social and Behavioral Research*. Thousand Oaks: Sage.

This edited collection follows Tashakkori and Teddlie's 1998 book and adds a great deal more detail and discussion of not only what mixed methods are and can produce, but what issues are involved in using mixed methods, how they are used in a variety of disciplines, and some speculation about where mixed methods will go in the future.

Thompson, Isabelle. 2006. "Writing Center Assessment: Why and a Little How." *Writing Center Journal* 26 (1): 33–61.

This is a wonderful article that lays out two essential arguments: externally mandated assessments can bring writing centers to the institutional and assessment tables and counting has limited impacts and uses as an assessment strategy. Thompson also provides a useful model for the development of assessment plans.

———, et al. 2009. "Examining Our Lore: A Survey of Students' and Tutors' Satisfaction with Writing Center Conferences." *Writing Center Journal* 29 (1): 79–101.

This is an interesting study for two reasons. First, it challenges the lore of writing centers, particularly non/directiveness in tutoring writing. Second, it uses surveys in a very smart way.

Thonus, Terese. 2001. "Triangulation in the Writing Center: Tutor, Tutee, and Instructor Perceptions of the Tutor's Role." *Writing Center Journal* 22 (1): 59–82.

This is a smart study of contrasting perceptions of the tutor's role. An assessment like this could be very useful in clarifying and fixing a more consistent and more reliable role for the writing center and its staff.

———. 2002. "Tutor and Student Assessments of Academic Writing Tutorials: What is 'Success'?" *Assessing Writing* 8 (2): 110–134.

This article uses discourse analysis as a means of describing tutorial successes and, by extension, a means of shaping tutorial interactions. The study showed that writing tutors are constantly negotiating between instructional directness and social goals such as politeness.

———. 2004. "What Are the Differences? Tutor Interactions with First- and Second-Language Writers." *Journal of Second Language Writing* 13: 227–242.

This article includes a meta-analysis of multiple studies regarding tutorials with non-native English speakers, all of which depend primarily on discourse analysis. The study showed differences between practices useful with native speakers and non-native speakers of English. By acknowledging these differences, tutoring practice can become more flexible and adaptable.

Walvoord, Barbara. 2004. *Assessment Clear and Simple: A Practical Guide for Institutions, Departments, and General Education*. San Francisco, CA: Jossey-Bass.

This book provides a very broad and simple agenda for assessment. Because it is so simple, it is easily adaptable to writing centers: set goals, gather evidence, and then use the information for improvement.

White, Edward M. 1990. "Language and Reality in Writing Assessment." *College Composition and Communication* 41 (2): 187–200.

This article provides a useful way to understand the conflicts between educational testing/assessment and writing assessment by looking at basic philosophical contrasts as well as resistance on both sides to acknowledging that resistance. This is a good piece to help WCDs understand and make informed decisions about how to access the ideology and language of psychometrics.

———. 2008. "Testing In and Testing Out." *WPA: Writing Program Administration* 32 (1): 129–142.

This piece is useful for writing center assessment because it is written for writing program administrators. The article contextualizes the roles of the writing program administrator and the writing center director from that perspective and provides a context for writing center assessment within the larger writing program administration and institutional context. Writing centers are mentioned only twice, and there is a lack of connection between what are outlined as writing program priorities and the work of writing centers. The article is constructed from a writing program administration focus on the balance between challenging students and enabling their success—letting people in (writing placement) and letting them out (graduating able writers). The writing center seems remote in this representation.

Whitney, Steve. 1997. "Down and Dirty Assessment." *Writing Lab Newsletter* 21 (7): 6–7.

This piece advocates unobtrusive exercises during staff meetings that can be used to elicit feedback from tutors about what the center does well and where it can improve.

Williams, Jessica. 2004. "Tutoring and Revision: Second Language Writ-ers in the Writing Center." *Journal of Second Language Writing* 13 (3): 173–201.

This article studies the impact of tutorials on L2 revision. The study focused on changes at the sentence-level when a tutor's advice is more directive.

Wolcott, Willa, and Sue M. Legg. 1998. *An Overview of Writing Assessment: Theory, Research, and Practice.* Urbana, IL: NCTE.

This book is exactly what it claims to be: an overview. This book focuses on methods with some discussion of theory and other writing-related research. For a practical guide to writing assessment, this is a great resource.

Yahner, William. 1993. "Explaining and Justifying Writing Centers: One MORE Example." *Writing Lab Newsletter* 18 (2): 5–7.

Although this article is not really about assessment per se, it does pro-vide a good example of using assessment data to develop and present cogent arguments about the value and impact of the writing center.

Young, Beth Rapp, and Barbara A. Fritzsche. 2002. "Writing Center Users Procrastinate Less: The Relationship between Individual Differences in Procrastination, Peer Feedback, and Student Writing Success." *Writing Center Journal* 23 (1): 45–58.

This is a very good example of using quantitative methods to do a cor-relation study between writing center use and procrastination. Findings indicate that writing center users procrastinate less in their writing than do non-writing center users.

INDEX

Sherwood, Steve, 6, 12
Simpson, Jeanne, 161
single-loop, 172–3
Smith, William L., 36–37, 59n1
Socratic Method, 35, 64
Sommers, Nancy, 119, 151
speculation, 2, 4, 66
stakeholders, 33, 35–36, 167–8
stakes, 2, 10, 66, 134, 137,
Stanford University, 172
statistics, 127, 146, 157, 159, 163
Stay, Byron, 28
Steward, Joyce S., 2
sticky ideas, 80, 177
strategic planning, 86, 122, 138, 140–1,
    143, 154–60, 175–6
strategy, 7, 17, 106, 123, 143, 146, 148,
    161, 176
"Student-Centered Assessment Research in
    the Writing Center," 17
"Study of Writing Center Effectiveness,
    A," 18
Stufflebeam, Daniel, 12, 16
summative, 32, 39, 48, 130
Swenson, Jeffrey, 19
Swing, Randy I., 14
"SWOT Analysis," 16

technical problem solving, 174, 177
Thompson, Isabelle, 12–13
Thonus, Terese, 11, 19
training, 10, 14, 18, 20, 36, 38, 73, 99–102,
    104, 117, 120–2, 128, 135, 154–5,
    158–60, 174–5
translation, 59, 64, 139, 162–5, 169
Tugend, Alina, 171–3
"Tutoring and Revision," 19
Tutoring Writing, 47n3
Tutortrac, 144, 153

United States, 8, 28, 64, 87
University Assessment Committee, 140
University of Louisville, 5, 144
University of Pittsburg, 36
University of Wisconsin-Madison, 6
"Using Focus Groups to Assess Writing
    Center Effectiveness," 12

values statement, 132, 145
vision statement, 40, 59, 67, 72–73, 76, 79

WAC. *See* writing-across-the-curriculum
"WAC Assessment and Internal Audi-
    ences," 138, 168
Walvoord, Barbara, 31–33, 38

WCD. *See* writing center director
WCenter, 25, 42, 78, 84, 97, 166
WEAVE, 142, 147–48
"What Do WPAs Need to Know about Writ-
    ing Assessment?," 10
"What Our Graduates Write," 10
What We Really Value, 9, 37
What Works In Student Retention, 14
White, Edward, 11
Whitney, Steve, 18
"Whose Idea of a Writing Center Is This,
    Anyway?," 161
Wikia, 6
Williams, Jessica, 19
Wolcott, Willa, 9
World War I, 8
writing-across-the-curriculum (WAC),
    87–88, 94, 96, 138–9
"Writing Center as Site for Cross-Language
    Research, The, " 12
"Writing Center Assessment Bibliography,"
    6
writing-center assessment scholarship, 26
"Writing Center Assessment: Searching for
    the 'Proof' of Our Effectiveness," 11
"Writing Center Assessment: Why and a
    Little How," 12–13
"Writing Center Data," 118
writing center director (WCD), 1–10,
    13–16, 20–22, 25–28, 30, 33–37, 41, 57,
    59–67, 75–78, 84, 87–88, 91, 96, 99,
    108, 111, 115–17, 122–4, 126, 133–4,
    136, 139, 140, 165–7, 169, 171–6, 178
Writing Center Director's Resource Book, The,
    28
Writing Center Journal, 6
Writing Center Research, 28
"Writing Center Users Procrastinate Less,"
    18
Writing Centers: An Annotated Bibliography, 6
Writing Centers Research Project, 5, 144
"Writing Centers: The Student Retention
    Connection," 14
Writing Centers: Theory and Administration, 3
Writing Lab Newsletter, 6
Writing Laboratory, 2
writing program administration, 88, 106,
    123–4, 162–3, 165, 176

Yahner, William, 15
Young, Beth Rapp, 18

Zhu, Jia, 19

ABOUT THE AUTHORS

ELLEN SCHENDEL is associate professor of writing and director of the Fred Meijer Center for Writing & Michigan Authors at Grand Valley State University in Michigan. At Grand Valley, she teaches academic and professional writing courses. Her scholarship focuses mainly on writing assessment and writing program administration and has been published in *WPA: Writing Program Administration, Assessing Writing, Writing Lab Newsletter, Journal of Advanced Composition, The Journal of Writing Assessment,* and several edited collections. She serves on the editorial boards of *Composition Studies, WPA: Writing Program Administration,* and *The Journal of Writing Assessment.*

WILLIAM J. (BILL) MACAULEY, JR. is associate professor and university writing center director at the University of Nevada, Reno. His recent publications include *Before and After the Tutorial: Writing Centers and Institutional Relationships* (coedited with Nicholas Mauriello and Robert T. Koch, Jr.) and *Marginal Words, Marginal Work? Tutoring the Academy in the Work of Writing Centers* (coedited with Nicholas Mauriello), which won the IWCA 2007 Outstanding Scholarship Best Book Award. His other scholarship has focused on student agency in writing, writing program/center administration, and first-generation/working-class students' acquisition of academic discourse.

NEAL LERNER is associate professor of English and writing center director at Northeastern University in Boston. His book *The Idea of a Writing Laboratory* won the 2011 NCTE David H. Russell Award for Distinguished Research in the Teaching of English. He is also the co-author of *The Longman Guide to Peer Tutoring* and of *Learning to Communicate as a Scientist and Engineer: Case Studies from MIT,* which won the 2012 CCCC Advancement of Knowledge Award. He has published on the history of teaching writing, the history of teaching science, and administrative and theoretical issues in writing programs and centers.

BRIAN HUOT is professor of English at Kent State University where he teaches undergraduate writing courses, writing teacher preparation courses, and graduate courses in the Literacy, Rhetoric and Social Practice Program. He is a former writing center director at two different schools. His published work has appeared in such journals as *WPA: Writing Program Administration, College Composition and Communication, and College English.* In addition, he has co-edited five collections, co-authored (with Peggy O'Neill and Cindy Moore) *The College Guide to Writing Assessment* and authored the monograph *(Re)Articulating Writing Assessment for Teaching and Learning.*

NICOLE CASWELL is finishing her dissertation at Kent State University on the role of emotion in teachers' responses and evaluations of student writing. In addition to teaching a range of university writing coursers at different institutions, she has held WPA and WCA positions at two different universities. Her scholarship includes writing assessment, writing centers, and emotions and has been published in the CEA Forum and the new East Center Writing Centers Association Newsletter.